A YEAR WITH THE
CATECHISM

365 Day Reading Plan

Donald Asci, STD

Petroc Willey, STL, PhD

Fr. Dominic Scotto, TOR, PhD

Elizabeth Siegel, MPhil

Catholic Truth Society

Our Sunday Visitor

www.osv.com
Our Sunday Visitor Publishing Division
Our Sunday Visitor, Inc.
Huntington, Indiana 46750

Nihil Obstat: The Rev. Fr. Marcus Holden,
            Diocesan Censor
Imprimatur: ✠ Most Rev. Peter Smith, L.L.B., J.C.D., K.C.*H.S.,
            Archbishop of Southwark
            December 1, 2017

ISBN 978 1 78469 197 4

Our Sunday Visitor Publishing Division, Our Sunday Visitor, Inc., 200 Noll Plaza, Huntington, IN 46750; 1-800-348-2440

ISBN: 978-1-68192-159-4 (Inventory No. T1876)
eISBN: 978-1-68192-166-2
LCCN: 2017961492

Contents

Preface

The *Catechism of the Catholic Church* is a glorious gift to the universal Church, but it can be intimidating. The division of the Catechism's text into a year's reading plan is intended to make the project of reading it from cover to cover a manageable and enjoyable experience. While this present work is a commentary upon the text, our sincere hope is that, through this work and the encouragement it gives to return to the Catechism, some of the riches of the Catechism itself might be discovered anew. Our commentary will have amply served its purpose if it leads readers to a greater understanding and love of the text of the Catechism and if it manages to echo and draw attention to something of the magnificent and beautiful "symphony of the faith" presented in that text. The riches of the Catechism are such that a commentary like this can only *begin* to uncover the treasures to be discovered in its pages.

Given the limitations of length, we have focused our attention on three things. First, we have wished to make the flow and "logic" of the text apparent by drawing attention to recurring themes and highlighting the "mountain ranges" in the landscape. Second, we have wanted to explain terms from the Tradition that may be relatively unfamiliar and provide a way of engaging with teachings that can appear strange, or even discordant, in relation to certain commonly held views today; the authors of the Catechism made the bold decision to present the faith in its fullness, knowing that the dangers of a lack of understanding on the part of modern readers would need to be met with an attentiveness and commitment to better explanations of the unified Christian worldview. Above all, we have wished to highlight some of the spiritual and pastoral elements of the text. We have wanted the reader to be able to read the Catechism as its authors desired — so as to come to *know* God the Holy Trinity in order to be able to *participate* more consciously and fully in his redemptive plan of loving kindness.

This commentary is a collaborative work. For the most part we have allowed the commentary on each of the Parts of the Catechism to stand under the authorship of one main figure, although we have worked to harmonize approaches as far as possible. Dr. Petroc Willey is the lead author for the commentary on the Prologue and Part One of the Catechism's text; Dr. Dominic Scotto, TOR, of Part Two; Dr. Donald Asci of Part Three; and Elizabeth Siegel of Part Four, Section One;, with a further contribution from Petroc Willey in Part Four, Section Two....

I have been blessed to be able to work with such able and committed collaborators in this project, and I am grateful also to the many who have offered invaluable prayer support for this project. It has been a special pleasure to work with the Catholic Truth Society and Our Sunday Visitor, and I would like to record thanks to Lisa Gregoire for her helpful coordination of the project. In addition, I would like to thank Justin Fortenot for his efficient transcription of part of the commentary that was handwritten and Carly Burke for her generous, skillful and perceptive review of the whole text.

Finally, a special thank you is owed to Katherine for her unwavering belief in this project and for the loving patience with which she accepted my frequent disappearance to write and to edit.

Petroc Willey

Make my soul your heaven,
your beloved dwelling and the place of your rest.

— Saint Elizabeth of the Trinity, "Prayer to the Trinity"

If a man
Should chance to find this place three times in Time
His eyes are changed and make a summer silence.

— *Edwin Muir, "The Sufficient Place"*

INTRODUCTION AND PROLOGUE

The Cover and Artworks

We begin our reading of the Catechism not from inside the covers of the book but *with the cover* itself. The Church has intended that the whole of this work proclaim Christ to us, including the small line drawing on the front cover. Inside, with the publication details, you will find a short account of the meaning of this picture.

You will see that it is a simple design, the symbolism easily decipherable and very familiar. It is a natural pastoral scene. We see in the center a shepherd seated, with a sheep at his feet looking expectantly up. This central figure is, of course, Christ the Good Shepherd, while the seated posture is the position taken, in the Jewish tradition, when one is speaking authoritatively. That understanding was carried over into the Christian faith, so that we now speak of a professor holding a "chair" in a particular subject, while a bishop teaches from his cathedral (from *cathedra*, Latin for "chair"). Here, then, is Christ as the Good Pastor of his people, teaching with authority and warding off danger. The sheep lies in the shade of a tree — the tree of the Cross, now bearing the fruit of an everlasting life of happiness won for us. The arching tree creates a frame, suggesting a window through which we look in order to see this summary of what the Catechism contains.

In addition to this graceful cover design, the authors asked for *four works of art* to be placed in the Catechism, one to introduce each of the Parts. Most publishers honored this intention (though not all did, for reasons of cost). Their presence is to manifest for us something of the indescribable beauty of Christ and of the Catholic faith, as well as to remind us of the capacity of art to attract us to the faith as we come to understand it through a contemplative gaze.

The Contents Pages

One feature of the drawing on the cover points us directly to *the importance of reading the contents pages carefully*. The shepherd is playing panpipes, and the Catechism's explanation of the logo informs us that the sheep is being held attentive by the "melodious symphony of the truth" being played. That symphony is presented in a concise format in the contents pages.

A review of the contents reveals *four Parts*, four "symphonic movements," which faithfully unpack each of the four dimensions of the Christian life identified in the *Acts of the Apostles*. There we see that the first disciples attended to the apostles' teaching, lived in fellowship together, and shared in the breaking of the bread and in the prayers (see Acts 2:42). The contents pages mirror these dimensions in the Profession of Faith, centered on the Creed (Part 1); in the Celebration of the Faith, gathered around the sacraments (Part 2); in Life in Christ, grounded in the commandments (Part 3); and in the Life of Prayer, at the heart of which is the Lord's own prayer (Part 4). The numerous headings and titles in the contents pages are gathered within the overall structure of these four Parts.

The *ordering of the Parts* itself is significant: the Catechism first presents us with the infinite, gracious God and then a consideration of ourselves in relation to him. We begin with the divine works of creation, redemption, and sanctification (Part 1), and then move to God's grace, healing, and elevating us in the sacraments (Part 2). From there we turn to our necessary response, in the obedience of a faithful life (Part 3) and constant prayer (Part 4).

We can think of the contents as a whole, the headings and the individual numbered paragraphs as bars of music making up the symphony. The contents pages invite us to a full reading, a full "listening," of the work. Only in this complete reception will the power of this heavenly music be appreciated.

Apostolic Constitution *Fidei Depositum*[1]

A *Letter to the whole People of God* from Pope Saint John Paul II introduces the Catechism. All official Church documents are known primarily by their Latin title and its abbreviation. The title is taken from the opening words of the document. The Latin title, *Fidei Depositum* (*FD*), is a term taken from the New Testament, from the first and second letters from Paul to Timothy, describing the precious heritage of faith that Christ has left with his Church. The young bishop is being exhorted to faithfulness in guarding and handing on this great treasure of the Church, in its fullness (see 1 Tm 6:20 and 2 Tm 1:14).

The Catechism offers us a definitive and inspiring account of this heritage for our own day. Its publication reflects the ongoing faithfulness to the Gospel of the successors of the apostles — the Pope, together with the whole episcopate. This Apostolic Constitution explains the process by which the Catechism was requested and composed and details the careful stages through which it passed, as befits this unique teaching document intended for use across the universal Church. *This is a work to guide the whole Church, every adult member of the People of God.*

Saint John Paul II explains that the Church offers us this account of the faith not in the format of a dictionary or an encyclopedia, as a list of definitions or as food for the mind only, but precisely as a *catechism*, as a work to assist in the *formation of God's people in the living faith of the Church* by making "the truth of the Gospel shine forth." Each of the four Parts has an essential role to play in this formation. Once you have read this important Letter, spend time making your own the prayer with which John Paul concludes it.

---

[1] In the reader's particular edition, this Letter may follow the other Letter of Saint John Paul II, *Laetamur Magnopere*, which we will read tomorrow.

Apostolic Letter *Laetamur Magnopere*

Today we read a second Letter. This Letter is again from Saint John Paul II and celebrates the publication of the definitive Latin edition in 1997. John Paul writes here of the lengthy and careful process of revision between the initial publication in 1992 and this definitive edition — a period almost as long as the initial period of its writing. Now, *the work is finally complete*, the last revisions concluded. The Letter from the Pope is fittingly titled "great joy." The desire of the bishops for this Catechism is now "happily fulfilled." One can sense the Pope's own happiness pulsating through every line of this short Letter. This, at last, is the work that was needed, showing the "totally reliable" way to present the Christian message.

It is not just that there is a natural sense of relief and satisfaction in good work masterfully completed. John Paul is also overjoyed by the reception and impact of the Catechism all over the world. The ongoing engagement of so many in this project means that this work witnesses to a *unique measure of agreement* in the "harmony of so many voices."

John Paul also writes here of the wider "extraordinary interest" the Catechism has raised, beyond the Church, and even among non-Christians. He sees here a deep confirmation of the need for this Catechism: this "extraordinary" interest, he says, must be matched by an "extraordinary" commitment to evangelization, urgently needed so that everyone can know and receive Christ's saving message. The Catechism, through which the "inexhaustible riches of the faith" can be rediscovered, is offered to serve this work of evangelization. As you read this brief Letter, note the energy and passion that John Paul expresses here for the true welfare, the "spiritual good," of all people.

CCC² 1-3
Prologue

The opening paragraphs of the Catechism contain guiding principles for reading the whole work.

First, we should note the importance of the three scriptural quotations that introduce the Catechism. The first highlights the fundamental focus of the entire Catechism — that we might all be helped into an ever-deeper *personal relationship with God*; the second emphasizes the importance of *knowing the truths of the faith* — we can enjoy this personal relationship only if we allow God to teach us who he is; the third reminds us that the Catechism is given for the sake of *handing on the faith to others for their salvation*.

The first paragraph is remarkable: it provides us with a summary of the faith. The whole of God's loving plan for our creation, our redemption, and our lifting to the new life of grace is proclaimed here in six elegant sentences. From creation to the final life of blessedness, the importance of God's unceasing call is emphasized.

The second paragraph reminds us of the apostolic foundation of the faith and surprises us with its statement about the gift of mission — the apostles were "strengthened" by the mission they received. To be given a worthwhile mission is one of the greatest of all gifts. The gift of mission provides us with purpose, with resolve; it calls us to discover new energies within ourselves, and so strengthens us.

Notice the warmth, sensitivity, and utter respect God demonstrates towards his creatures. He "calls," he "invites," while we are called to "welcome" and "freely respond." There is no compulsion — only a loving God calling to his children, seeking their good and their happiness.

Finally, note the fourfold means of formation, of handing on the faith, reiterated in the last lines of CCC 3, and footnoting Acts 2:42.

---

² *Catechism of the Catholic Church.*

CCC 4-10
Handing on the Faith: Catechesis

Today's reading explains the essential nature of catechesis and its importance in the Church.

CCC 7 reminds us that *catechesis is essential for the healthy growth of the Church*, both numerically and in her authentic development. Each new soul, freshly drawn into Christ's Body, is to be fed with the pure nourishment of God's truth through the work of catechesis. As Saint Paul puts it, once attached to the Body, the child is to move from milk to solid food, so that a healthy growth is maintained (see 1 Cor 3:2; Heb 5:12-13). Thus the great periods of renewal in the Church, in which God inspires the bishops anew in their zeal for souls and for sanctity, are also necessarily "intense moments of catechesis" (8). In CCC 8-10 the Catechism draws our attention to the prevalence of bishops who are also saints in these times of renewal. It is not coincidental, then, that the initiating bishop of this Catechism, John Paul II, and the bishop who called for the Church council from which this Catechism derives its trajectory and proximate inspiration, John XXIII, have both, since the publication of the Catechism, been declared saints of the Church.

Because catechesis is so essential to the healthy development of the Church, these paragraphs take great pains to *define* it very carefully. CCC 6 carefully distinguishes catechesis from related areas of the Church's work, while CCC 4-5 provide central points of definition. The goal of catechesis is to initiate each new member into "the fullness of Christian life" (5) — that is always the target. As we have seen, this fullness has a fourfold nature, reflected in the four Parts of the Catechism. The teaching given for our initiation into this fullness is to be systematic and organic — it is to be planned and sensibly sequential, emphasizing the links between the different elements being taught, so that those receiving the teaching can understand that this is *one* faith, *one* truth, in its many aspects.

CCC 11-12
Aim and Intended Readership and Index of Citations

CCC 11 tells us that the Catechism provides *an account of the essentials* of the faith. What is given here is only that which it is absolutely necessary for us to know, the essential truths that have been handed on to us through "the whole of the Church's Tradition." The presentation of these essentials is *synthetic* — care is taken to impress upon us how the truths of the faith belong together through the organization of the contents of the faith. The presentation is also *organic*, a vital point we shall discuss when looking at CCC 18.

The sentence on the "principal sources" might strike us as oddly placed in a paragraph concerned with the aims of the Catechism. We might remember though that in *Fidei Depositum*, Saint John Paul celebrated the Catechism's publication precisely because he saw it renewing our contact with the "living sources of the faith." These living sources are found in the footnotes on every page, and they are gathered in the Index of Citations at the end of the Catechism. Take a moment to find in that Index the categories of sources mentioned in CCC 11 — Scripture, the Fathers, the liturgy, the Church's Magisterium. The authors of the Catechism want us to be directly acquainted with these.

CCC 11 also reminds us that the Catechism is intended to be *fruitful* — to inspire the writing of other catechisms and act as a solid anchor and reference point for their composition.

We have seen that all of the bishops of the world were involved in writing this Catechism, and from CCC 12 we see clearly why this was the case: the Catechism is intended primarily for them, to assist them in their responsibilities as the chief catechists. Through the bishops, *it is offered to all the faithful*, as a sure norm for understanding the faith. The Catechism has been published as an aid for helping the bishops reach all of their flock with the good news of Christ.

CCC 13-17
Structure and Subject Index[3]

We had occasion to view the structure of the Catechism when we examined the contents pages. These paragraphs provide us with a short summary of the content of each of the four Parts.

CCC 13 refers to the *four pillars*. These are not equivalent to the Parts but rather make up Section Two of each Part. Using the analogy of pillars, then, these provide the main structural "bones" to the building. The presentation of Section Two in each Part provides the detailed content of that Part, in the form of Creed, sacraments, commandments, and the Lord's Prayer.

If Section Two provides us with the pillars, Section One in each Part lays the necessary *foundations* upon which the pillars are erected. Thus, before we reach the details of the Creed, we learn of God's revelation of himself; before we unpack the sacraments in Part Two, we ponder the work of the Father, Son, and Holy Spirit in the liturgy and our grace-led participation in this work; prefacing the concrete expositions of the commandments in Part Three is a reminder of the principles of Christian living common to the keeping of all the commandments; and the first section in the prayer Part of the Catechism leads us beautifully into a consideration of the petitions of the Lord's Prayer through profound reflections on the nature of prayer.

You may want to note that the Parts are explicitly related to the great theological virtues which define the whole of the Christian life — *faith, hope and love*. Thus Part One is concerned with the fostering of faith in our lives, Part Three with the inculcation of love, and Part Four with the development of hope. Part Two, treating of the liturgy and sacraments, is the wonderful integrating center to the whole Catechism: here, faith, hope, and love come together — we profess our faith in the Creed, reach out in hope through the "Our Father" and receive all the grace needed for lives of Christian love.

---

[3] This is also referred to as the Index or the Analytical Index in different editions of the Catechism.

CCC 18-22
Practical Directions

The practical directions are simple to understand and yet radical in their nature. CCC 18 makes clear to us that the Catechism is a rare text in that it is intended to be read, not just sequentially, but also across the Parts. Numerous *cross-references* have been placed in the margins in order to facilitate this special kind of reading, together with a Subject Index at the end of the Catechism. While it might appear that topics belong only in one Part of the Catechism, related aspects appear in numerous places, and every topic always belongs, in some fashion, to all four Parts. For an adequate understanding of a topic, therefore, we are asked to use the cross-references and Subject Index to range across the whole Catechism.

We are being invited, then, to a slow reading, to take our time, pondering how different areas of the faith relate to one another. The Catechism calls this an *organic* reading. "Organic" indicates the living interdependence of parts on one another, just as the different parts of a body work together for the good of the whole and can only be understood in relation to that whole.

Practiced with persistence and diligence, *reading organically will transform our relationship to the Catechism*. As a simple exercise, to get the idea, read CCC 218 and then the single cross-reference to CCC 295. CCC 218 explains the special revelation to Israel as being the result of God's gratuitous love. The cross-reference to CCC 295 reminds us that God's love is also the source of all creation. So we are led to a profounder truth through the cross-reference; we see that God's actions, in creation and in history, are always consistent with this one principle: that they flow from his love. God's love for his people Israel is harmonious with his love for all nations, indeed with the whole of creation.

CCC 23-25
Necessary Adaptations

Each paragraph in the Catechism makes a single point, the three points here making a fitting climax to the Prologue. Each paragraph speaks of a different "necessary adaptation."

The first necessary adaptation is of *our lives to the truths of the faith* (23). The faith we study in the Catechism wants to put down roots in our lives, and the authors of the Catechism are intending that the truths we find here will "shine forth" in our lives. This will happen if we read attentively, deepening our understanding of these truths, as God works to transform us through our understanding. And so we will find we are learning to make our lives faithful to God.

The second necessary adaptation is of *our teaching of the faith to those whom God sends to us* (24). Each person is unique, and so we have to assist each person to receive these same truths in a way unique to them so that their lives, also, can be fully "adapted" to the truths of the faith, according to who they are. Thus we will find we are learning to make our lives faithful to the souls God sends to us.

Finally, *everything is to be adapted to charity* (25). Charity, the love of God, is the eternal, unvarying measuring point to which we "adapt" everything in our lives and in our teaching. In our ongoing seeking to be faithful to God and to the human person, we will consciously and persistently seek to make visible the love of the Lord. In our lives and in our teaching, we are to strive to understand that intrinsic connection to God's love more and more deeply.

PART ONE
The Profession of Faith

CCC 26-30
Introduction and the Desire for God

So we begin the First Part of the Catechism. After an introductory paragraph outlining the structure of Section One in this First Part, these opening paragraphs remind us of our fundamental orientation to God. The human person is defined here as a *"religious being"* (italicized words and phrases often indicate the key point being made). The word "religion" is probably derived from the Latin "bond." We are to understand ourselves, therefore, in the light of the bond God has "written in the human heart." We are defined by our capacity for a relationship with the infinite, personal God who created us, the deepest truth about us being that we belong to God. Cross-references to CCC 27 explain that this is because we carry God's image (355); that we are made in the image of the eternal Son, the only One who can truly claim to be *the* Image of his Father (1701); and that we find our happiness in conforming our lives to this truth of who we are (1718).

These paragraphs go on to speak about how we revolt against this basic truth of our belonging to God, straining against the bond, fearful of an imaginary god we make in our own image, and also out of a fruitless desire to hide ourselves in our misery and sin. On top of this, we are confused and scandalized by our broken world, a world in which sin is deeply set — even in the lives of believers. But the bond remains. It is unbreakable, even when rejected by us. The call of God is unceasing. This drama of our troubled, deepest relationship is the context for all of the teaching in the Catechism which is to follow. And the introductory text prepares us for the rigors of the journey that lies before us, a journey that will demand "every effort of intellect," as well as a focused will and a firm heart.

DAY 12

CCC 31-35
Ways of Coming To Know God

The opening line of CCC 35 summarizes this section: *"Man's faculties make him capable of coming to a knowledge of the existence of a personal God."* From the world around us we can gain knowledge of a Creator God (32), and from a reflection on ourselves as persons we can realize that the Creator God must be personal, for a Creator cannot be less than his creation (33). God is always greater.

The Final Explanation for the universe must be able to "contain" in itself, and account for, all that is in the universe, or it is no explanation at all. Where does *beauty* come from? It can only be from the Beautiful One, as Augustine said (32). What is the source and origin of my *personal* being? It must be from an ultimate Being that is itself Personal. Where does my *moral sense* come from, my capacity for indignation at wrongdoing, my attraction towards the unselfish act? I cannot be morally superior to the Source and Explanation of my own being. All that is in an effect must be in its cause.

Moment by moment, all that is flows from a Personal Source who contains all Beauty and Goodness. As the Catechism rightly insists, any reflection on the world and ourselves must take us in this direction. How, in each concrete instance, this conviction of a personal God takes root in each of our lives the Catechism sees as emerging through a series of "converging and convincing arguments," a phrase from Cardinal John Henry Newman. A reading of a Gospel, the witness of Saint Teresa of Calcutta, a stunning sunset, the moment one knows the beloved must be immortal, a Church vibrating with the Real Presence in the reserved Host — all of these can make up, in a single life, the converging arguments that finally bring a person to "attain certainty" about this truth of God's existence. The evidence lies all around us, its configuration in each life unique.

CCC 36-38
The Knowledge of God According to the Church

Today's reading makes two complementary points. First, *God gives to each person the capacity to know of his existence and to know how to act well.* The Catechism emphasizes that we can come by our own understanding, by the "natural light of human reason" (36), to a certain knowledge of the existence of a personal God and, together with this, to the understanding of fundamental principles of what is good and of how to act (the "natural law"). It is this natural capacity that makes it possible for us to "welcome God's revelation" (36) — to look for his revealing of himself. God's revelation is a crowning of our natural capacities. If our nature did not have this capacity, how could God reveal himself to us?

Second, *the need for God's revelation of himself to us is made clear.* Revelation is needed because although we have this capacity, it is nonetheless challenging for us to reach this knowledge and to attain this certainty. In part, this is because we have to go beyond sensory knowledge to attain such truths, since God is spirit. We are capable of this, but it demands effort. The challenges in reaching these truths also lie in our disinclination to discover them: God's existence complicates my desire to govern my own life, to live as I wish, to pattern my life after my immediate desires. If God exists, if there are objective truths, then I must give up control. These truths call for "self-surrender." I must relinquish my kingdom.

God's revelation is of things beyond our natural understanding, of course, truths about himself that we would not have been able to attain without him revealing them to us; but he also, alongside such truths, confirms those things of which our natural understanding is capable — for example, in giving us the Ten Commandments. He strengthens our natural understanding so that we can know these truths "with ease, with firm certainty and with no admixture of error" (38).

CCC 39-43
How Can We Speak about God?

These paragraphs are intimately connected to those we read yesterday. Then we examined what we can *know* of God; today we review how we can *speak* of God. The Catechism emphasizes the unity of the acts of knowing and speaking: "In defending the ability of human reason to know God, the Church is expressing her confidence in the possibility of speaking about him" (39). We speak as we know.

The Catechism emphasizes that *our ability to speak of God is real, but very limited.* "Since our knowledge of God is limited, our language about him is equally so" (40). The foundation of this limited, but nonetheless real, knowledge and ability to speak of God lies in his creation. Created things are the work of his hands. We can reflect on all that lies around us, on his creatures, and reach up from them to their Creator, who must be more than his creatures. Since we know creatures exhibit beauty, for example, we can speak of God as the All-Beautiful.

What we mean by "the All-Beautiful God" lies beyond our full comprehension; there is always more to know about God. *The meaning of the words we use of God lies in proportion to the reality of who he is.* God is the perfection of all beauty, and this perfection corresponds to his being which is infinite. Thus we are speaking of an infinite, unlimited, unbounded Beauty. We can be confident that we have said something true here, that we are indeed speaking of his reality; yet we hardly know what we are saying.

It is no coincidence that the Catechism, having begun this chapter with the definition of the human person as a "religious being" (28), turns at the end of the first chapter to the language of worship, with a quotation from the Liturgy of Saint John Chrysostom. In the Liturgy we stand before the mystery and beauty of God, worshiping "the inexpressible, the incomprehensible, the invisible, the ungraspable" (42).

CCC 50-53
God Reveals His "Plan of Loving Goodness"

CCC 50 deserves special attention, for it introduces the whole of Chapter Two. If you leaf through this wonderful chapter you will see that it contains three articles: "The Revelation of God," "The Transmission of Divine Revelation," and "Sacred Scripture." CCC 50 explains that the whole chapter describes *"another order of knowledge."* Chapter One was concerned with the *natural* order of knowledge, with what we can know by using our senses, our imagination, and our powers of reasoning. Beyond this is the *supernatural* order, the "order of divine Revelation."

The order of revelation cannot be grasped by our natural powers, for it lies far beyond them. *Revelation exists because of God's free and loving decision to give himself to us, introducing us to his mystery.* In the case of human persons, we can only truly know others if they choose to reveal themselves; how much more this must be true in the case of divine Persons! God lies infinitely beyond us, yet he wants to introduce us into his own life. The Catechism employs the New Testament image of adoption here to remind us that this is an act of love lying far beyond what is natural (see 52).

The Catechism uses a beautiful word to describe this process of our introduction into his own divine life — "pedagogy," which literally means *leading the child.* As children are gradually introduced to the adult world, so we are introduced to the world of the divine Persons, with the capacity to take the steps being given to us at each new stage (53). God lovingly prepares us for this new life through what he does and says in the history of mankind, a history which culminates in the full gift of himself in the Person of Christ. In each of our lives, today, God follows this same path, leading us through his actions in our lives and speaking to us, so that we can share in the life of his Son.

CCC 54-64
The Stages of Revelation

As God the Father leads each one of us, gradually and in stages, by his "divine pedagogy" (53), so *he leads all the peoples* on the great platform of the world's history. Today's reading traces the major "stages" through which God leads human beings, as he prepares them to receive his full revelation of himself and the definitive act by which our salvation is won.

The *ultimate purpose of God's acts in history is to bring all peoples together into the unity of his kingdom.* The self-exile from God's care and solicitude at the beginning led to the shattering of human relationships, to disunity and mutual antagonism. Just as God calls each individual person to a life of integrity and wholeness under his grace, so he calls the whole human race into a unity of love after this shattering. The "stages" of which we read here all form part of this overarching plan.

The stages are marked by "covenants" — with Adam and Eve, with Noah, with Abraham, with the People of Israel under Moses, with David and his house — with God preparing people for "a new and everlasting Covenant intended for all, to be written on their hearts" (64).

More than simple agreements, these *covenants are God's pledges of his unwavering gift of himself and his love.* When they are broken from the human side, God renews them — "Again and again you offered a covenant to man" (55). God's plan for the salvation of humanity is thwarted by none of the disfigurements and distortions caused by human pride and sin.

Finally, *there are always some, in every age, who respond,* who understand something of God's plan, who keep alive the hope of salvation. The last paragraph in each section of today's reading (58, 61, 64) speaks of them, of the faithfulness of those who live, often in a hidden way, at the heart of history, responding to God's loving pedagogy.

CCC 65-67
Christ Jesus — "Mediator and Fullness of All Revelation"

God's plan has a center. It is a stage in the plan so decisive in its impact, so full in its implications, that all subsequent history is simply an unfolding of this supreme act. The beautiful quotation from the Carmelite saint, Saint John of the Cross, speaks of this stage in the plan as being like an immense gathering together: all the parts of God's plan, all the elements in his revelation, are brought together in one single Word — and the Word is a Person. The divine Person of God the Son appears in history to enact and seal the everlasting covenant, the final expression of God's faithfulness to his plan of salvation, and the everlastingly fruitful source of grace to bring all the peoples of the world into the happiness and unity of God's kingdom.

The whole of the Catechism can be seen as an extended meditation and teaching on this appearing of God among us, drawing together how the significance of this event has been grasped "over the course of the centuries" (66). While it is obvious that nothing further can be added to the very words and acts of God himself in human flesh, that this is the decisive point to which we return and the foundation of all meaning in history, CCC 67 writes of the value of what are called "private revelations." These do not add to the public "deposit of faith," but they can be helpful in assisting individuals in particular situations and periods of history.

CCC 74-79
The Apostolic Tradition

In his self-revelation, God appears *in* a particular place and *to* a particular people, *for all peoples*. He appears *in* a particular time, *for all times*. *God's revelation of himself, which is particular, unique, and contained in time and space, is for all times and places.* This next section of the Catechism explains how the precious deposit of faith is handed down in history, from one generation to the next, each one receiving and meditating upon the wonder of God's visiting his people. There are four main points today's reading makes:

- Because it is the transmission of *divine* revelation, it is necessarily *God's* own continuing work. This transmission to all peoples in all times is *the work of the Blessed Trinity themselves* (79).

- Because God has revealed himself in order to save us, *the transmission of this revelation is for the sake of the salvation of all peoples* (74). The purpose of this transmission is to bring all peoples together, in unity as children, around their divine Father.

- Because revelation is of God's personal nature, *the transmission of revelation is centered on persons,* those whom he personally called and sent (76-78). It is centered on the apostles and on their successors whom they in turn personally call and send.

- Because the divine Persons act by "*deeds and words* which are intrinsically bound up with each other" (53), the apostles transmit divine revelation in the same way, through their life and teaching, through the institutions they establish and their writings (76, 78). In the Church, the pedagogy of God is continued, with his revelation and gift of himself being transmitted from age to age in the words of the Holy Scriptures and in the living Tradition of the Church.

CCC 80-83
The Relationship between Tradition and Sacred Scripture

Christ promised to remain with his Church until the end of the age. Today's reading beautifully explains how Christ is *made present* in his Church and is handed down from generation to generation.

Every new generation receives Christ in a twofold way: from Tradition and from the Sacred Scriptures. The two are intimately connected, since the apostles, and those closely associated with them, not only committed the message of salvation to writing (83), but also handed on the message through their lives, their prayer and worship, and their teaching (see Acts 2:42) — through what is described here as "Apostolic Tradition."

Christ is *fruitfully* present in his Church *because of this combination of sacred words and holy acts.* Holy Scripture and Sacred Tradition are both handed down in the Church, from age to age, under the guidance and inspiration of the Holy Spirit, flowing from the witness of those who knew and touched and lived with Christ himself, in the flesh. We have already seen how the Catechism emphasizes that God's saving work is characterized by the union of words with deeds. This is the unwavering pattern of divine activity. The two come together perfectly in the Person of Christ, who is the Word made flesh. Thus we can rightly expect Christ to be present in his Church today in this dual way.

CCC 84-95
The Interpretation of the Heritage of Faith

We have been offered the beautiful image of Tradition and Scripture flowing together from a single source, intercommunicating with each other and making their way to the same goal. Their flow and communication are possible because of the banks that support and enable their movement. Without such necessary containment they would all too easily spill out and waste themselves. The importance of containment, which is, in truth, a service, is the topic of today's reading: the Church herself receives and hands on the great stream of the Sacred Deposit, and she does so under the authoritative guidance of the Magisterium (from Latin, *magister*, meaning "teacher"). The great dogmas of the faith are placed like marker-points in the flowing waters — or, as the Catechism puts it, "lights along the path of faith" (89), making the travel secure. These three — Scripture, Tradition, and Magisterium — belong together; they "are so connected and associated that one of them cannot stand without the others" (95).

This portion of the Catechism also deals with growth in understanding the faith (94), or what we might call the "development of doctrine." This is a matter of the Church making *explicit* things that were once just held *implicitly*. The deposit of faith was given once, for all, in its fullness, and the Church has always embraced this fullness and taught it as a whole. She has always grasped what the Catechism calls "the whole of the Revelation of the mystery of Christ" (90). But only gradually does the Bride of Christ make explicit her understanding of different elements in this fullness. The text refers us to Jesus' promise that the Spirit would guide the Church into all truth (Jn 16:13) — there is always "more truth" to discover. But Jesus also told his disciples that this would not be "new" truth — rather, the Spirit would be reminding the disciples of what Jesus had told them (Jn 14:26).

CCC 101-104
Christ — the Unique Word of Sacred Scripture

Having established that Scripture, Tradition, and the Magisterium belong together, supporting each other like the three legs of a single stool, the Catechism now moves on to provide us with the Church's understanding of the Scriptures.

The description of what the Scriptures are is a beautiful and moving one. Here we see God our Father wanting to speak to his children and accommodating himself to their language in order to do so. In eternity, God speaks just one Word; he says everything, all at once. This Word is Jesus, who is also everything that the Father wants to say *to us*. The Father speaks his divine Word to us, addressing us fully and completely, keeping nothing back.

God is not in time, so he holds all truth as a single Word. This is reflected in time in the multitude of words, syllables, phrases, and sentences that we find in the Scriptures. However, the Catechism says, quoting Saint Augustine, they are all part of the "one Utterance," the same single divine Word that is beyond time. All of the words and phrases we find in the Scriptures, then, in both the Old and the New Testament, point to him (see Jn 5:39-40; Lk 24:25-27).

We might think of it this way: sometimes we "just know" that something is true — we have the "whole truth" in our mind; but we still have to take time and care to patiently spell this out, for ourselves or for others. Considered another way: if I fall in love, I "just know" that this love is everything and forever, and that is what my marriage vows then make explicit; but there is still the day to day living out what that "whole truth" of love actually means. We are creatures who *live in time*, and so God spells out for us the "whole truth" of Christ over all of the pages of the Bible so that we can come to know him gradually, day by day.

CCC 105-108
Inspiration and Truth of Sacred Scripture

In today's reading we can find, first of all, a general truth about how God works with us, his creatures. God is described as the author of the Sacred Scriptures. *How* is he the author? He is so, in the first place, by his creation of *human* authors. The Christian writer George MacDonald put it like this: "Would God give us a drama? He makes a Shakespeare." God loves to involve us as full agents in his creative work.

God's authorship of the Sacred Scriptures must mean even more than this, though; otherwise every novel and poem would be on the same "level" as the Bible. In the case of the Scriptures, then, we find something more, something unique. The Catechism, following the Scriptures themselves (see 2 Tm 3:16; 2 Pt 1:19-21, 3:15-16), teaches that God "inspired" the human authors (106). Literally, the word means that he "breathed" into them. And in doing so, he does not make the human authors less human, as though they had to be robots to be used by him; rather, he makes "full use of their own faculties and powers" (106). When God works in our lives, he makes us *more*, not less, human. This is why we must study the Scriptures also as human documents, seeking to understand what the human authors intended to say in their writings.

Because the Scriptures are divinely inspired, in them we find whatever God wanted written, and no more, entirely free from error. We also find there *the truth needed for the sake of our salvation* (106-107). We find *that* kind of truth in the Scriptures — the truth that he needs to provide for us in order to save us; the truth that we need to hear and to receive in order to be able to respond to his loving invitation.

CCC 109-119
The Holy Spirit, Interpreter of Scripture

The Christian Tradition gives us a beautiful phrase for the way we read this unique book: "divine reading" (in Latin, *Lectio Divina*). Reading Scripture is always a divine reading, since "Sacred Scripture must be read and interpreted in the light of the same Spirit by whom it was written" (111). The Holy Spirit, who inspired the human authors to write the Father's saving truth for his children, also enlightens us to understand that truth. Without the Holy Spirit's assistance in interpreting the text, it remains a "dead letter."

The Spirit's interpretation builds on our human reading of the text. We use our natural faculties to try to understand what the human authors wanted to say. The many types of writing in the Bible — proverbs, poetry, codes of conduct, historical passages, prophecies, and so on — communicate truth in different ways.

Passages in Scripture always mean what the human authors meant to say. However, because God is *the* author of Scripture, passages can also mean *more* than this. The Scriptures — and the realities they convey — have a rich meaning within God's loving plan. They can have many "senses," or meanings: they can illuminate our *faith* in Christ and in God's plan; they can encourage us to greater *love*; and they can inspire us by supporting our *hope* (116-118). These three virtues are connected to the "allegorical," "moral," and "anagogical" meanings, as you can see. The Catechism asks us to be guided by three overarching principles of interpretation as the Spirit helps us discover this richer meaning:

- *the unity of Scripture:* the single loving mind and heart of God has inspired the whole text, so we can read different parts of Scripture in the light of other passages;
- *the unity between Scripture and Tradition:* Tradition shows us how the Church has interpreted the Scriptures through the centuries;
- *the analogy of faith:* the teachings of the Church across the ages are grounded in the Scriptures and cohere with each other (see also 89-90).

CCC 120-130
The Canon of Scripture

The center of the Holy Scriptures is unequivocally presented here: *the four Gospels*. Because Christ is the fullness of revelation and the center of God's saving plan, the Gospels that narrate his life and teachings, death, Resurrection, and sending of the Holy Spirit are the heart of the Holy Scriptures (125-127).

The Scriptures have a center; but this does not mean that the "edges" are unimportant or merely peripheral. All Scripture speaks of Christ — the New Testament in an obvious way, the Old Testament more subtly. It is by and from Christ's life and teachings, therefore, that the Church reads and interprets all of the Scriptures. Nothing is redundant. The Church uses "typology" to connect the Old Testament to the New; all of the realities in the Old Testament are images (or "types") of Christ, his redeeming work, and the Church (128-130). Thus the waters of creation point to the re-creating water of Baptism and the water that Christ turns into the wine of his new life, while David the Shepherd-King is an image, or "type," of Christ, and Jerusalem an image of his Church-Bride. Why does the Church read the Scriptures in this way? In answer, we remember the unity of God's plan, revealed across the centuries, in which his promises were fulfilled beyond expectation in the reality of his coming in the flesh. God reveals his plan gradually to us. The text uses the word "pedagogy" again (122) — God is leading us as his children who need to be introduced slowly into the full, glorious truth he wants to give us.

Having established the "Canon" of the inspired Scriptures, the Church has firmly resisted all attempts to add or remove any books. "Canon" means "rule" or "measuring point" — the Church used her ancient "rule of faith" to decide which writings constituted the inspired Scriptures (120). The books are listed here in detail since the full Canon, agreed upon around the year 400, is not accepted by all.

CCC 131-133
Sacred Scripture in the Life of the Church

As you read today's paragraphs, notice how many words in these brief paragraphs convey the sense of how *God's transforming power* is present in the Holy Scriptures. The Church "forcefully" (133) exhorts all of us to read the Scriptures regularly, precisely because of the "force and power" of those same Scriptures (131).

We are encouraged both to a *personal* reading of the Scriptures and to an attentiveness to hearing them read and explained to us in the *liturgy and sacraments and in catechesis*. We are being reminded that the Scriptures have been entrusted to the Church and that we are being invited into a reading and understanding of them that flows from our membership of the Body of Christ. It is as "children of the Church" (131) that we are fed with the inspired Scriptures.

We have already mentioned the *Scriptural Index* at the end of the Catechism. You may want to make it your practice, when reading a passage from the Scriptures, to turn to the Index and find the passage there, following the references found there to the paragraphs in the Catechism. For example, for Mark 1:1 you would go to CCC 422 and 515. In this way, you will find yourself being constantly referred to the way in which the Church has been "reading" the Holy Scriptures across the centuries, informing her prayer, her faith, and her life with this "pure and lasting fount of spiritual life" (131).

CCC 142-149
The Obedience of Faith

Let us begin with the title. Through the use of this simple biblical phrase, "The obedience of faith," we are gently steered beyond any thought that we should choose between faith and works. One who listens to the Lord is called to respond, to act (see Jas 1:22ff). Faith, if it is authentic, always seeks what the Catechism calls "embodiment" (144). It seeks to express itself, to "become flesh" (Jn 1:14).

Because of this, when the Catechism wishes to help us understand faith, it chooses to do so, not abstractly, but by presenting us with *living examples* — of saints from the Old and New Testaments and from the rich history of the Church. Here we find a great "cloud of witnesses" (Heb 12:1; see CCC 165) who help us to understand the nature of faith by the way they lived. Abraham and the Blessed Virgin are offered to us as the models of this faith.

The obedience of faith, therefore, involves our "whole being" (143). It entails both the *assent of the mind* and the *determined commitment of the will*. The mind assents to God as the supreme reality, as the firm foundation for our lives, while the will gladly embraces God as our supreme happiness.

The challenge of faith is that it seems too good to be true. Can we *really* trust that the bedrock of our lives is a heavenly Father who wills and can bring about our complete good if we place ourselves wholeheartedly into his hands — even if through sacrifice and suffering — since "with God nothing will be impossible" (Lk 1:37)? It is precisely this obedient faith that enabled Abraham to move towards the Promised Land and Mary to welcome the divine Savior into her life.

CCC 150-152
"I Know Whom I Have Believed"

We might think that faith primarily means believing in certain true propositions. This short section reminds us that *the truths of faith are ultimately about the divine Persons.* We believe in the Father, in Jesus the only-begotten Son, and in the Holy Spirit.

This is not as strange as it might sound. All beliefs *that* some*thing* is the case ultimately turn out to involve belief *in persons.* For example, let us say that I have a belief that honey is a healing substance. Ultimately, this belief rests on my own experience and that of many others, together with various tests that have been performed; and the veracity of such tests lies, in part, in the reliability and honesty of the persons conducting them and in the human powers of unbiased observation and reasoning.

We rely on such natural faith in persons countless times every day, though we are also aware of the weaknesses that can afflict any part of this chain of evidence, so that — as the Catechism says — it would be "futile and false" (150) to entrust ourselves absolutely to any human person. Ultimately, though, we believe in the whole "system" of evidence collection, and in the capacity of the mind to discover truth, and such a belief must point us to the ultimate personal ground of the universe — to the One who finally says, *"I am Truth. Believe Me."* All seeking must end in our finding the personal Being who is the Source of all truth-seeking and finding.

The whole Christian life, then, can be summed up as our daily walk of faith with each of the divine Persons. Notice how the Catechism describes the life of faith: it is only by sharing in the *Holy Spirit* that we are able to believe in *Jesus* (152), and only by faith in *Jesus* that we can come to the *Father* (151). Thus we are led to entrust ourselves "wholly to God" (150), the unshakeable bedrock of our lives.

CCC 153-165
The Characteristics of Faith

In this rich section, the Catechism places three essential points before us.

First, *faith is a divine gift* (153). It must be so, because God is so far beyond us. Just as God's revelation of himself is his gratuitous free act, so he lovingly cleanses our sight and gradually enlarges our heart so that we can respond in faith.

Second, *faith involves the full use of all our powers* (154-159). Faith is the *work* the Lord asks of us (see Jn 6:29), and it is work that stretches our mind and involves every ounce of will. There is immense satisfaction in this: just as physical exercise leaves us feeling tired but fitter, so the spiritual exercise of acting out of faith fittingly employs all of our natural powers of imagination and understanding, of desire and will. Through the exercise of the gift of faith, we experience God calling us forth and crowning all of the natural powers with which he created us.

Third, *the exercise of faith is necessary for salvation* (161-165). This is not an arbitrary requirement. The obedience of faith is our response to the Lord's gracious invitation to us to share in his divine life. It is to the happiness of an eternity of trusting love and self-gift, mirroring his own gift of Self, that we are invited — what Jesus conveys to us in the image of a *banquet* of fine food (see Lk 14:15-24). God will not force us to enter the banqueting hall or to eat. Through the work of faith, he teaches us to want and to have the taste for the rich fare he has prepared. But what of those who have never heard of this invitation? Will they be denied entrance? No, there is a way — the way of conscience (see 162 and the cross-reference there) — and the Catechism will look at this later. The heavenly Father gives every person a means of responding to his call.

CCC 166-169
"Lord, Look upon the Faith of Your Church"

Today's reading helps us to grasp a simple, but essential, distinction: faith is a *personal* act, but never an *individual* one.

It is *personal* in the sense that I must freely believe for myself; no one can believe for me. Only I can give my heart, my very self, to God, in response to his gift of himself to me. My heart is mine alone to give (see 160, and also 368 and 2563).

But the personal nature of faith must not lead us to think of ourselves as isolated in this act of self-gift. It is not as individuals cut off from others that we come to believe. On the contrary, *we are carried and supported by the faith of others.* The text speaks of how each of us is "a link in the great chain of believers" (166), echoing the famous words of Blessed John Henry Newman in one of his meditations written in 1848: "I am a link in a chain, a bond of connexion between persons." Or, as another great English believer put it, "No man is an island, entire of itself." Just as each of us receives life itself through others, and is then supported day by day by others in that life, so it is with faith — the new life of the soul is brought to birth in us through the Church, who then nourishes us and feeds us, raises us and educates us.

CCC 170-171
The Language of Faith

In CCC 170, the Catechism helps us to understand how to think about *the relationship between words about God and the reality of God himself.* What it says here is paralleled in CCC 2132 in a passage concerned with religious images. When we look at an image of Jesus — a painting, or a statue, for example — we do not adore the statue itself. The statue is not Jesus, but rather points us *to* Jesus. It *helps us* to adore him. Just so in the case of words: we do not believe in the words themselves, but in what they point us to. Like images, they help us to "approach" divine realities and also help us to "express" these realities. Words and images are both precious to us for this reason. But they are not to be mistaken for God himself.

CCC 171 reminds us of how we learn language, how we learn to speak and express ourselves. In their home, children hear language spoken and gradually learn to express themselves; they realize how to use phrases and which words refer to different objects around them. In God's adopted family, the Church — our spiritual mother — is the primary teacher of the "language of faith." The language she teaches us comes from Jesus himself; it is God's own language, expressed in human words. Received from Jesus by the apostles, this language of faith is now handed on to each new generation who are spiritually born in the waters of Baptism and raised in the household of the Church.

CCC 172-175
Only One Faith

This short group of paragraphs has immense importance. Three of the four paragraphs are taken from a single Church Father, Saint Irenaeus of Lyons, from his work *Against Heresies*, probably written around AD 180. Irenaeus could trace his spiritual lineage back to the first apostles — to Saint Polycarp and thence back to Saint John the Evangelist.

From the very birth of the Church, as we find in the teaching of those first apostles, the central proclamation was that God had worked in his beloved Son, Jesus, to *restore the unity* that had been lost since the world had preferred self to the loving will of the Father. Pentecost was the great event of the unleashing of the unifying power of the Holy Spirit so that the confusion reigning since Babel could be reversed and all could hear the one Gospel in their own language. Through the grace of the Holy Spirit, the diversity of languages and cultures was able to be united in a rich, single Tradition so that "the same way of salvation" (174) might be preached and received in all the nations.

The very opening paragraph of the Catechism, summing up the essence of the Gospel, makes this intention of God clear to us: through the sending of his Son and Spirit, the Father was calling together every person "scattered and divided by sin, into the unity of his family" (1). This was the Father's work from the beginning: "The gathering together of the People of God began at the moment when sin destroyed the communion of men with God" (761). The work reaches its culmination in the death and resurrection of Christ and the pouring out of the Holy Spirit. Now there is one "deposit of great price" (175) handed down through one unified Tradition "with a unanimous voice" (173), calling every person into the single home of the Church, to be united there with one heart and soul.

CCC 185-197
The Creeds

This short section is particularly important for helping us understand all that will follow in the rest of Part One of the Catechism, because here we have the introduction to the Creeds, and it is on the Apostles' Creed that the remainder of this part is built. If you glance ahead to CCC 199, 430, 456, and 571, you will see in each case that these paragraphs mark the beginning of "articles." There are twelve in all, corresponding to the twelve divisions of the Apostles' Creed. CCC 194 explains the origin of this Creed and that it is "rightly considered to be a faithful summary of the apostles' faith."

You will see that both the Apostles' Creed and the Nicene Creed, reproduced in the Catechism alongside today's paragraphs, are structured around the three Persons of the Trinity. When we profess our faith, we are professing faith in the Father and the Son and the Holy Spirit. The foundation of our faith is in the divine *Persons*. After that we profess our faith in their *acts*. The Persons make up the other main structuring principle of this part of the Catechism — it is divided into three chapters. You may find it helpful to spend a little time looking back over the contents pages for Part One and identifying the chapter and article headings.

This rich section explains the *character* of the Creeds. They are deliberate *summaries* of the faith — compact, memorizable syntheses needing unpacking and explaining. That is what the Catechism does for us here, in addition to showing that the elements in the Creed are *connected* — that they belong together. The word "article" derives from the Latin "*articulus*" — a joint or connecting part of the body. Notice how the Creeds are described in CCC 186 as "organic and articulated summaries" — they are summaries in which everything is linked together, making up a single whole. Finally, notice the emphasis placed on their immense *spiritual* importance: read CCC 197.

CCC 198-202
"I Believe in One God"

In Lewis Carroll's *Alice in Wonderland*, the King explains to Alice how to tell a story: "'Begin at the beginning',,the King said, very gravely, 'and go on till you come to the end: then stop.'" The Creed tells the story in just this way. It begins at the beginning, and the beginning is God; everything else flows from this. Notice that the same is said of the commandments: every commandment is an unpacking of the first one (see CCC 2083).

At the beginning, then, we find God. We also find his *oneness*. The remainder of today's reading is concerned with this. First, the importance of this element of our faith is emphasized — believing in God's oneness is "equally fundamental" (200) to believing in his existence. Why? The answer is given in the following paragraphs which present the two meanings of "one" God.

- "God is one" means that he is the *only* one (201). God has no rival; he is the "one and only God." Because there is only one God, our lives belong entirely to him. We owe him everything. We do not divide our loyalties.

- "God is one" means that there is *no division* in him (202). We believe in three Persons — the Father, Son, and Holy Spirit — but that does not mean we have divided God into three parts and shared him among the three. In the case of human beings, we all share in the one human nature; none of us possesses human nature in its entirety. But each divine Person possesses the whole of the divine nature fully. The word in the Tradition which expresses this is the final word in our section — God is entirely *simple* — from the Latin *simplus*, meaning undivided, not made up of parts. In the created order we find qualities separated out — wisdom, love, beauty. But in God they are one — God's wisdom is always loving and always beautiful because he is one.

DAY
34

CCC 203-213
God Reveals His Name

When we wish to know another person, we ask his or her name. To give one's name is to allow for friendship and intimacy. *Because God wants to be known by us, he gives us his name.* Because he is infinitely beyond us, his name is necessarily deeply mysterious, but it nevertheless allows us to know him in his unchanging majesty.

Out of reverence for the divine Name, it was replaced by the word "Lord" in the Jewish reading of the Scriptures, and so "Lord" came to signify God's name (209). "Jesus is Lord," therefore, became the way in which the first Christians expressed their faith in Jesus' divinity (see Rom 10:9; Phil 2:11).

The Catechism gives us the literal rendering of the Tetragrammaton (206) and helps us see what this implies for our understanding of God.

First, we understand that *he is faithful through time.* He is the one who keeps his promises, who has remained steadfast in the past, who is present to us now and will be in the future. He is unshakably faithful (205, 207).

Second, we understand that *this faithfulness remains even in the face of our sin and the death it deserves* (210-211). Jesus reveals that, precisely as the one who bears our sins (see Jn 1:29; Mt 26:28), he is the bearer of the divine Name (Jn 8:28, 58), and is accused of blasphemy for this claim (Jn 8:59; Mk 14:62-64).

Third, we understand that *God is eternal and unchanging* (212-213). God is "beyond space and time" (205). As we have seen, he is entirely simple. He contains in himself all Being. All creatures are some-thing — they have a nature and a share in existence. God, on the other hand, is utterly beyond all created reality. As the Uncreated, he simply IS — without beginning or end — the fullness of Being.

CCC 214-221
God, *"HE WHO IS,"* Is Truth and Love

The name of God, "HE WHO IS," is now explained as being able to be expressed "summarily" (214) as Truth and Love. These two terms sum up who God is. They are explained separately, but the Catechism makes clear that they are inseparable in God. God is *truthful love*; he is *loving truthfulness.* What is finally *true* about God is that he is *love* (221).

When we look at the world God created, and at his revelation of himself, this notion of truthful love is the interpretative key we can always rightly use, because everything in creation and in revelation is an expression of who God is.

God's loving *truthfulness* is explained in CCC 215-217. It means that we can always trust that God means and will do what he says; we should never doubt him (215). It means he made the world to be *known* by us, and for us to come to know *him* by this world — "for from the greatness and beauty of created things comes a corresponding perception of their Creator" (Wis 13:5). It means, finally, that he will lead us to understand who he is by sending his Son (216-217).

God's truthful *love* is explained in CCC 218-221. It means that God's choices are *always* and *only* the result of his love (218). It means that all earthly loves, however powerful or insistent, are only a *shadow* of his love. If we really want to understand his love, we must learn it from *the most precious gift* he has offered us, his only Son (219). Finally, his love is the *unmovable reality* in which each of us is called to *share* (220-221).

CCC 222-227
The Implications of Faith in One God

Faith must be connected to life. What we believe must have consequences for our lives. If we do not live according to our beliefs, we cease to believe. Beliefs must be acted upon, or they wither. Beliefs take root and flourish only in the rich soil of our everyday choices, responses, and actions.

The Catechism makes this point the key to how we are to read it. We can recall that in CCC 18 we were given practical directions for reading the Catechism, and the single element highlighted there was to read *across* the Catechism, following the cross-references. This is because the cross-references link our beliefs together and link them also to our life, to our prayer and to our celebration of the sacraments. The cross-references show us the *significance* of our beliefs, helping us to take seriously their *implications*.

Often, as it does here, the Catechism will pause in its presentation of a doctrine in order to explore the implications of a belief. When it does this, the Catechism usually takes us to the life and sayings of a *saint*, because a saint is someone who did exactly this, who *lived out* the implications of faith. Look out for this feature in the Catechism — for example, you will find it at the end of the presentation on the Trinity (260), on that of God's almightiness (274), of God as creator (313), and so on.

Spend time prayerfully with today's text, pondering how believing "in God, the only One, and loving him with all our being has enormous consequences for our whole life" (222).

CCC 232-237
"In the Name of the Father and of the Son and of the Holy Spirit"

The title of today's reading — the formula we recite when we make the Sign of the Cross — reminds us that the *deepest mystery* of the Christian faith is also the *most common* profession of faith that we make, and also that this most common profession of faith is the most profound *entry into prayer* that we have.

In the Sign of the Cross, all that is most profound in the Christian faith is translated into the simplest of all actions. This action is made over us at the *very beginning* of the Christian life, at Baptism (232), and so marks our entire life. It is thereafter the entry point into *every* encounter God wishes to have with us in his sacraments.

Through the wording of the formula, we express the profound truth that God is both One and Three, for we speak of three Persons with a single Name (233). This truth is the *central mystery* of our *faith* and of the Christian *life* (234), and we show its centrality for our lives by making the Sign over the *body*. Our actions, as well as our prayers and beliefs, are placed under the governing protection of the Blessed Trinity. It is he, Father, Son, and Holy Spirit, whom we ask to direct our ways.

The movement of the hand as it traces the Sign of the Cross over the body reveals to us not only the innermost mystery of the Blessed Trinity (the *theologia*) but also the economy (the *oikonomia*) of the Three-in-One (236). "Economy" is the term given to the loving plan of God (235-236). The descending hand evokes the sending of the Son from the Father, and then the tracing of the Sign of the Cross is completed — the costly work of our redemption — with the movement of the hand to the shoulders also expressing the sending of the Holy Spirit to strengthen and seal the work of Christ.

CCC 238-248
The Revelation of God as Trinity

The final paragraph in yesterday's reading explained the term "mystery of faith" (237), and this understanding underpins all that we discover today. When the Church uses the term "mystery," she does not mean to signify a puzzle that is unclear. "Mystery" signifies, rather, the *truth* that God and his ways are utterly beyond us, are "hidden." Mysteries "can never be known unless they are revealed by God" (237). The Blessed Trinity is the greatest of all mysteries.

The term mystery proclaims both the *transcendent* nature of God — that he is beyond us — and God's *personal* nature. God's mystery can be *revealed*, but only in a *free relationship* with us, a relationship of trust and faith into which we must choose to enter.

Today's paragraphs are concerned with that gracious revelation of himself. They explain that the divine Persons do not reveal themselves, but rather each reveals the other. A beautiful "giving way" characterizes God's revelation. The *Son* introduces us to the *Father* (238-241), while the *Holy Spirit* reveals the *Son* and his *relationship with the Father* (243-248). The Holy Spirit is sent to guide us into the whole truth about God, completing the revelation of the life of God (243).

Only One who is God can reveal God to us. We can *trust* Jesus' revelation of the Father because Jesus is God (242); and we can *trust* the revelation given by the Holy Spirit because the Spirit is God (245).

The detailed account of this revelation in the Catechism may surprise us, but it is vital for us to appreciate, because the Son invites us to share in *his* relationship to the Father — we are to be adopted as children in the Son. Jesus wants to introduce us to "*my* Father and *your* Father" (Jn 20:17). Jesus has come to show us the face of the Father, to show us what his relationship is with the Father, so that we may enter into this same relationship (Jn 14:1-14).

CCC 249-256
The Holy Trinity in the Teaching of the Faith

That which is *most precious* is what we *love* with the most passion and seek to *guard* the most closely. The faith of the Church in the Blessed Trinity underpins the whole of the Christian life. Nothing is more important.

This sense of having been entrusted with a priceless jewel is beautifully expressed in the quotation from Saint Gregory of Nazianzus cited in CCC 256. Saint Gregory "lives and fights" for this belief. It is his beloved "companion" whose dear company enables him to "bear all evils and despise all pleasures." This apt quotation explains why so many councils of the Church appear in the footnotes to today's passage. The bishops, gathered together, wanted to deepen their own understanding of this mystery and to defend it against error (250).

The question was, in part, how to do justice in language to the greatest of all mysteries which God had so graciously revealed. A *renewed language* was needed, and from this new language of the faith, as Christianity spread, a *renewed culture* took shape which expressed the central truths of the Holy Trinity. The terms "person," "substance," and "relation" took on new meanings as they were used in service of God's revelation (251).

In today's reading, the *meaning* of each of these central terms is, first of all, helpfully explained (252), and then a paragraph *unpacking* each of the terms is presented (253-255):

- *Substance* designates the Oneness of God and that each of the Persons is truly God.
- *Person* (Greek: *hypostasis*) designates the fact that Father, Son, and Holy Spirit really *are* distinct in God. It is not just that there are three human "ways" of looking at God.
- *Relation* explains that the distinctions between the Persons lie *solely* in their relation each to the other.

CCC 257-260
The Divine Works and the Trinitarian Missions

We have seen that the Creeds are typically structured according to the divine economy, the divine plan. This plan is normally presented as having *three main parts* — creation, redemption, and sanctification (235). These three great works are then, in turn, associated with one of the divine Persons in particular. Thus the work of creation flows from the Father, redemption from the Son, and sanctification from the Holy Spirit. Such a presentation records *the order in which the Persons were revealed* (238-248).

Today's reading reminds us that because there is only One God, the whole divine plan is in fact the *common work* of the three divine Persons (258). Creation, redemption, and sanctification all flow from the Father and are unfolded in the "missions" of the Son and the Holy Spirit, with each Person contributing to this loving plan of God according to what is "proper" to each (258-259).

What is this "common work" to which each Person contributes in a perfect union of love? The answer is given in a wonderful statement at the heart of today's reading: "the whole Christian life is a communion with each of the divine persons, without in any way separating them" (259). The vision with which we are presented is that of a daily walk with each of the Persons, coming to know, to love, and to trust them more and more deeply. The whole Christian life, then, consists in the overflowing grace of the Father, the Son, and the Holy Spirit, each of whom is working to make in us their dwelling place on earth so that they might finally dwell in us as in heaven, *forever* (260).

CCC 268-274
The Almighty

The importance of this core belief in God's almightiness is stressed in the opening sentence. The Catechism draws our attention to the fact that this is the only attribute of God that we profess in the Creed. The final paragraph of this short section returns to this theme of the vital significance of this belief — once we believe this, all other beliefs follow easily (274).

Is it so difficult, then, to believe in an *almighty* God? No; this follows naturally from the accompanying belief that he is the Creator of all things from nothing (269). But what is more challenging — and *life-changing* — is to believe in an almighty *Father*, to believe in the all-powerful *love* of God; and that is what we profess in the Creed. We believe in God the *Father* almighty (270). God's might is entirely fatherly.

His might is therefore *mysterious* to us, for we look for it in the wrong places. Like Elijah, we look for God in the earthquake, while he is to be found finally in the still voice (1 Kgs 19:9-13). The Catechism takes us to where the almighty love of the Father is most fully revealed: in the Incarnation, where God the Son comes among us as a little child, and then in "the voluntary humiliation and Resurrection of his Son, by which he conquered evil" (272). The heart of the Father is *almighty in love*, and nothing can overcome him in this. It appears to be weak, but in fact nothing is stronger. The Catechism reminds us to look to the saints, who knew this, and especially to the Blessed Virgin who, in embracing the Child Christ, embraced the truth of God's power being made perfect in weakness (273; also see the scripture references to which this paragraph of the Catechism takes us).

CCC 279-281
The Creator

Today we begin a major new theme in the Catechism, that of God as Creator. It is a theme that, in one aspect or another, will take us right up until the end of the first chapter in the Catechism (up to CCC 412).

These introductory paragraphs present us with what seems like a paradox. On the one hand, creation concerns the *beginning* of all things. The Bible *opens* with the account of the creation of heaven and earth. Creation is what comes *first* (279); creation is the *foundation* on which God builds his saving plan (280).

But then the Catechism reveals that there is, in fact, something that comes even *before* creation, something even *more* foundational. Creation itself is founded on *the mystery of Christ*: the Father creates all things through and for his beloved Son. For, ultimately, "no other foundation can anyone lay than that which is laid, which is Jesus Christ" (1 Cor 3:11). We understand what God *created* in "the beginning" only if we search for the purpose of creation in what is *uncreated*: the love of God that has no beginning. In the eternity of the Father's loving will, creation was destined for glory in Christ (280).

The Catechism points us to the Scriptures and to the liturgy to learn these things, to Saint Paul who wrote of the glory awaiting the whole of creation (Rom 8:18), and, above all, to the central liturgy of the Church, the *Easter Vigil*. There, in the darkness and stillness of the night as the Church awaits the burst of the new life of Jesus' resurrection, the beauty of God's plan is unfolded for us in the readings that lead us from the first creation and garden to the re-creation of all things in Christ and the garden of the Resurrection. The seven days of creation are crowned with the "eighth day," the eternal day of Christ's victory (281).

CCC 282-289
Catechesis on Creation

God speaks to *every* person, *every* day; every day "pours forth speech" from God (Ps 19:2). The mercies of the Lord are "new every morning" (Lam 3:22). God speaks to us in the creation around us; this is where *every person* can go to listen to God, as attested to in the opening words of the Bible. There we have a magnificent series of acclamations — "God *said* ... " and the clear realities of light, earth, sun and moon, stars, trees, animals — and finally man himself — appear in their goodness (see Gn 1).

These words from God can raise in us the most *basic* questions of all, as the realities of creation force us to consider the source and meaning of our own existence (282-284). Saint Augustine says in his *Confessions*, "I have become a question to myself." As the Catechism illustrates, the question concerning the "truth about creation is so important for all of human life" (287) that it has given rise to many different philosophies and attempted answers (285). And so God has provided *another book* to be read alongside the "book of nature," the "book" of his revelation in Tradition and Scripture. This book provides a *trustworthy interpretation* of the "words" we find in nature. The two books must be read together (288).

Many *scriptural passages* on the subject of creation appear, therefore, in the footnotes of today's reading. The Catechism reminds us of the *principles for interpreting the Scriptures* that it has already presented in CCC 109-119. Notice in particular the clear assistance given to us in CCC 289 on how to interpret the *first three chapters of Genesis* (the Catechism will return to this point in CCC 390). These chapters are "uniquely important" and "remain the principal source" for teaching on creation since they express certain key truths about creation: (i) its origin and end in God; (ii) its order and goodness; (iii) the vocation of man; and (iv) the drama of sin and hope of salvation.

CCC 290-292
Creation — Work of the Holy Trinity

We are *radically* dependent on God. Every breath of air we draw into our lungs is *given to us* by God in his unceasing love, moment by moment. Every part of creation we see around us — the children playing in the street, the clouds above us, the humming bird outside of the window — is *held in being*, second by second, by God in his faithfulness.

The crucial point to which the Catechism draws our attention here is the thoroughgoing difference between God and his creation. The word "create," it notes, is only ever used in relation to God. *God's relationship to us* is one of *creating*. *Our relationship to other things*, on the other hand, is always one of *making*. We do not "create" anything, but rather "make" things from that which God creates. God is *eternal*. Unlike God, every created thing at some point *began to be*.

How are we to think of this absolute dependency? The medieval English mystic Julian of Norwich recorded in her *Revelations of Divine Love* a vision of the whole of creation as being like a small acorn lying in the palm of her hand: "I marveled how it might last, for I thought it might suddenly have fallen to nothing for littleness. And I was answered in my understanding: It lasts and ever shall, for God loves it." The Catechism draws on a similar image here, taken from Saint Irenaeus of Lyons: the Father creates and holds all things in existence in his two hands, the Son and the Spirit (292). We are held and loved every moment by the Father who creates and "holds us together" by his beloved Son and pours out upon us every good thing in his Holy Spirit (291).

CCC 293-294
"The World Was Created for the Glory of God"

These wonderful paragraphs *dispel the misunderstanding* that is so prevalent, the idea that creatures can be of benefit to God, that God can gain from us.

That the world is made for God's glory *cannot* mean that it increases his glory, for he *is* the *fullness* of *every* perfection and good: "And from his fullness have we all received, grace upon grace" (Jn 1:16). Our goodness adds *nothing* to God. Our praise *cannot* be useful to *him*.

What, then, is the "glory of God"? It is the "manifestation and communication of his goodness" (294). God, who is All-Good, wills to share his goodness. Our goodness, our love, and our praise, then, do not *benefit* God. But they are *important* to him because *we* are important to him. God longs to draw us to himself, nurturing our virtue and goodness; he longs for the beauty around us, and his own perfect beauty, to awaken our praise because *he wants our happiness.* He wants us to be "fully alive" (294). Jesus said, "I have come that they may have life, and have it abundantly" (Jn 10:10). The world was created so that it might point us to this abundance, through the natural glories around us and finally through being the home for the Incarnate Son who came to bestow his grace on us. The Father longs for us, to make us able to participate in every way in what he has to give — *himself.* This is why God creates, so that he can fill creation with his goodness and so draw us to himself, to become "all in all" (294).

CCC 295-301
The Mystery of Creation

This section of the Catechism wants us to see that creation is a *mystery*: it is luminous with a *spiritual, personal presence*. It is not a flat, self-subsisting intricate mechanism, but has depth and carries meaning.

The Catechism speaks of creation being "addressed" to us (299), like a letter. And because God creates everything out of love (295), it is a *love letter*. Saint Augustine described creation as the ring given by the Beloved. Whenever we see creation, we also "see" the love of God. God did not *have* to write this letter or give us this ring. He *chose* to, because he loves us. And he needed no help to do so — it is a pure expression of who he is. Everything in it comes directly from him (296).

We can read the letter because, although we are creatures, he has made us in his image, with a share "in the light of the divine intellect" (299). When God wrote us the letter, he knew he would also need to teach us to read it, for it would be indecipherable otherwise, a mere jumble of symbols. But God has given us the ability to rise to a unified intellectual understanding of his world. In his poem "Frost at Midnight," Samuel Coleridge beautifully expresses the hope that his sleeping child will come to be able to understand the language of God:

> … so shalt thou see and hear
> The lovely shapes and sounds intelligible
> Of that eternal language, which thy God
> Utters, who from eternity doth teach
> Himself in all, and all things in himself.
> Great universal Teacher! he shall mould
> Thy spirit, and by giving make it ask.

In the end, even love letters are not enough. The divine Lover and Letter-writer himself comes and finds us in the midst of his works. The letters are only meant to prepare us for that. But that is the topic of Chapter Two of this first Part of the Catechism (422).

CCC 302-314
God Carries Out His Plan: Divine Providence

Today's reading can give us great confidence. "Providence" refers to God's plan and ability to bring us to the happiness for which he has created us. "He who calls you is faithful, and he will do it" (1 Thes 5:24).

God might, of course, simply have placed us in a position of perfection from the beginning (310); he might have planned to bring us to this state by himself, without involving us. But what shows his delicacy and utter respect for us is that he will bring us to everlasting joy only in, through, and with our free collaboration (306-307). He will never force us to be happy. But he has promised to give us everything we need to reach happiness (308).

The cooperation he seeks from us is simply our "childlike abandonment" (305) to his providence. This abandonment asks us to move forward, not because we always see the way ourselves, but because we trust the Father. The Scriptures were given to educate us in this trust (304).

If the way were easy there would be no need for trust. But as we know, trust is needed every day in the face of the evil and suffering which lies all around us in a world terribly disfigured by sin. The lure of compromise and the temptation to despair are always present. What enables us to patiently resist both of these dead ends is the conviction that in *every* situation God never for a moment abandons us. Nothing falls outside of his providence, or his ability to use all that happens to draw every person into the happiness to which he has called us (311). The central event of our faith demonstrates this. There we see the greatest of all evils — the murder of the Father's beloved Son. There, in the midst of this sin, Christ *bore* all, *forgave* all, and *triumphed* over death, bringing us "the greatest of goods" (312).

CCC 325-327
Heaven and Earth

These paragraphs introduce us to the two "orders" of creation — the invisible world of the angels (328-336) and the visible world (337-349).

Both orders of creation are equally real. Because reality received through the senses is so important for us, we have a natural tendency to measure reality by what we can feel and see and touch. And precisely because of that, God came to show himself to us in a way that accommodated the senses. The apostle John cries out in wonder and delight, "We have *seen* with our eyes ... *touched* with our hands" (1 Jn 1:1). God the Son lovingly came among us in the full reality of visible creation. But the visible is not an end in itself, or the final word in reality. Rather, it is given in order to lead us to the invisible. The visible world is a great sign, pointing us on to the greater reality of what is spiritual. In the case of Jesus himself, the Catechism will explain that "what was visible in his earthly life leads to the invisible mystery of his divine sonship" (515).

As human beings, we live in both worlds — the angelic, invisible world and the corporeal, visible world (327). Our nature is made up of both orders. In the Church's Tradition a term given to this understanding is that *the human person is a "microcosm,"* a small world, because in our nature we sum up all the levels and types of being — we share intelligence with the angels, the life of the senses and the capacity for movement with animals, simple life with the plant kingdom, and existence itself with all that is inanimate. When the Son of God took human nature to himself, he thereby embraced the whole of creation in that nature. In his redemption of our nature, he restored the whole world (see Eph 1:9-10).

CCC 328-336
The Angels

This beautiful text takes us through *the ways in which angels appear in the three main periods of salvation history,* using a structure frequently used in the Catechism because it corresponds to the revelation of the Persons of the Trinity. The *first* period — when the Father is revealed, but the Son and Spirit are more hidden — is the time before Christ. It is described as the time of the Old Covenant, or Old Testament, or of "the promises" (since the Son, who fulfills all the promises of God, has not yet come). The *second* period is that of the Son, when he takes on flesh and dwells among us. It is often called the period when time was fulfilled, the time of the New Covenant. The *third* period is our own, in which the Spirit is fully revealed. It is the age of the Church, or the "end times."

You will see that this section on the angels follows this basic structure. After explaining who angels are (328-330), we have teaching on angels in the time of the Old Testament (332), then the New Testament (333), and then the time of the Church (334-336). You will find this structure is used often to help us into *God's way of looking at things* – by learning about different aspects of the faith in this way, we follow *his* timing of how he reveals himself and his plan of love.

One other point you will have noticed in this teaching on angels is that they are always to be understood *in relation to Christ* (331). The Church's teaching, we remember, "speaks of God, and when it also speaks of man and of the world *it does so in relation to God*" (199). We are not so much learning about angels, as about *God's* angels, *Christ's* angels. CCC 331 makes this explicit: angels can be understood *only* in relation to him. *We*, also, can be understood only in relation to him, as we shall see.

CCC 337-349
The Visible World

This passage helps us to understand the opening chapter of the Book of Genesis with its account of the seven "days." The passage is to be read *symbolically*, not literally. Truths can be taught in many ways, and the passage is rich with truths "revealed by God for our salvation" (337).

The truths are divided into three: first, those associated with the account of the six days (338-344), each given to us in an italicized phrase; then the truths concerned with the seventh day, the day of God's rest (345-348); finally, a paragraph on the eighth day — a day not included in the Genesis account, but a new day, towards which the original week is pointed, the day of the new creation and the fulfillment of all that God intended (349).

The seven days belong together. They are described as unfolding in interdependence, solidarity, and harmony, and in a "hierarchy" (342), which literally means a "sacred order." It is a sacred order of *value*, moving from the inanimate to those creatures that have life; then to creatures that experience their own life, have emotion, movement, and sensation; and finally to the human person in whom the spiritual order is united to the visible order. On the seventh day, the divine Author of this order is formally acknowledged and worshiped.

The New Testament is the great account of the appearance of the *eighth day*, which is the fulfillment of the old order, the perfecting of its goodness (339, 349). And so the first chapter of John's Gospel is presented as a series of *seven new days*, with the wedding at Cana appearing on the *eighth* day. Jesus comes as a bridegroom to win his bride. After the Resurrection is the period of espousal (see 1617), a period that is to find its fulfillment in the marriage feast of heaven.

CCC 355-361
Man: "In the Image of God"

We now begin a rich set of teachings on the human person, the creature who is at once "distinguished" from all other creatures (343) and who is "unique" among them precisely because he *sums up* and *unifies* in his own person the whole of creation (327).

There are *four fundamental relations* that make up the human person, and these are introduced in CCC 355 and form the heart of the presentation that follows. They are: our relation to God; the relation we have in ourselves between soul and body; our relations to other human persons; and the relation we have to the rest of visible creation. It is the fact of these four relations that make the human person unique.

The great worth of the human person depends entirely upon his *primary relationship*, which is to God, his Father and Creator, in whose image and likeness he is made (356). It is this primary relationship that gives us our dignity and our basic identity. We call human beings "persons" because they are made in the image of the divine Persons (historically, the term was applied to human beings only because of this conviction). *Our nature is God-like* because God intends that we share his eternal life (356). Because we are God-like, each person is "capable of self-knowledge, of self-possession and of freely giving himself and entering into communion with other persons" (357).

There is a radical *equality* between all people because of their being made in God's image. Parents and their children stand together to say "*Our* Father." All are "truly brethren" (361), forming a unity (360) in Adam, and in Christ who came to share our nature (359).

CCC 362-368
Man: "Body and Soul but Truly One"

You will have noticed the very careful way in which this is written. We are *embodied souls* — that is, souls who have bodies. Soul and body *together* make up the *whole* human being (359). So close is the relationship between soul and body that we are a *single unified nature* (365).

Yet there is a *hierarchy of value* here, too. "Soul" refers to that which is "of greatest value," the spiritual principle (363, see also 2289). We are "most especially" (363) in God's image because of the soul. In fact, the soul is so *centrally* who we are that the term is also used to refer to the whole person. Because of our being a spiritual soul, every human being is literally a "new creation" coming straight from the hand of God. The human soul is not "made" by creatures. Only God can make a soul (366).

We do not neglect the body, though. The body shares in human dignity precisely *because* it is united to the soul. In fact, the body is a *temple*, because we worship God in the body (remember CCC 28). *We* are the place where God is worshiped (see 1179, 1695, 2794), and physical churches remind us of this (1180). Temples are sacred places and are treated with loving reverence, and the Catechism will draw many implications from this point (for example, 2297-2298, 2300).

Finally, just as churches have a center, the altar, so human beings also have a center, the *heart* (368). As in a church, the new covenant — Christ's sacrifice that saves us — is made present on the altar for us, so for each of us personally, that covenant is renewed in the heart (see 2563).

CCC 369-373
Man: "Male and Female He Created Them"

God created us for communion, not only with himself, but also with other human persons. We have been created to *need* others and also to *need to give ourselves* in love and service to others. Our lives are not self-sufficient and closed in on ourselves. They are turned *outwards* towards others. The phrase the Catechism uses is that God created us to be a "communion of persons" (372).

It is because we are made in God's image that we have this call to receive and give ourselves to others as the very heart of our nature, since God himself, as we have seen, lives as a communion of divine Persons in an eternity of loving self-gift (255, see also 1702). From God's love flows *life*; love and life are united in him. Male and female mirror this as well, as new life is transmitted through their loving union (372). Just as the divine Persons are *equal* (242, 245), so also are male and female human persons made in his image (369). And just as the divine Persons are *distinct*, and their distinction lies in their *relation* to each other (254-255), so this, too, is mirrored on the level of creatures. The distinction between male and female is real and is willed by God as something good (369), and the distinction lies in the way in which male and female can be "for" the other, each a "helper" fitted for the other and finding fulfillment in this (371-372).

Finally, this section speaks of the *fourth relation* that makes up our nature — that of dominion over the earth. This is described as a sharing in God's providence (373) — in other words, being intelligent cooperators in God's plan of love for his creation.

CCC 374-379
Man: In Paradise

We are presented in today's reading with the picture of the world when it was "very good" (Gn 1:31). It is a world of happiness, without death, without suffering, of friendship with God, inner integrity, a loving and fruitful relationship between man and woman and the enjoyment of a harmonious relationship with creation. As the Catechism says, "This entire harmony ... will be lost by the sin of our first parents" (379).

For man in paradise, each of the four fundamental relations is unharmed; "all dimensions of man's life were confirmed" (376). The two phrases that the Church uses to describe this state are *original holiness* and *original justice*. The first describes the friendship between God and man before the first sin ruptured this. The second describes the harmonious state of the other three relations, where all is in order as it is meant to be. CCC 377 speaks of original justice as a "mastery over the world" and notes that by this "world" God meant especially over *oneself*. The Church, you will remember, sees the human person as being like a "little world," a microcosm. *This* is the domain over which we are given the challenge of kingship or queenship, and we establish our rule precisely by putting ourselves under the greater rule of God, the only Lord and King.

You will have noticed, then, that *original justice depends entirely on original holiness*. It is precisely by the "radiance of this grace" that "all dimensions of man's life were confirmed" (376). To love the Lord our God is the greatest and the first of the commandments (see Mt 22:37-40). The others "make explicit the response of love that man is called to give to his God" (2083). Because man's happiness depends entirely on his friendship with God, it is the restoration of this alone that can mend his brokenness. What could not be guessed was that the restoration would involve a *surpassing* of the original state of paradise (374).

CCC 385
The Fall

Today's reading is unusually short — a single paragraph. Its importance for all that will follow in the Catechism's proclamation and explanation of the faith, however, justifies our spending all our attention on this today. As so often in the Catechism, this is an *introductory paragraph* to lead into a major section of doctrine (for example, 199, 268): CCC 385 is a *summary of key points* to help us understand the Church's teaching on the Fall.

The paragraph begins with the reminder of the *infinite goodness of God* and of the *essential goodness of all his creation*. Everything that is, *without exception*, is fundamentally good (299) since all that exists has no other source of its existence than God, who is goodness and love without end (293, 296). Even though the world is fallen from the state God had intended for it, this is still the case.

The second point in this paragraph is the *inescapable experience of suffering and of moral evil*. This seems to contradict the opening sentence. Yet the Catechism shows us that the opposite is the case, and gives us the example of Saint Augustine wrestling with this question in his autobiographical book, *Confessions*. Evil throws us into the arms of the God of love since we know that by naming evil we are measuring it against the good. Without knowledge of the good how could we even identify an action as evil? Without a straight line how could we judge something to be crooked?

Thus we reach the third point — that *only in the light of the good is evil seen for what it is*; only in the light of "the mystery of our religion" is the "mystery of lawlessness" seen for what it is (385). We only see in the light. Darkness shows us nothing. We find the response to evil, therefore, only in the light of the revelation of divine love. We fix our eyes on Christ, the King of Love.

CCC 386-390
"Where Sin Abounded, Grace Abounded All the More"

Today's reading follows closely on the point we saw being made in CCC 385. We saw there that *only goodness reveals evil* since goodness is the measuring point against which we make the judgment that something is bad. We know when a plant is sickly only because we know what a healthy plant looks like. And so it is seeing man in relation to God, who is infinitely good, that "unmasks" evil (386).

When God's revelation is ignored or denied, therefore, there is no point of measurement left and "we cannot recognize sin clearly" (387). This is why, as Saint John says, "Everyone who does evil hates the light, and does not come to the light, lest his deeds should be exposed" (Jn 3:20). Without the revelation of Christ's love, evil appears just as a mistake, a weakness, and so on. It is the absolute love of Christ, who loves us to the end (Jn 13:1), which reveals evil for what it is — a radical *choice* against *love* (387).

The unmasking of evil is not for its own sake, but *for the sake of the conversion of the person*. Only when we see evil for what it is can we turn to the light and be saved. The Holy Spirit convicts the world of sin by revealing the *Redeemer*, the one who saves from sin (388). With the unmasking of evil comes its solution. The diagnosis of the illness is made by the doctor who gives the cure.

A final important point is made in this section: *the Fall is a historical event*. The biblical account in Genesis uses "figurative language" (390) — in other words, not all of the details are to be taken literally — but the *event* is real enough. And every age lives with the impact of that event.

CCC 391-395
The Fall of the Angels

Following the principle that we saw expressed in CCC 385, that only light reveals darkness for what it is, this section on the fall of the angels focuses our attention on *Christ's victory over the devil*: "The reason the Son of God appeared was to destroy the works of the devil" (394).

The Catechism warns that the devil *appears as an intimate friend.* His is a "seductive voice" (391), and it was his "mendacious seduction" (394) that led our parents into disobedience. He proposed the way of disobedience and distrust as the means to achieve a godlike status — whereas, as we saw in the very first sentence of the Catechism, God *wants* to bring us into intimacy with him, making us his friends, through obedience and trust (see 1).

The devil is "a *liar* and the father of lies" (392), and Christ came as the *Truth* to "unmask" the lies. The final paragraphs of the Catechism speak of how the devil "mendaciously attributed to himself the three titles of kingship, power and glory" (2855), and even tried to "divert Jesus from the mission received from his Father" (394) by tempting him with these, as though they were in his power to give (see Mt 4:1-11). And so when at Mass we say to God the Father, "For the kingdom, the power and the glory are yours, now and forever," we are affirming the truth that Christ, through his temptations, his passion, death and Resurrection, has restored them to the Father (see 2855).

The devil is the one who came to bring *death* to us. He is a "murderer from the beginning." His voice leads to death through disobedience, and he speaks out of envy of man's blessings and hatred of God and his kingdom. "Now the prince of this world will be driven out" (Jn 12:31), Jesus cries as he approaches the time of his passion. His *resurrection* reveals his victory over death.

CCC 396-401
Original Sin

In a single sentence at the beginning of this section, the Catechism sums up the nature of the human person in a way that allows us clearly to understand what original sin is: "A spiritual creature, man can live this friendship only in free submission to God" (396).

Remember:

- Man is a *spiritual* creature: made in the image of God, as an embodied *spiritual* soul, man has freedom. God will not force man's submission. He only ever *invites*, his respect for our freedom absolute.

- God calls us to *friendship*: he gives his love freely and in return *seeks our trusting love*. Friendship cannot be established through anything less than mutual love.

- Man is a *creature*, not the uncreated God. God is infinite, without bounds or limits. Man is created good, but is *limited*. Man is not all-knowing or all powerful. He cannot "create" from nothing, but can only "make" things out of what God has already created (see 296).

What, then, is original sin? Our first parents *lost their loving trust* in God's call to friendship (397). Letting trust die in the heart, through the seductive voice of Satan (391), they *disobeyed* God and rejected their creaturely state — they sought to be "like God" without God. It is impossible, of course. Seeking to win by disobedience what God wants to give in love, and what can only be received in trusting love, man falls into the utter misery called original sin.

This is the character of every sin: "All subsequent sin would be disobedience toward God and lack of trust in his goodness" (397). Sin is fueled by the unreal picture we have of God, a "god" of whom we live in fear and whom we think we must resist (399). Cut off from our true source of life and nourishment our lives run wild in confusion and sin and finally wither as we desperately seek, among creatures, what only a return to our true God can give (400-401).

CCC 402-412
"You Did Not Abandon Him to the Power of Death"

The impact of original sin on the whole human race reminds us of our *profound unity* (402-403). God created us as one human family, with one nature and one destiny. He wills to save us, not as isolated individuals, but *together*, as a single body (look back to CCC 360). He has made us dependent upon each other. Our sin affects others, as do our prayers and our striving to live in grace in response to Christ. For good or for ill, we affect each other deeply. We often experience this deep mutual impact as unjust. We can remember that the Church describes our "relationality" in precisely the opposite way, as original *justice*. It is Adam who has corrupted our relationality, turning original justice into a state of original *injustice*.

The Catechism clarifies that, as transmitted to us, original sin is not to be thought of as "sin" in the sense of a personally willed wrongful act. It is rather "sin" in the way that the Greek word for sin, *hamartia*, means the term — we are like an arrow that is "missing the mark," missing the target (404).

Baptism puts us back "on target" (405), but we are now living in a "battlefield" state (409). It is a dramatic image — the danger of serious spiritual injury and death could not be emphasized more. The ignoring of our condition is one of the greatest dangers, for then we live blindly, unaware of the perils (407).

The final image with which we are left, as this chapter concludes, is that of the promise of Christ, who will join us as our brother and Savior on the battlefield. His coming will make *everything* worthwhile, and the "inexpressible grace" he brings will communicate *unimaginable blessings* after the definitive victory he will win for us. His coming will be preceded with the finest fruit of his victory, in the form of his mother, freed from original sin.

CCC 422-429
I Believe in Jesus Christ, the Only Son of God

With today's reading we begin a new *chapter*, a new *focus* — the Second Person of the Blessed Trinity, Jesus Christ — and a new *period* in salvation history, the "fullness of time." Three headings introduce this second chapter to us.

The first heading reminds us that *the Father's sending of his Son is the heart and center of the Christian faith* (422). The purpose of his sending his Son is to redeem us and adopt us as his children. This is the "Good News" of the Christian faith.

A word on terms used here: "Good News" is our translation of the Greek New Testament word, *euangelion*, which literally means good (*eu*) message (*angelion*). We also translate this Greek word as "evangelization." So, to evangelize is simply to bring "good news"; and the good news is that the Father has sent his beloved Son to redeem and adopt us. This paragraph from the Catechism also quotes from the first line of Saint Mark's Gospel: "the gospel of Jesus Christ, the Son of God" (422). "Gospel" is *another* translation for this Greek word, only now it has come to us via old English — *god spell*. The important thing, then, is to realize that "Gospel," "evangelization," and "Good News" are all translations of the same Greek New Testament word.

The next two headings remind us that the work we are reading is a *Catechism* — it is a work to help us transmit and tell others about the faith, the Good News. The Catechism has been written to enable us to share its contents with others. What people will find, when we share with them, is not just a wonderful message, but the *Person of Jesus Christ* (426). Christianity is more than principles to live by, more than a philosophy of life. God might have given us just this, but he has "acted far beyond all expectation — he has sent his own 'beloved Son'" (422). The Christian faith is God's invitation to know him *personally*.

CCC 430-435
Jesus

Names in the Bible are not mere labels. "A name expresses a person's essence and identity and the meaning of this person's life" (203). Jesus' name tells us both *who he is* (God) and *what he does* (saves). His name expresses both his identity and his action.

God can forgive sins since all persons belong to him — he is their Father and Creator. And because every creature belongs to him, all sin is a sin against him. "Because sin is always an offense against God, only he can forgive it" (431). When Jesus forgave sins, therefore, he was manifesting his divinity in the clearest possible way as the beloved Son sent from the Father for this purpose. Those who rejected him called him a blasphemer for this claim (see Mk 2:5-7; CCC 587).

Jesus saves us by coming among us as God. The Catechism teaches here that he saves us by his *Incarnation*, for here he united the whole of human nature and every person to himself so that he could work his salvation in them (432); by his *death*, for here he took upon himself as God made man all the offense of sin and forgave it (433); and by his *resurrection*, for this manifests the power of God's loving forgiveness to overcome death, the result of sin (434).

Two other points are worth mentioning. First, the Catechism provides the rich background to this whole section in the *biblical references* given at the foot of the pages. We are encouraged to read these for a deeper understanding. Second, notice that Jesus' *name* is the focus of *every* paragraph. Jesus hands himself over to us by making his name known, and speaking his name in love and from the heart is how we enter into intimacy with him (see also 203). Speaking his name is the "heart of Christian prayer" (435).

CCC 436-440
Christ

Unlike "Jesus," "Christ" is not a proper name. It is a *title*. However, because Jesus perfectly lived out the meaning of this title, it has become his name (436). We rightly refer to God the Son as "Jesus Christ."

Christ, or Messiah, literally means *anointed*. In the Old Testament, kings, priests, and sometimes prophets were anointed with oil to symbolize their consecration to God's work. The title became the way in which all Jewish hopes were summed up as they looked for one who would be anointed with God's Spirit to save them.

Jesus was anointed not with oil, a symbol of the divine blessing and commission, but with *the Holy Spirit himself.* The Holy Spirit consecrates him at his conception (437), comes down upon him at Baptism to reveal him as the Anointed One, the Christ (438). We can look forward to an extended section later in the Catechism on Jesus and the Spirit (702-741). As "Christians" we are members of Christ's Body, anointed by the same Holy Spirit.

Finally, we can note that the title "Christ" is *the description of a mission.* Kings, priests, and prophets were anointed for a *purpose*: kings to rule a kingdom; priests to sanctify a people; prophets to speak God's truth. Jesus is anointed as *the* King, the Ruler of God's eternal kingdom of love and joy. He is anointed as *the* Priest, offering himself as the one true sacrifice to save and sanctify us. He is anointed as *the* Prophet, to speak and live the full truth that sets us free and brings us happiness. Because some understood this mission in too political a way, Jesus also referred to himself by other titles from the Old Testament, especially the Suffering Servant and the Son of Man.

CCC 441-445
The Only Son of God

The text of the Catechism here carefully explains how this term, "son of God," which was applied to many in Israel, as well as to Israel as a whole, came to be used of Jesus to express his divinity. "Son" clearly indicates a relationship, but in all other cases, when applied to creatures — whether angels or human persons — it signifies an "adoptive sonship" and a "relationship of particular intimacy" (441). How, then, do we see this title being used to express Jesus' unique status?

First, it is because he refers to himself as the *only* Son of God. There were clearly others called "son of God," and so the claim to be the *only* one marks Jesus out. We shall see that there is a connected doctrine in the fact that Mary was *ever*-Virgin: "Jesus is Mary's only son" (501).

Second, we see this because in the Scriptures *we hear the voices of Father and Son expressing their unique relationship*. The Father speaks of Jesus as the "beloved" Son (444), while Jesus distinguishes his own relationship to the Father from that of others (443). It is *his* Father who reveals to Peter this unique relationship. In a later part of the Catechism, CCC 571-591, we will see how Jesus expressed his unique claim to divinity in a number of ways.

We can also see the unique application of the title to Jesus when we consider *his role in relation to us*. It is *in* Jesus, the only-begotten Son, preexistent and of one being with the Father, that *we* are able to be adopted as sons and daughters of the Father. It is precisely because Jesus shares in the fullness of divinity that, by his grace, we can be given a share in his own relationship with the Father. *Jesus can make us partakers in the divine nature precisely because he is fully divine.*

CCC 446-451
Lord

As with the title "Son of God," the title "Lord" — as a way of addressing Jesus — could be taken as a simple expression of human respect, an elevated way of saying "Sir." When we read the Gospel accounts, then, not every instance in which Jesus is called "Lord" need necessarily be read as an act of faith in Jesus' divinity (448).

However, it is clear from the New Testament that oftentimes either Jesus himself, or those who address him, *do mean much more than this* (for example, Jn 9:38; 21:7). As we have seen, "Lord" is also the way of referring to the divine Name which God himself revealed (209). For the faithful Jew, wishing to honor the mystery of God's Name expressed by the Tetragrammaton, "Lord" is the acceptable alternative (see Mk 12:29; Lk 4:12). Jesus is also addressed as Lord in *this* sense, of carrying the divine Name; and one of the earliest Christian proclamations of faith was simply "Jesus is Lord" (Rom 10:9; 1 Cor 12:3; Phil 2:11; Acts 2:36; 10:36; Rom 6:23). We can see from these early New Testament texts how the belief in Jesus' divinity is placed alongside the obedience of faith due to God the Father; thus we find it expressed that God is *Father* of the *Lord* Jesus (Col 1:3; 2 Cor 1:3). These expressions of faith were hammered out in the Councils of the Church by the successors of the apostles and have emerged into the forms of faith we have today in the Creeds.

The Catechism concludes this section on the title "Lord" with a reminder of the prominent place it has in Christian prayer. The acclamation "Lord!" is a cry of *adoring love*. The Catechism reminds us — as it did with the section on the name "Jesus" (435) — that *the Church believes as she prays*. Her beliefs are expressions of her worship. We will further explore this principle when we read about the centrality of liturgical prayer (see 1124).

CCC 456-460
Why Did the Word Become Flesh?

For the first time, the Catechism introduces a section by *asking a question*: Why did the Word become flesh? The content of the question is taken from John 1:14: "And the Word became flesh and dwelt among us." It is as if the Catechism's authors paused before the awesome reality of the Word, who is God, taking flesh, and asked: "How could this *be*? Who *is* this God of ours that he would stoop to the level of a creature and appear among us, in human form? *Why* would he do this?"

The answer comes in four stunning statements of faith, each italicized in CCC 457-460. They appear in an *ascending pattern*, speaking first to the lowest state of the human person and taking us through to our highest calling.

The only Son of God, the divine Word, became flesh first *because of our sins*, to save us from our misery and disintegration into death. He took our human nature in order to share in and rescue us from the distress of our poverty, pain, and death. In this *he revealed the great love of God for us*, who does not want *anyone* to perish. *Jesus rescues us by changing us*: as our true image, he calls us to live as he lives. The salvation he brings is not a surface-level change, but *a radical call to holiness*, to be perfect as the Father is perfect. And so the final goal of Word taking flesh is to raise us to live with God, in his eternity of joy, *to share as sons and daughters in his own relationship with the Father*. By his grace we come to know and love him as he is in himself.

The truths we have contemplated transform our understanding of ourselves and others, providing us with the solid foundation for our Christian lives. Read CCC 1691 — the content of today's reading is the substance of the opening to the part on the Christian life.

CCC 461-463
The Incarnation

Today's reading seems mainly concerned to impress upon us the absolute importance of this belief. "Belief in the true Incarnation of the Son of God is the distinctive sign of Christian faith" (463). Holding to this belief is what marks out the Christian. Veering from this belief, or losing a sense of its central place, marks the loss of authentic Christian faith.

There are also important points in the phrase "the Word became flesh" clarified for us here. When the Church, following John 1:14, speaks of the Word becoming "flesh," she intends us to think of more than just the bodily matter of our skin, our tissues, and so on. She means *human nature* as a whole, body and spiritual soul (461). CCC 470-478 will discuss this at length. In New Testament Greek, the word translated "flesh," *sarx*, additionally carries the connotation of weakness, of helplessness, which is also communicated here in the quotation from the hymn in Saint Paul's Letter to the Philippians. Jesus humbled himself, he became a servant and "obeyed" death, receiving in himself all the effects of sin (461).

Again, in the phrase "the word became flesh," "became" is not to be understood as implying a change in God. As we have seen, God is unchangeably faithful and loving (see 214). He does not change. He does not take on a new character at the Incarnation. Rather, it was then that he "revealed his innermost secret" (221). *The change brought about by the Incarnation is not in God but in human nature*, which is lifted up and united to the Godhead, and brought into the presence of the Father, reconciled and redeemed through the work of Christ. And so the Church speaks of Christ "assuming" human nature, in the sense of adopting it, taking it on. In Christ, every aspect of my nature has been united to God; every element of my being has been adopted.

CCC 464-469
True God and True Man

The readings for the next two days belong together. They are both concerned with the Church's understanding of the Incarnation. Today we see how this understanding was fashioned in the crucible of history, with its personalities and Councils, and with all the struggles involved in grasping the full truth of how God has acted "far beyond all expectation" (422). Tomorrow, this same path is followed, but through a consideration of all of the elements that make up a full human nature, seeking to understand better how each is united to the divine Son of God.

CCC 464 is a crucial paragraph: it summarizes the truth of the Incarnation. The Incarnation of the Son of God is "unique and altogether singular" — in other words, there is no comparison point we can make. Jesus is not simply the very greatest human being, or a human person filled with God's grace and presence to an exceptional degree. The Lord Jesus is "one of the Trinity" (468) who assumed a complete human nature. The Catechism draws the implication very clearly: "Thus everything in Christ's human nature is to be attributed to his divine person as its proper subject, not only his miracles but also his sufferings and even his death" (468). This means that when we read the pages of the Gospels, every sentence which has Jesus as the subject in reality has "one of the Trinity" as the subject. When we read, "Jesus called his disciples to himself and said ..." this is "one of the Trinity" calling the disciples and speaking to them. When Jesus weeps, one of the Trinity weeps.

Every heresy (see 2089) the Church has faced concerning the mystery of Christ has in some way rejected the view that *God fully assumed complete human nature*. In every heresy one of those terms is removed. Instead there is the fastening onto some limited aspect of Christ's mystery, while denying the full truth of the faith.

CCC 470-478
How Is the Son of God Man?

Once again, the Catechism provides us, in a single paragraph, CCC 470, with an excellent summary of the section we are reading before unpacking it in some detail. CCC 470 explains that only gradually were the *implications* recognized of the truth that a complete human nature was assumed by the Son of God. Jesus had everything that belongs to our humanity. The paragraphs following speak of Christ's human *soul and intellect* (471-474), his human *will* (475), his human *body* (476-477), and his human *heart* (478). The Church is saying that "one of the Trinity" thought with a human mind; chose with a human will; ran, ate, slept, and suffered in a human body; and loved with a human heart. Jesus is only one Person — that is, only one individual Being knowing, acting and loving — the divine Person of the Son of God. *In the Person of Jesus we meet the human expression of one of the Trinity; we see into the life of God.*

As part of a complete humanity, the Divine Son united a human intellect to himself. CCC 472-474 explains this. It means that Jesus had to learn *naturally* as all human beings do, gradually through experience — what hot and cold feel like, how to tend plants successfully, and so on. As the Divine Son, though, he also had *supernatural* knowledge of all that the Father had given him to reveal for the sake of his mission of salvation — the Father and his loving plan and also the "secret thoughts of human hearts" (473). His human will, like his human intellect, is entirely turned over to the service of his saving work (475).

This section also helps us understand why the Church venerates Christ's human heart, his Sacred Heart, and images of Christ's body (476-478). Because his heart and body — indeed *every* aspect of his humanity — *belong* to the divine Person, in venerating them we are venerating the eternal Son.

CCC 484-486
Conceived by the Power of the Holy Spirit

The Persons of the Blessed Trinity act together in the work of *creation* (258, 292). Here we see how they act together in the even greater work of the *re-creation* of all things. In this short, delicate section we see how the Father prepares and invites the Blessed Virgin (484), the Holy Spirit overshadows her (485), and the Son is conceived in her (486). The Incarnation is truly a Divine work of the Persons *together*.

The Incarnation is a work of the divine Persons in *cooperation with the Blessed Virgin* (488). We can notice the importance of the *free assent* that Mary gives. The Father "invites" Mary (484); he does not force her. The work of our redemption at all stages is something that is to be humanly and freely welcomed and embraced, as our divine Lover God wants nothing less.

As well as providing her free assent, Mary also offers her *human nature* to the divine Son. It is human nature taken from Mary that is assumed by the Son. The Holy Spirit causes her to "conceive the eternal Son of the Father in a humanity drawn from her own" (485). It is in and through the humanity drawn from Mary that the eternal Son reveals the Father and rescues us from sin and death. It is in and through the humanity drawn from Mary that the eternal Son rises glorified from the dead.

Finally, we see in these short paragraphs the secret of the whole Christian life: *that it is brought about by the Holy Spirit*. It is the Holy Spirit who comes upon Mary (484), who causes Mary to conceive Christ (485), and who anoints the humanity of Christ with power (486). The Christian life is a divine life, lived "in the Spirit" and made possible only by the anointing power of the Spirit who is sent upon us and upon all of the Church (see Gal 5:25; Acts 1:8).

CCC 487-494
Born of the Virgin Mary

Saint John Paul II, in his greatest work on catechesis, described Mary as a "living catechism" (*Catechesis in Our Time*, 73). And what we read in her life always leads us to her Son. The Catechism gives us this principle at the beginning of today's reading: "What the Catholic faith believes about Mary is based on what it believes about Christ, and what it teaches about Mary illumines in turn its faith in Christ" (487). This is the key to understanding each of the doctrines about Mary — the Church asks us to look for what they teach us about Jesus and his saving work.

Mary's *predestination* is the first doctrine presented here (488-489). It teaches us that *God's plan of salvation fully embraces our freedom.* "The Father of mercies willed that the Incarnation should be preceded by *assent* on the part of the *predestined* mother" (488). God has a plan "formed from all eternity in Christ" (50). His predestination does not mean that he coerces us into his plan, but rather that he provides all that is needed for us to make our assent.

Mary's *Immaculate Conception* is the next doctrine presented (490-493). Mary was conceived without original sin, without the disorder that affects all human beings. Does this unique condition mean that she did not need a Savior? On the contrary. While Christ has rescued you and me *out of* the misery of sin, in the case of the Blessed Virgin, he has saved her *from entering into* this condition. She was "preserved" from sin, perfectly redeemed from the moment of her conception.

Mary's *obedience of faith* is the third doctrine (494). Reading this paragraph helps us understand what a perfect act of faith looks like — a wholehearted offering of ourselves in trust to the God who wishes to espouse us and for whom nothing is impossible, that we might be his "handmaid" in whatever situation he places us for the sake of Christ's work of redemption.

CCC 495-507
Mary's Motherhood and Virginity

These two doctrines, concerning Mary's motherhood and virginity, appear to be opposites. In fact, they are two sides of a single coin, *both of them affirming Christ's uniqueness and divinity.*

The Council of Ephesus, in AD 431, solemnly declared that Mary was the *Theotokos*, the Mother of God (495). While this is a title given to Mary, the declaration primarily says something about Jesus. The cross-reference to CCC 466 explains the truth about Christ that is confirmed here: that Jesus is a *single divine Person*, God the Son who took to himself a complete human nature drawn from the Blessed Virgin Mary. The Person whom Mary carried in her womb was the divine Son. The title preserves for us the mystery of the Incarnation.

The *virginity of Mary* (496-498) and her *perpetual virginity* (499-501) both affirm the unique nature of Jesus. Jesus had no earthly father; Joseph is his earthly *foster* father. The proclamation of Mary's virginity protects the truth that Jesus is the consubstantial Son of the Father.

The virginity of Mary is a historical truth; her miraculous conception of Jesus is a given fact of history. As we saw with the affirmation of the essential historical veracity of the Gospels (126), and as we will see with the miracles of Jesus (548) and his bodily resurrection (639), the Church holds firmly to the historical truths of these events — and seeks to answer any objections to their historicity (498, 500). They are not only symbolic of deeper spiritual truths.

However, all of these historical events do *also* carry rich spiritual significance. We see this in the next section of the Catechism, which concerns the meaning of Mary's virginity in God's plan (502-507). The Church wants us to develop those "eyes of faith" (502) that can begin to perceive *why* God acts as he does, that can "read" the meaning of the events around us in the light of God's plan for our adoption into the mystery of his eternal love.

CCC 512-513
The Mysteries of Christ's Life

In today's reading the Catechism makes the important observation that the only two points about Christ that are mentioned in the Creed are his *sending from the Father* in the Incarnation and his *return to him* in the events of the Paschal mystery. The focus for the Church's catechesis on Christ, therefore, will always be on these two topics.

The Gospels, as we know, give us much more than this, though they, too, have a clear focus on the last three years of his time on earth, and a particular concentration on the final week of his earthly life. There is much that is "hidden" in the life of Jesus.

The Catechism notes that these two points in the Creed, however, provide all the "light" (512) we need to understand *everything* else in Jesus' life. You may have noticed that the Catechism is often helpful in providing this guidance as to which doctrines and teachings shed light on other beliefs that we hold (for example, 89, 388). It is helping us to remember to read the faith as a *unity*, as a single coherent set of teachings that make sense to us *together*, as one *whole*. The Catechism is also reminding us by this that there is a *hierarchy of truths*. This does not mean that some teachings are truer than others; it is rather that some are more fundamental and essential and that they help us to understand the other truths (see 11, 90, 199, 234).

In the celebration of Christ's life in the liturgical year these two teachings are marked by Christmas and Easter. In the liturgy we *celebrate* the great truths that we proclaim in the Creed. And it is again these great feasts and seasons that shed light on the rest of the Church's liturgical year. "Beginning with the Easter Triduum as its source of light, the new age of the Resurrection fills the whole liturgical year with its brilliance" (1168).

CCC 514-521
Christ's Whole Life Is Mystery

The essence of today's section lies in the opening two paragraphs. The Catechism first *distinguishes mystery from curiosity* (514). Curiosity is only appropriate for earthly matters — it can lead to mild interest. The revelation of God's mystery, on the contrary, concerns the "divine sonship and redemptive mission" of Christ (515), and the only appropriate response to this is our wholehearted belief and commitment — to *believe* that Jesus is the Christ and God the Son so that through this belief we may have *life* in his name (see also 203, 430). The Gospels reveal this mystery. The materials in the Gospels were selected for this reason, so we read the Gospels for the sake of *deepening our belief in Jesus* and to *ground our lives securely* on his loving and saving presence.

CCC 515 explains how this revelation of Christ's mystery occurs: through Christ's humanity which is a *sacrament*. The Gospels record Jesus' "deeds, miracles and words," which lead us to recognize that we are in the presence of the invisible reality of the divine Son and his work. The word "sacrament" is taken from the Latin *sacra*, "sacred," and applied to Jesus' humanity it means that his humanity was both the *sacred sign* and the *sacred instrument* of his divinity.

Because Jesus is the divine Son who assumed our humanity, everything he says and does reveals God. CCC 516-518 explain three aspects of this: Christ's whole earthly life is *revelation* of the Father, is *redemptive*, and *recapitulates* human life, restoring it to its "original vocation" (518). *Recapitulates* means that, as the "head" (in Latin, *caput*) of the human race, Jesus represents us, living human life in all its "stages" and dimensions as it is meant to be in God's plan. We can now join ourselves to Jesus, becoming members of his Body, with Jesus as our true head. Then it is not only *we* who live the Christian life, but *Jesus himself* who, as our head, *lives in us* (519-521).

CCC 522-534
The Mysteries of Jesus' Infancy and Hidden Life

How do we now live the new life of Christ? How do we join ourselves to his redemptive work? Or, to put this in a better way: How does *Christ join us to himself* in and through our daily life, inviting us to respond, so that we can benefit from his having assumed our humanity and united it to his divinity? The Catechism begins to walk us through the answer to this question, starting from Jesus' infancy and hidden life. Everything in Jesus' life, we remember, is *revelation of the Father,* is *redemptive,* and is a *recapitulation of human life and history for the sake of its restoration.* This includes those early years and the times before Jesus began his public ministry.

The first thing you may have noticed is that he accomplishes this through *the work of the liturgy and the sacraments.* Look through these paragraphs and notice all of the sacraments, the feasts, the seasons, and the holy days. This is where his life is communicated to us now. This is where the grace to live the new life in Christ flows out upon us.

The second place where he joins himself to us is in *the most ordinary events* of "daily life" (533). When we are poor (525), are called to "become little" (526), are persecuted (523, 530), are learning obedience to our parents (532), are living out our family life (533) — and also when we learn that the Father's call invites us to a response that takes us *beyond all earthly loyalties and commitments* (534), since Jesus living in us is, above all, always about his "Father's work."

In these ways, then, we become "sharers in the divinity of Christ who humbled himself to share our humanity" (526).

CCC 535-540
The Baptism and Temptations

As we read these passages concerning Jesus' baptism and his temptations, we remember that the Catechism wants us to read these as *mysteries of Jesus to which he joins us* so that *we* live them and *he* also lives them *in us* (521).

Jesus' baptism and his temptations *belong together,* for the Holy Spirit who descended upon Jesus during his baptism immediately drove him into the desert to be tempted by the devil (Mk 1:12-13; CCC 538). His baptism is his voluntary identification with us in the misery of our sins so that through his faithful obedience to the Father *as one of us* "in all things but sin" we might be adopted as beloved children of God. The Father delights in the Son and in this ministry of mercy and redemption (536). The Holy Spirit immediately drives him into the desert to endure the temptations facing humanity, so that Jesus might recapitulate the temptations that Adam faced (539).

The meaning of the two events together can be summed up in the verse from the Letter to the Hebrews, "For we have not a high priest who is unable to sympathize with our weaknesses, but one who in every respect has been tempted as we are, yet without sinning" (Heb 4:15; CCC 540). The baptism concerns his entering into our weakness; the temptations, his rebuffing of all attacks testing his "filial attitude toward God" (538).

The Letter to the Hebrews goes on to invite us to have utter confidence that we will receive all the grace we need to have this same "filial attitude" in the face of temptations that assault us in our daily lives (see 4:16). We can know that it will be *Jesus,* who has already "vanquished the Tempter *for us*" (540) who will be living in us. He has united us to himself so that we never need face difficulties on our own or through our own strength.

CCC 541-553
The Kingdom

Today we continue reading of the way in which Jesus draws each of us to share in the mystery of his life. As the Catechism will explain, the single Greek word for "mystery" has two dimensions to it and so came to be translated into Latin by two terms, *mysterium* (mystery) and *sacramentum* (sacrament): "*sacramentum* emphasizes the visible sign of the hidden reality of salvation which was indicated by the term *mysterium*" (see 774). Jesus' whole life is *the* mystery in both these senses, for all that he said and did, all that is visible in him, is the *sacramentum* that draws us into the hidden *mysterium* of his divine sonship and saving work.

This mystery is expressed in "the Kingdom of God," a phrase which depicts the Father's will to save all people by gathering them around God the Son into the family of God. Jesus' preaching and miracles, his acts of love and healing, his eating with sinners, and his casting out of demons are the *sacramentum* that reveal the kingdom, the hidden reality, or *mysterium*, of salvation.

From the very *beginning* of his ministry Jesus proclaimed this kingdom (541), for he was sent from the Father to "draw all men to myself" (Jn 12:32), and the proclamation of the kingdom was the entire focus of all that he said and did during his earthly life. The hidden work of salvation was achieved and revealed above all in the "Easter mystery," the "Paschal mystery," in which the *sacramentum* of the Cross and Resurrection express the *mysterium* of God's redeeming love, and Jesus' kingdom overthrows the kingdom of the devil (550).

Today *we* enter into that kingdom, and are joined to the work of salvation, through the Church — the gathering of people around Jesus that the Son established through his appointment of Simon Peter and the Twelve. Jesus associated these men *forever* with his kingdom, and it is through them that he "directs the Church" (551).

DAY 77

CCC 554-560
The Transfiguration and Entry into Jerusalem

The *more* we understand, the *more* God can show us. As soon as Saint Peter understood that Jesus was the Christ, Jesus could begin showing him what this really meant, the King of unconquerable love who would suffer and die but rise triumphant and undefeated.

But every act of understanding is hard won, for the fallen mind is dull, the heart obtuse (see 37): "Peter scorns this prediction, nor do the others understand it any better than he" (554). As we saw, God's pedagogy is gradual and in stages (53), and the Blessed Trinity works always to open the eyes of our mind to understand the true nature of reality. And now "for a moment Jesus discloses his divine glory" (555). Jesus *reveals more* of his divinity in order to help the disciples *receive more* fully the depths of love in God's saving plan (see the quotation from the Byzantine Liturgy in 555). In the end it is only children, the angels, and "God's poor" who will have the simplicity and insight to see Christ's glory, revealed in his humility, and welcome him into Jerusalem as the true King, bringing salvation (559).

All that the Father reveals to us, through Christ and the Holy Spirit, is for the sake of our *own* entering into the new life of grace made possible by the Son's Incarnation. Jesus has united his life to ours so we might unite ours to his (521). In the Transfiguration we are shown a glimpse of our blessed *future* in Christ — the glorious resurrected body — and by this glimpse we are given the added strength we need *now* to follow the way that Christ has shown us. Again we notice the double way in which this whole section invites us to share in the life of Christ — through the events of everyday life in which the perfect will of the Father may be received and through the grace of the sacraments and the liturgical year (556, 559-560).

CCC 571-573
The Passion, Death and Burial of Jesus

These short introductory paragraphs lead us to the *center of the Good News*. That center is the "Paschal mystery": the events concerning Jesus that took place around the Jewish Feast of Pasch, or Passover — his passion, death and burial, and then his resurrection. We are at the very center here because, the Catechism tells us, these events mark the *accomplishment of God's saving plan*. The final and definitive nature of this accomplishment is underlined by the phrase taken from the Letter to the Hebrews: "once for all" (9:26). With the death and resurrection of Jesus, God's plan is complete. As Jesus said, "It is finished" (Jn 19:30). Jesus, having loved his own, has loved them *to the end*. Having been obedient to his Father, he has been obedient *to the end*. In the words of Saint Irenaeus, quoted in CCC 518, Jesus has now "experienced all the stages of life" and by this has made possible the gift of "communion with God to all men."

These paragraphs impress upon us that this accomplishment was achieved in a "historical, concrete form" (572). God's plan is not accomplished in the realm of ideas or ideals; its accomplishment was achieved at a particular time and place. It took place in the flesh. There are historical records that record the events (573). In the pages to come, the Catechism will refer time and again to the factual nature of this completion of God's plan.

A final point worth noting is the reference to the Church's faithfulness to *the interpretation Jesus gave* "of 'all the Scriptures'" (572). We know that "all divine Scripture" speaks of Christ (134). We see here that he is also its *interpreter*. It is Jesus himself who taught the disciples, and it is the Church's faithfulness to this interpretation that underlies her God-given teaching.

CCC 574-576
Jesus and Israel

The paragraphs we read today explain the religious reasons for the conflicts which led ultimately to Jesus' death. They center upon three points in particular, points which are summarized in CCC 576: Jesus' attitude towards the *Law*, towards the *Temple*, and towards faith in the *One God*. As you can see, these are taken up as the main headings following these paragraphs, and we will spend time on each area over the next few days.

We sometimes express doubt by saying that a message or an account sounds "too good to be true." In each of the areas of conflict in Jesus' life, those who opposed him were facing a reality that must, to them, have seemed too good to be true. God acted "far beyond all expectation" (422) in sending his own beloved Son. Because of who he is, Jesus sums up and fulfills all of the "institutions of the Chosen People" (576). Jesus is *the* priest, prophet, and king; he is the *true* Temple and the *real* sacrifice; he is the giver of the *new* Law, the meaning of *every* feast and celebration; he is the revealer of what it *means* to say that God is One, as a Trinity of Persons in an eternal communion of love.

When Jesus came, sent from his Father, he acted in ways that made sense in the light of his identity and mission, but they were "far beyond all expectation" and so-called for a decision on the part of those who witnessed or experienced them. The Catechism lists some of his actions, signs of "contradiction" (Lk 2:34; CCC 575), that led to conflict (574). He called for a radical conversion in the light of these signs of the in-breaking kingdom he was establishing. The Catechism notes how understandable it was, in the face of "so surprising a fulfillment of the promises" (591), that many rejected him. In Jesus, they experienced the *limitless nature* of God's love.

CCC 577-582
Jesus and the Law

Jesus will not allow us to oppose law and grace, or the New Testament against the Old Testament. Jesus is not a "soft option" set against a stern, unyielding Old Testament law. He does not overthrow what has come before. He *fulfills* it, *completes* it, *strengthens* it, *builds* on it. Jesus *keeps* all the promises made in the time of the Old Covenant. He is the "Yes" of God (see 2 Cor 1:20), the Confirmation of the truth of what his Father has been revealing gradually by stages (see 53, 65).

The Sermon on the Mount — the collection of Jesus' teachings gathered in Matthew 5-7 — both *affirms* and *radically deepens* what was given to the People of God in the Old Testament. Jesus wants for us not only the good action but the *pure motivation*, not only what the hand can give but what the *heart* can release. His teaching is truly "radical" in the etymological sense of "going to the root." We have already seen that in biblical and Christian teaching the heart is central to an understanding of the person (368, 478; see also 2562-2563).

Jesus not only affirms the goodness of the whole Law, but *keeps* it fully and in every respect (578-580). In Jesus, God the Son lives the very Law that has its origin and source in him. He lives it in and through the human nature he assumed. Through his words and actions he *shows* what the true Law looks like.

The conflicts over the Law lay in Jesus' claim to be its authoritative interpreter, in both word and deed (581). As the divine Son he *taught with absolute authority*, correcting, where needed, certain human interpretations that were current, especially in the area of laws on the Sabbath and on dietary regulations (581-582). For example, he taught the true "pedagogical meaning" (582) of the dietary law through explaining what it is to be truly *clean of heart* before God.

CCC 583-586
Jesus and the Temple

Jesus is not only the fulfillment of the Law. He is also the fulfillment, in his own Person, of all of the *worship* of Israel. Jesus had *zeal* for the Temple (584); it is "my Father's house" (see Jn 2:16-17). Nonetheless, the physical Temple was only ever a dim image of his own Body, and all of the sacrifices offered in the Temple only ever a poor shadow of his perfect sacrifice of obedient love to the Father for all mankind. Upon Christ's coming, "Types and shadows have their ending," as Saint Thomas Aquinas wrote. As in the case of the Law, Jesus did not overthrow the sacrifices and worship, the feasts and holy seasons of the Old Covenant. He came to *perfect* and fulfill them (583-584), although — as in the case of the Law — the meaning of his words and actions were distorted (585).

Jesus refers to himself as the true Temple of God because all worship now takes place "in him" and "through him" (586; see the footnote reference to Jn 2:21). He is the one over whom the cloud of God's presence, his *shekinah*, rests (see Mk 9:7), and it is through his sacrifice of love that access to the Father is made possible (Mt 27:51).

For ourselves, we are now being "built" into the Temple of Christ's Body. Each of us is placed as a jewel (Rv 21:18-21), a "living stone" (1 Pt 2:5), in the new Temple of Christ, in which the Holy Spirit dwells as our true life (Eph 2:21; see CCC 1695), teaching us to pray *in* the Son, as members of his Body united to him, *to* the Father (see 797).

CCC 587-591
Jesus and Israel's Faith in the One God and Savior

With this third element in the conflict between Jesus and some of the religious figures of his time, we reach what the Catechism calls the "real stumbling-block" for those who opposed him: his claim to be able to *forgive sins* (587). The scandal of Jesus' actions was based on the fact that "only God can forgive sins" (Mk 2:7; CCC 589, see also 1441). While I can forgive a person those sins committed against *myself*, no one else has the right to do this; no one, that is, except *God*, to whom I belong. Likewise, I cannot forgive a person's sins committed against a *third party*; again, only *God* can do this, for all of us belong to him.

God alone can forgive everything since *all sin* flows from disobedience towards God and expresses distrust in his goodness (397). Jesus never contradicted this fundamental truth. He never claimed that anyone other than God could declare sin to be forgiven; he simply *exercised* this divine authority himself — "Your sins are forgiven" (Mk 2:10) — and left it to his hearers to draw the conclusion as to his union with the Father (589). His divinity was further expressed in the fact that he gave to his apostles this same authority to forgive sins (Jn 20:21-23). Clearly, *only one who himself had the power and the authority to forgive sins could share this with others.*

The forgiveness of sins, then, is described in the Catechism as the "divine work *par excellence*" (587). An appreciation of this phrase from the Catechism, together with our understanding of the meaning of the name "Jesus" as "God saves" (see 430-432), helps us to realize that the *forgiveness of our sins* and our *liberation from evil* is the focus of Christ's work in our *own* lives (see 1741).

CCC 595-598
The Trial of Jesus

Today's reading is particularly hard-hitting. The answer to the question "Who was responsible for Christ's crucifixion?" is quite simply, "I am responsible, because I sin, and Christ died to rescue me from my sin." *All sinners collectively are responsible for Christ's death.*

The section begins by noting that if we seek to answer that question, "Who was responsible for Christ's crucifixion?" purely on the level of history, looking at the various actors during the trial and death of Jesus, we face a certain "historical complexity" (597). Some religious authorities in Jerusalem clearly wished him dead, on a charge of blasphemy. But this antagonism towards Jesus was not characteristic of all of the Pharisees (595-596), nor of all the Jews in Jerusalem. In any case, it is difficult to identify motivation. While the charge against him was blasphemy (Mk 14:64), the fear of Caiaphas appeared to be that Jesus would bring disaster upon the Jewish people through Roman aggression. Ultimately, the "personal sin of the participants (Judas, the Sanhedrin, Pilate) is known to God alone" (597).

In considering this question of *responsibility*, the Catechism also wants us to appreciate the difference between objectively sinful acts and the accompanying subjective guilt. Notice the side reference to 1735, which speaks about how far the guilt of bad acts can be "imputed" to a person. Many elements — fear, ignorance, pressure — can lessen the guilt and blameworthiness of a person who acts badly. On the cross Jesus said that his enemies did not know what they did, for they were ignorant of who he was (see Lk 23:34).

Of course, *we* do not have such an excuse, for we profess to know him and to be his disciples (597). And notice the present tense: "our sins *affect* Christ himself" (598). They do so in two ways: they "crucify" him anew *in our hearts*, where he now lives, and they "crucify" him *in the members of his Body* (see the scriptural references in footnote 390).

CCC 599-605
Christ's Redemptive Death in God's Plan of Salvation

From the consideration of the historical circumstances surrounding Christ's trial and death, we now turn to the place of Christ's death in God's plan. Jesus' death on the cross was part of *God's deliberate plan* (599), *foretold* in the Scriptures (601). That God has a plan does not make our actions into those of robots or mere puppets (600). It might help to look back to CCC 306-307 on Providence and secondary causes: God uses *our free choices* to achieve *his plan*. God never *causes* evil, but he does *permit* it, even the evil of the Crucifixion, so as to achieve redemption (311-312).

The Catechism also wants us to understand that the fact that this is God's plan does not imply for a moment that the Father has no care for his Son. On the contrary, *the Father, the Son, and the Holy Spirit are one God*: they have one name (233), one substance (242), with each wholly possessing the Godhead (253) and sharing together the same mission (258). It is not that "God's plan" is that of the Father only. It is the common plan of the Persons. Moreover, we remind ourselves that in his innermost being *God is love* (221). The three divine Persons live in a perfect unity of love (255). Christ's redemptive death is therefore an expression of this Trinitarian unity and love.

Christ's death is the divine answer to the disorder, hate, sin, and disunity of fallen humanity, the common divine response of the three Persons who are One almighty, unifying Love. As we saw in the section on the Fall, sin is a lack of harmony, of love, and of truth, and so the Son "assumed us in the state of our waywardness of sin" (603). He totally identified himself with us in our fallen state, experiencing the effects of sin, and even death, in order to mend what was broken in us. His healing love is offered for *each person without exception* (606).

CCC 606-612
Christ Offered Himself to His Father

In our readings for the next two days we see that Christ's *free offering of himself* is out of *love for the Father* (606-612) and out of *love for humanity* (613-618).

The *freedom* of Christ is a key theme in today's reading. Jesus freely chooses what the Father wills — he exercises "sovereign" freedom (609), being free as only a true king is free. And Christ's kingly freedom is gained, paradoxically, through his total, loving *obedience* to the Father — "I do as the Father has commanded me."

Jesus does not obey only externally, or halfheartedly; he *embraces* the Father's plan and will — "I *love* the Father." He is *whole*hearted in his obedience, holding nothing back. The term "embrace" is used of Jesus' obedience whenever there is mention of the Father's loving plan of salvation (606, 607, 609).

This embracing of the Father's plan allows him to "accept" the suffering that is an inevitable dimension of love in the fallen world in which deep sin and the distortions of self-will oppose the Father's plan. Perfect Love faces the opposition of sin and its consequences, experiencing the horror of suffering and death. This can't be "embraced," for it is not itself a good, but an *agony*; but it can be — and is — fully *accepted*. "By accepting in his human will that the Father's will be done, he accepts his death as redemptive" (612).

This free and loving embrace of the Father's plan, even in the face of suffering and death, is supremely expressed in the Mass. Jesus takes the very heart and center of who he is — his free and loving union with the Father — and gives *this* — gives *himself* — to us. The Catechism describes it this way: "Jesus transformed this Last Supper with the apostles into the memorial of his voluntary offering to the Father for the salvation of men" (610). The Last Supper, in the body *given* and the blood *poured out*, perfectly expresses and incarnates his total self-offering (610-611).

CCC 613-618
Christ Offered Himself for Our Sins

A sacrifice is an offering. Why are offerings made to God, who is infinite Being? They add nothing to him, give him no joy that he does not already have, provide no complement to his already boundless love.

Offerings are made, not for his sake, but for *ours*. Because we are made to give ourselves over into his perfect happiness and enjoy him forever, we seek every means by which to express this. We want to offer ourselves in love, so we symbolize this by giving things that belong to us — tithes of crops, of animals, of time. But they only symbolize the gift God *really* wants: the heart. And when the heart is not given along with the offering, we see the reaction in the Sacred Scriptures: "'What to me is the multitude of your sacrifices?' says the Lord; 'I have had enough of burnt offerings of rams and the fat of fed beasts'" (Is 1:11); "'Do I eat the flesh of bulls, or drink the blood of goats?'" (Ps 50:13).

The heart of the human person that turned away in Adam, and continues holding itself back and defiling itself, must be turned back to the Lord in a pure and perfect offering of love. *This* is the work of the New Adam, the Son of God who, in the humanity he took from Mary, gives himself wholly. This offering "completes and surpasses all other sacrifices" (614); it repairs the broken relation of disobedience by substituting the New Adam for the Old (615), thereby creating a new humanity in his own Person. The objective language of the Church's teaching — "satisfaction," "atonement," "made righteous," "reconcile" (614-616) — communicates the full reality of what Jesus achieved. This is *God's work* — he has *remade his creation* by the life of Christ, especially in the final act of self-offering on the cross. Now the privileged invitation extends to us all: join ourselves to Christ and be "made partners" in this new creation (618).

CCC 624-628
Jesus Christ Was Buried

This short section offers us a wonderfully clear catechesis on what the Church means when she teaches that Jesus *died* and was *buried*. The Catechism wants us to understand the full significance of these two truths, both of which are specifically proclaimed in the Creed.

The Catechism reminds us what death is: the separation of the immortal soul from the body (624). The immortal soul is the active principle of the living unity of the body (365). The soul "does not perish when it separates from the body at death" (366), but this separation is nonetheless a horror to us; it is experienced as something unnatural, as an evil, for God did not intend this for the human person (400). When Jesus died, then, God the Son experienced the separation of the immortal soul from the body. In Jesus, *God experienced human death.*

God is the Author and Giver of life, and Jesus himself proclaims, "I am the Way, and the Truth, and the *Life*" (Jn 14:6); and so, uniquely in the case of Jesus, both the human soul and the human body which God the Son assumed remain united to the divine Person, even though in a "dead" state, separated from one another. Because Jesus' body remained united to the divine Person, it did not become corrupt: the Catechism quotes from Saint Thomas Aquinas who taught that "divine power preserved Christ's body from corruption" (627). Thus it is that God the Son descends into hell in the state of one who has died and yet is alive to proclaim the message of redemption to the dead there (see 632-635).

As always, the Catechism is concerned to show how we might join ourselves to God's mysteries, and in this case it is through our Baptism (628). Through Baptism we die to sin and are "buried" in the waters of the font so as to rise to new life with him (see 535-537; 1214).

CCC 631-635
Christ Descended into Hell

We will focus today on the meaning of Christ's descent into hell, but before we do so it is significant to note that this falls under a single article with the Resurrection. CCC 631 introduces *both* truths. Christ rises from the *lowest* place: "it was precisely out of the depths of death that he made life spring forth."

"Hell" in this article does not mean the place of those who eternally turn away from the loving mercy of God. CCC 633 explains that it refers to the place where all await the Redeemer of mankind. It was not for his own generation alone that Christ came, but *for the whole of humanity.* Christ's death is an extension of his mission, from the time and space of his life on earth to "all men of all times and all places" (634). It is the "holy souls" whom Christ thus freed from death, the "just who had gone before him" (633). Before Christ's incarnate work of redemption, the vision of God, *that vision which perfects the happiness for which we have been made* (27-30), was not available.

Death, we remember, is the result of sin. Jesus, having lived in obedience to the Father, resisting sin, freely took on himself for the sake of humanity the consequence of sin — death — and "tasted death" (624) so that the Gospel of salvation might be preached "even to the dead" (634). This is *his* choice; death does not bind him. In this act he took complete power over death and destroyed it. He brought the hope of the Gospel to those in the bondage of death who were deprived of the vision of God and the happiness of heaven by Adam's sin. The Catechism provides us with an extract from a beautiful homily from the early Church which has come down to us describing this final aspect of the work of salvation (635).

CCC 638
On the Third Day He Rose from the Dead

With this paragraph we reach the "central truth" of the Christian faith. Look at the words used in this paragraph: "fundamental," "essential," "fulfilled," "crowning." When a king is crowned, he is recognized as the *authentic ruler*. The crowning is the act that establishes finally and without doubt the validity of his claim to the throne. The Catechism gives the Resurrection this role in the life of Jesus: this is the "crowning truth of our faith in Christ." *This truth confirms finally, definitively, and completely all that Jesus said, did and suffered.* Now we know that Jesus is indeed God the Son, the one with the authority on earth to forgive sin, the one who can rescue us from every evil, the one in whom we can place all our hope and faith. Now we know *for certain* that "we can believe in Jesus Christ because he is himself God" (151), whereas it "would be futile and false to place such faith in a creature" (150).

The sections on the Resurrection following this paragraph are therefore *among the most crucial* in the whole of the Catechism. Saint Paul emphasized the stark alternatives in his First Letter to the Corinthians: "If Christ has not been raised, then our preaching is in vain and your faith is in vain.... If for this life only we have hoped in Christ, we are of all men most to be pitied" (15:14-19). Paul then continues: "But in fact Christ has been raised from the dead, the first fruits of those who have fallen asleep" (1 Cor 15:20). *In fact* it is *true*, Saint Paul emphasizes. We will find, therefore, that this next section highlights the *factual* and *historical* nature of the Resurrection. This great chapter of Saint Paul on the meaning and nature of the Resurrection will lead the Catechism's account (see footnote 490) and is quoted no fewer than fifty times in the Catechism text as a whole.

**DAY
90**

CCC 639-647
The Historical and Transcendent Event

The Resurrection of Christ *really* happened. This is the key emphasis of this section. This central teaching of the Church certainly requires of us an act of *faith* — nothing *compels* us to believe in Christ's resurrection. But the Catechism wants to show us that it is *entirely reasonable* to believe. "Christ's resurrection is a real event, with manifestations that were historically verified" (639). It points us to two facts in particular: the *empty tomb* and the *appearances* to the disciples. The empty tomb is not a "direct proof" (640), and the disciples who saw Jesus "are still doubtful, so impossible did the thing seem" (644). There are other possible explanations. But two things are clear. First, that the Resurrection is the *best* explanation we have for the empty tomb and the appearances; and second, that it is not a phenomenon that took place only on the level of the "experiences" of the disciples. The New Testament might have presented this as a mere vision, or a spiritual insight, but it is absolutely clear that it is not of this nature. When one looks at the evidence, "it is impossible not to acknowledge it as an historical fact" (643).

Certainly it is a *unique* fact. This is not surprising given that the Incarnation was a "unique and altogether singular event" (464). The Resurrection is not a return to earthly life (646). It is the same body, yet it is different, for it is a glorious one with new powers and properties (645). And although Christ's resurrection is undoubtedly historical, it also "surpasses history" (647), for Jesus' body can no longer be confined to earth but now "passes from the state of death to another life beyond time and space" (646).

CCC 648-650
The Resurrection — A Work of the Holy Trinity

Today's reading invites us to *view things from God's perspective*. The Fathers of the Church, the Catechism teaches us, contemplated the Resurrection precisely from this vantage point, taking a God's-eye view of things (650).

The Resurrection, then, is *a work of the Persons of the Blessed Trinity* who reunite the human body and soul of Christ which death had separated. This reuniting could take place because the divine Person of the Son remained present to both of these separated elements. God the Son *freely* allowed death to work the separation (649), and equally freely reunited the body and soul. In fact, because of the unity of God, the three divine Persons act *together* to raise Christ the Lord from the dead. They act together, the Catechism teaches, each Person manifesting "their own proper characteristics" (648).

The Catechism again uses two terms, "transcendent" and "historical," to describe this action (see 648). God is *transcendent* (that is, he lives beyond our understanding and our categories, and beyond our time and space), and yet he acts in *history*. God acts at a *particular* time and place for the sake of *all* times and places.

Because Christ's resurrection is a transcendent act, it reaches across all time and space. What does this mean for our *own* life and death? Christ, we know, has united each of us to himself through his assuming of human nature at the Incarnation and now calls us "to become one with him" (521). We can begin to glimpse how this means that by his divine power he can also reunite *our* body and soul, overcoming death's separating powers in us as well. Through Christ's union with us, he enables us to *share* in his Resurrection. We will need to wait until the end of the Creed to pursue this point in detail (see 992-1004). Nevertheless, the next section in the Catechism develops these points further (651-655).

CCC 651-655
The Meaning and Saving Significance
of the Resurrection

The significance of the Resurrection is not easy for us to grasp because the Resurrection takes us *beyond* this present life. We know what this life contains. We experience a natural life, with its many joys and sorrows. We know some of the high points of what our lives on earth can yield. But the Resurrection "opens for us the way to a new life" (654), a "new creation" (2 Cor 5:17).

We can catch *glimpses* of this new life even *now* because of our union with Christ. We have "tasted" the "powers of the age to come" (Heb 6:5; see CCC 655). The new powers that belong to the Risen Christ, we pray, will be ours in the life of the resurrected, and are already revealed in lives filled with God's grace in which the divine life shines out even in our weakness. Therefore, just as the Catechism urges us to *contemplate things from God's perspective*, so it also urges us to see ourselves — those whom Christ has united to himself — from this perspective. The Resurrection of Christ has brought about our adoption as children of God, giving us a "real share in the life of the only Son" (654). "From now on, therefore, we regard no one from a human point of view" (2 Cor 5:16).

We can confidently embrace the new life into which we are being drawn because the Resurrection confirms everything that Christ taught (651), all the promises God has ever made (652), and all that the Church believes about the identity of Christ concerning his divinity (653). The Resurrection is the *ultimate confirmation* of the faith.

CCC 659-664
He Ascended into Heaven

In the Gospel of Luke, after Jesus ascended it is said that the disciples went back to Jerusalem "full of joy" (Lk 24:52). Does this surprise us? Do we tend to imagine them being full of sorrow because he has left them? Perhaps we think of the Ascension as Jesus leaving us, as our being left to continue the journey of faith without him. This is not how the Church understands the Ascension, though. One of the great Fathers of the early Church, Pope Saint Leo the Great, said that the disciples realized that "he had not left his Father when he came down to earth, nor had he abandoned his disciples when he ascended into heaven." *Jesus did not leave us when he ascended.* In fact, he said to his disciples, "I am with you always, till the close of the age" (Mt 28:20).

The Catechism emphasizes that the Ascension is not about Jesus leaving us, but about his *bringing us home,* into "the Father's house" (661). Jesus ascends to the Father, to be seated at his "right hand" (663). The divine Son now *brings the humanity he assumed into the place of authority and glory.* He is making "a place" for us in his Father's house, as he promised (Jn 14:2), and he said that he would bring us to this place. This he is doing through the exercise of his priesthood, making permanent intercession for us as "the center and the principal actor of the liturgy" (662).

The "glory" of the *exalted Christ,* ascended to heaven, differs from the glory of the *Risen Christ.* While on earth after the Resurrection, as a concession to our limited ability to see him as he truly is, Christ's glory was "veiled under the appearance of ordinary humanity" (659). Now ascended to heaven, Christ's humanity is no longer veiled. It is "hidden" in the brightness of the Godhead until he "appears" in his glorious Second Coming (see Col 3:1-4).

CCC 668-677
He Will Come Again in Glory

Christ is already the exalted Lord of the *Church*, of his Bride who recognizes his loving Lordship. But Christ's Lordship extends over more than the Church. "Jesus Christ is Lord: he possesses all power in heaven and on earth" (668). He is the Lord of the *whole world*, of history, and of the cosmos. The period in which we now live is when we wait for his return, for the time when his *actual* Lordship will become *fully effective*, not only in our own lives, and not only in the Church, but in the *whole of creation*.

This could take place at any moment, for "the final age of the world is with us" (670). Christ the Risen and Ascended Lord is to be manifested in all his glory. The King will return to earth; but for now he waits. Why? Because of his mercy. Jesus asked his disciples, "When the Son of man comes, will he find faith on earth?" (Lk 18:8). The current period, of watching for his coming, is also the time when *the Church is called to evangelize*, to proclaim the Good News to the whole of creation. The Catechism reminds us that the Jews will come to recognize Jesus as the Messiah before he returns (673-674).

It is also the time when Christ the Lord gives us the grace to follow in his footsteps so that we pattern our lives by him (see 521). The Church is called to follow him through his suffering and death into the glory of his resurrection: "the present time is the time of the Spirit and of witness, but also a time still marked by 'distress' and the trial of evil which does not spare the Church" (672). The Catechism warns us especially of the temptation, in this difficult waiting period, of yielding to a "pseudo" messiah — one who promises salvation and ultimate "solutions" without Christ (675-676). This is the figure of the Antichrist.

CCC 678-679
To Judge the Living and the Dead

In these compact and challenging paragraphs the Catechism explains first what we will be judged upon (678) and then who will judge (679).

There are two aspects to judgment on the Last Day: our *choices and intentions* will be judged, as will our *actions*. Our choices and intentions do not always reveal themselves clearly in how we act; nonetheless, they are *most deeply who we are*. The Catechism goes so far as to speak about the *secrets of hearts*. We remember that "heart" here does not mean "emotion" or "feeling" — the heart is "the depths of one's being, where the person decides for or against God" (368). Do I choose to act out of love for God and for others in every small event of the day? Do I choose to make myself available to others in service, seeking their well-being? Or do I keep to myself? Do I maintain only an *appearance* of love while *really* seeking my own good and fulfilling just what I narrowly want for myself? God is calling us out of ourselves, to love and to give at every moment, especially through the needs of those closest to us, our neighbors. On the Last Day our hearts will be "revealed" in how we respond to that call of divine grace.

There is only one judge (679), Christ himself. His is the right to pass definitive and full judgment — no other judgment counts for anything, whether how we judge ourselves or how others judge us. Only Christ has plumbed the depths of the human heart, through resisting temptation and living the life of perfect love to the end. Christ offers us nothing but mercy and salvation from the misery of our sins if we will accept this. But if one will not recognize the truth of Christ's merciful judgment, one ends by judging oneself. The heart that refuses mercy, "rejecting grace" (679), is hardened — it chooses the hell of condemnation instead, including self-condemnation (see 1033).

CCC 683-688
I Believe in the Holy Spirit

With today's reading we begin a major new section on the Creed, centered on the Third Person of the Blessed Trinity. Throughout this section we will see that the work of the Holy Spirit in our lives is to *lead us to Jesus*. The Catechism beautifully speaks of the "divine self-effacement" that characterizes the Holy Spirit (687), who does not draw attention to himself and "does not speak of himself." He is wholly "for" the Son, pointing us to him, "unveiling" Christ to us.

The Fathers quoted in this section are lyrical in their descriptions of how the Persons of the Blessed Trinity each refer to the others; thus the Holy Spirit leads us to the Son, who in turn "presents" us to the Father (683). The Holy Spirit is the first in this "progression": it is he who awakens faith in us, leading us to the Truth incarnate. In fact, the Catechism teaches, *we come to faith only through him*: "No one can say 'Jesus is Lord' except by the Holy Spirit" (683).

The Holy Spirit is thus the *first* in the order of our coming to faith, and the "beginning" in another sense as well: *the beginning of the final stage in the work of salvation*. With the revealing of the Holy Spirit we enter a "new era," the "age of the Church" (see 1076) — the end times when God completes the gathering of the community of the redeemed.

The whole of this third chapter on the Creed concerns the work of the Holy Spirit in the "economy of salvation," and CCC 688 lists where the invisible movements of this work of the Spirit can be seen. If you read this list carefully, you will notice that the Holy Spirit is the source of the new life of Christ in *each* of the four dimensions of the Christian life — in prayer; in the liturgy; in the life of faith; and through fostering holiness and communion among God's people.

CCC 689-690
The Joint Mission of the Son and the Spirit

As we move into this catechesis on the Holy Spirit, let us first appreciate *the inseparability of the Holy Spirit from the Son*. The Spirit's mission is a *joint* one with that of the Son. The Catechism draws from a beautiful text of Saint Gregory of Nyssa who compares the Holy Spirit to oil covering the whole body. Just as we would touch any part of the body through the oil, so we touch Jesus *through* the Holy Spirit. Jesus has no part "that is not covered by the Holy Spirit" (690).

In this section and the pages to come, you will also notice how much the mission of the Spirit is written of in terms of his *uniting* us — to each other and to the Father's beloved Son. The Holy Spirit is a Spirit of *union*, of communion. And we are reminded again that union does not erase distinctiveness; true union, rather, *depends* upon it. So, "In their joint mission, the Son and the Holy Spirit are distinct but inseparable" (689).

This passage also reinforces a point we saw when we were contemplating the mystery of the Blessed Trinity. CCC 236 wrote of the relationship between the inner life, "theology" or "mystery" of the Trinity, and the "economy" of the Trinity — the works by which the inner life of God is revealed. It is *through* the "economy" that the mystery of God is revealed. The Father's sending of his beloved Son and Spirit reveals something of the eternal Self-gift the Father makes of himself in eternity.

Finally, we must note that, through the gracious action of the Blessed Trinity, *we* are brought to share in this joint mission of the Son and Holy Spirit. We are called to participate in the Father's "sending" of the Son and Spirit for the sake of the salvation and re-creation of his world: "this joint mission will be manifested in the children adopted by the Father in the Body of his Son" (690).

CCC 691-701
The Name, Titles, and Symbols of the Holy Spirit

You will have noticed that the Catechism regards "naming" as a crucial element in its presentations. When we introduce a person, we give his or her name. When the Catechism wishes to "introduce" us to the Father (203-221), or the Son (430-451), or the Spirit (691-701), it begins through a consideration of their names and titles. (Later we will find a similar interest in naming the Church and the individual sacraments, since as the *works* of the divine Persons, they are named "after" them.)

This section helpfully distinguishes between the name, titles, and symbols of the Holy Spirit. The *name* of the Holy Spirit, joining two terms used for God — "Holy" and "Spirit" — makes clear that we are speaking of a distinct divine Person (691). The *titles* of the Holy Spirit each emphasize his character as *Gift*, as *being for others*: he is "of the Lord," "of adoption," "of God," and so on. The title "Paraclete," likewise, associates him with others, with the work of consolation or of advocacy (692-693).

With the *symbols* of the Holy Spirit we are faced with a rich and beautiful range of imagery (694-701). Each symbol *helps us grasp something of the nature of the Holy Spirit*. It is worth noting, for each of the symbols, which distinct aspects of the life of the Holy Spirit they assist us in understanding better. For example, water signifies birth and fruitfulness; fire, the "transforming energy" of the Spirit; and so on. The other point to which you may wish to attend is the relationship of this symbol to Christ. Here we see the "joint mission" at work, under the guise of a particular symbol. So, for example, when Jesus lays his hands on the children who come to him, *he is blessing them with the Person of the Holy Spirit* (699). When he casts out demons by "the finger of God" (Lk 11:20), he is doing so *by the divine power of the Holy Spirit* (700).

CCC 702-716
God's Spirit and Word in the Time of the Promises

Over the next three days we will be reading about the mission of the Holy Spirit in creation over the three "eras," or "times," of God's plan of loving goodness. Today the Catechism presents the mission of the Holy Spirit in the period *before* the coming of Christ. We can notice again that, although this whole section of the Catechism is a catechesis on the Holy Spirit, the figure of Christ is equally prominent in the text, for the Catechism wishes to remind us that *the Spirit's mission is to introduce and lead us to Christ.*

There are five main sections in today's reading, each concerned with a different time period in this era of "the promises." We begin with creation itself, and the sections take us right up to the birth of John the Baptist. In the whole of this era, the Catechism teaches, both the Holy Spirit and the Son are *perpetually at work*, but in a *hidden* way. The Son and the Holy Spirit are spoken of under figures, symbols, "types," and images. In due course, in "the fullness of time" (see 717), the Son will be manifested in the flesh through the overshadowing action of the Holy Spirit. But that time is not yet. This era is a time of hiddenness in which the activity of the Son and Spirit are known by their *effects*. Their work is focused on making ready, through the message of inspired prophets, a Remnant of God's People, "prepared for the Lord" (716). This period of preparation looks forward to both a promised King, or Messiah, and a new Spirit (711). It is a period marked by incompleteness and gradual revelation, by patterns of sin and renewal and exile and return, as God teaches his People to *long for the solution* which will appear only in the fullness of time.

CCC 717-730
The Spirit of Christ in the Fullness of Time

Today we reach *the culmination of the period of expectation*. This beautiful section of the Catechism takes us to *two figures* who were filled with the Holy Spirit and intimately connected to the mission of Jesus: John the Baptist and Mary.

The work of the Holy Spirit in *John the Baptist* marks the *completion* of one era: the completion of making ready the precious Remnant of the poor ones who were awaiting the Lord (718); the completion of the Spirit's speaking through prophets announcing the coming Messiah (719); and the completion of the long wait for the restoration of the divine likeness in man (720). The work of the Holy Spirit in John also marks the *opening* of a new era: CCC 717 carefully explains how the Visitation of Mary to Elizabeth marked the *beginning* of *God's* visitation of his people, as Jesus is carried to the hill-country where he greets John the Baptist, bringing the gift of the Holy Spirit.

In the section on the Holy Spirit's work in the *Blessed Virgin*, note the italicized words: the Holy Spirit *prepared* Mary as the *dwelling place* for the Son; he *fulfills* the Father's plan of loving goodness in her; he *manifests* the Son in her; and through her, he brings the nations into *communion with Christ* (721-726). In tomorrow's reading we will see the repetition of these same words in CCC 737 when the Catechism teaches us about *the Holy Spirit's work in the Church.*

In the final section of today's reading (727-730), the Catechism invites us to pause and think back over all we have read so far in the text about Jesus. We are reminded that Jesus is the *Christ* (see 436-440) — that is, the one *anointed by the Holy Spirit*. His mission of salvation was from the beginning a *joint mission* with the Holy Spirit. He came in order to *bestow the Spirit upon us for the restoration of the divine likeness in us.*

CCC 731-741
The Spirit and the Church in the Last Days

In today's reading we see how the Holy Spirit is at work in our *own lives*, as members of Christ's Body, the Church. As we noted from yesterday's reading, the Holy Spirit's work is comparable in both Mary and in the Church because Mary is not only the *dwelling place* for her Incarnate Son on earth, but she also, at "the end of this mission of the Spirit," became the *fruitful mother* of the "whole Christ" (726) — a term that the Christian Tradition uses to designate *Christ, Head and members together* (we will see this discussed further when we reach CCC 795).

The mission of Jesus and the Holy Spirit, hidden in the era of the promises, and brought to glorious fulfillment in "the fullness of time," is now "completed" in the bestowing of the Holy Spirit upon the Church at Pentecost. The *restoration of the divine likeness* in each person, the calling of each to *share in the life of the Blessed Trinity*, the *new life* of the children of God — all of this now begins in the Church as the Holy Spirit comes as flame and wind and power.

The three paragraphs at the end of this section (739-741) are particularly significant, as the Catechism gives us an "advance" reminder of the parts of the Catechism still to come — liturgy and the sacraments (Part Two); the new life we have in Christ (Part Three); and the gift of prayer (Part Four). You will notice how, in each case, these dimensions of the life of the Church and of the life of every Christian are made possible by the gracious gift of the Holy Spirit whom Christ bestows upon us to underpin and flow into every area of our lives, sanctifying them and drawing us into the heart of God through them.

CCC 748-750
"I Believe in the Holy Catholic Church"

The opening words on the Church *refer us immediately to Christ*, "the light of humanity" (see Lk 2:27-32). They are taken from the Second Vatican Council document on the Church, written in 1964. The first words of that document, from which its title was taken, are *Lumen Gentium*. *Lumen* is Latin for "light" and *Gentium* means "peoples," the whole of humanity. The Church, then, is given her identity here at the beginning: she is the place of Christ's light, *a place where Christ's light "shines out visibly"* (we will return to this *visible* shining later).

The second paragraph (749) gives us another aspect of the Church's deepest identity, as *a place of holiness*, the holiness of the Holy Spirit. We can say that just as she has no other light than the divine light of God in Christ, she has no other holiness than the holiness of the Holy Spirit.

The third paragraph reminds us of the four great "marks" of the Church's identity (one, holy, catholic, and apostolic) which the Catechism will explain in later paragraphs. Here, at the beginning of this section, it wants us to know that these "marks" are from God and are not merely the work of the Church's human members. They are inseparable from belief in the Blessed Trinity, because they are *all* gifts of divine goodness.

It is worth returning briefly to the contents pages of the Catechism to see where this section on the Church fits into Part One as a whole. You will see that the twelve articles of the Apostles' Creed fit into three chapters, one for each of the three Persons of the Blessed Trinity. Articles nine to twelve, following in the chapter on the Holy Spirit, tell us of the works of the unquenchable love of the Father, Son and Holy Spirit for us. We do not believe "in" them in the same way we believe "in" God, because they are not God himself but his "works" (750).

CCC 751-757
Names and Images of the Church

Notice first that today's paragraphs come under the larger heading: "Paragraph 1. The Church in God's Plan." There are three main sub-headings under this, to help us discover the Church's place "in God's plan." In other words, *the Catechism wants us to know who the Church is in God's "eyes,"* in his plan, his "mind," as he has revealed it.

We tend to be more accustomed to thinking about what the Church is in "my eyes," or "my mind," according to our limited knowledge and experience; so these are important paragraphs for opening us to the *greater and deeper reality of the Church* as she is in *reality* — which is another way of saying "in God's plan"!

The first section is concerned with the significance of the *names* used for the Church. The Catechism here takes us to some of the rich imagery the Scriptures use, to help us begin to delve a little into the Church's "inexhaustible mystery" (753). CCC 751 and 752 give us the *names*, and CCC 753-757 give us the *images* or *symbols*.

The *names* communicate different aspects of the Church's reality. All the names given to the Church *describe what God is doing.* He is calling, gathering, drawing into a relationship of belonging to him, and providing his body and blood in the Eucharistic liturgical gathering. The Church is "called out" by the voice of God's love — called out of the secular world, out of our individual and small-minded worlds, out of our merely personal opinions. She is called "to gather together," to assemble, to be a congregation: she is called to *belong to the Lord.* All the *images* of the Church are given to help us understand more deeply *the unity, the goodness, and the beauty of the Church in God's plan.*

CCC 758-769
The Church's Origin, Foundation, and Mission

CCC 758 is a simple introductory paragraph that provides an outline of what is to follow and gives us two things to look out for: the origin of the Church in the *Holy Trinity's plan*, and the Church's *progressive realization in history*.

You can see the *Trinitarian structure* in three of the subheadings: "A plan born in the *Father's* heart"; "The Church — instituted by *Christ Jesus*"; "The Church — revealed by the *Holy Spirit*."

Then, from the six subheadings together, you can see a perfect summary of the *progressive realization in history* of the "Holy Trinity's plan," called "the Church."

CCC 760 begins with a sentence that turns our view of the world upside down because it places the Church at the *center* of all things. It is a view, in fact, that Christians have held since the very first centuries, as the footnotes reveal — that the reason for the creation of the entire universe is so that God might draw mankind, a microcosm of creation, to himself; and that he does this in the Church.

CCC 761 and 762 speak of the stages of preparation for the Church: her beginning; then a "remote" stage when Abraham is called and promised that he will be "the father of a great people"; then a time of "immediate preparation" — the forming of the people of God in the desert with the giving of the Ten Commandments. After this we find an important point of clarity about the relationship between the kingdom and the Church. It is sometimes mistakenly said that Christ spoke only about the kingdom, not the Church, and that the Church is therefore a man-made institution and not in the Holy Trinity's "plan" at all. The Catechism explains that in fact the Church is the "little flock," called and gathered around Jesus, and that she is "the seed and beginning of the kingdom" which is "fully achieved" when that flock, the Church, is "united in glory with her king" (763-769).

CCC 770-776
The Mystery of the Church

What does it mean to say the Church is a *mystery*? In this section of the Catechism we find the answer given in *three vital truths*, provided for us in summary form in the three subheadings.

First, the Church's mystery consists in the fact that *she is always a visible and invisible reality at the same time.* She is both "visible and spiritual," "human and divine" (779). She is never merely what we can see, feel, or experience. The second point builds on the first. The Church, which is both visible and invisible, is also *the place of God's "nuptial union" with man* in a love that "never ends" (772-773; also refer to 25).

The third heading leads us to another level of the mystery: the Church who is both visible and invisible, and is a nuptial union between God and his beloved people, is also *the universal sacrament of salvation.* As we have seen, "sacrament" means both *sacred sign* and *sacred instrument.* The Church signifies and communicates the sacredness and efficaciousness of the saving work of Christ — especially his passion, death, and resurrection (774).

The two italicized phrases in CCC 775 tell us *what God is doing* in a sacrament — he is *bringing about union between God and man* and he is *bringing about unity with each other.* The phrases help us to appreciate why the Church is called the universal sacrament of *salvation* — because we need to be saved from the fatal wounds of our self-centeredness, from what separates and divides. The Church is Christ's instrument of salvation in which he brings us from disunity into unity and from separation into union.

CCC 781-786
The Church — People of God

Over the last few days we have been studying the Church in the Holy Trinity's plan. This came under the heading "Paragraph 1." For the next three days we read through "Paragraph 2." Since the Church is from God the Holy Trinity, she lives in relation with each of the three divine Persons. This and the next two sections, therefore, explain how the Church is, at the same time, the *People of God* (living in relation to the Father), the *Body of Christ* (living in relation to the Son), and the *Temple of the Holy Spirit* (living in relation to the Holy Spirit).

Today's reading on the Church as the People of God has three subheadings to guide us. CCC 781 explains who are the People of God; CCC 782 lists this People's *unique characteristics*; and CCC 783-786 present this People's *call and mission.*

One of the first points to notice, because it is perhaps difficult for us to grasp in our individualistic world, is that God "willed to make men holy and save them, not as individuals . . . but rather to make them into a people . . . which would be one, not according to the flesh, but in the Spirit" (781).

This truth of being *one* People, with *one* Body, the Body of Christ, as *one* Temple, the Temple of the Holy Spirit, with *one* set of characteristics, *one* vocation, and *one* mission has far-reaching implications for us as members of the Church. It is why we come *together* for the liturgy, join *together* for fellowship and charitable works, and are encouraged to pray *together*, with memorized prayers to enable us to pray together out loud with one voice as one People, one Body, one Temple of Praise. It is, of course, important to pray one's own spontaneous prayers and pray in one's own home, but the importance of God's saving us *as a People* helps us understand the supreme importance the Church attaches to liturgical prayer and worship.

CCC 787-796
The Church — Body of Christ

CCC 789 offers us three extraordinary aspects of the Church as the Body of Christ and links us back to CCC 521 to help us ponder the great mystery of what it means to be really and truly *in* the Church. By faith and Baptism, then, we are *united to each other* and *united to Christ*, who is, distinctly, the Head of the whole, the Head of the members. Christ is the *Head* of *his Body*, the *Church* (792; see Col 1:18). Notice the number of footnotes from the Scriptures (from footnote 215 onwards) and especially from the letters of Saint Paul. This is not a late, or uniquely Catholic, development of doctrine; it has been there from the beginning.

In this connection, CCC 795 introduces us to the ancient phrase, *Christus Totus*. It is a phrase worth remembering and repeating frequently. Look at the four quotations from the saints, men and women from different times in the history of the Church, who have taken up these scriptural references with a single unchanging interpretation.

Finally, after appreciating the communion with Jesus that we are given by being in the "one Body" of Christ; by appreciating the salvific "reign" the Head has over us, "providing for our growth" (790-794), we come to the nuptial love of a personal relationship between the Head and the members and the reason why the Church is referred to as "she." The final quotation from Saint Augustine (and notice that the Catechism puts it in italics to emphasize it for us) follows directly after key passages from the Scriptures (see footnotes 240-242) and gives us a clear way of understanding and pondering the exquisite beauty of the mystery of the Church and of our faith: "*as head, he [Christ] calls himself the bridegroom, as body, he calls himself 'bride'*" (796).

CCC 797-801
The Church Is the Temple of the Holy Spirit

To help us deepen our understanding of the Church as the Temple of the Holy Spirit, the side references alongside CCC 797 take us in two directions: back to the significance of the *Temple* (586) and forward to the *unity* of the Church (813).

You have already read about the significance of the Temple in Judaism and Jesus' identification of himself with the Temple as "God's definitive dwelling-place among men" (586), and it is worth following the Scripture references to glimpse the range of its meaning here. For example, look up the beautiful passages of Exodus 29:43-46 and Ezekiel 37:26-28. There you will see the constant refrain that God has chosen to "dwell in the midst" of his people, to abide, to *stay* with us.

God's "dwelling in the midst" of his people is seen in the "tent of meeting," or "tabernacle," established in the desert. His presence continued in the Temple of Solomon in Jerusalem that was eventually destroyed, then in the second Temple that was also destroyed — and then in the *Temple of Christ's body*, which was put to death. But, of course, Christ rose from the dead, and now his risen Body, the Church, is the *permanent dwelling-place chosen and established by God*. There the Holy Spirit, who we know is the "Lord and giver of life," animates "every vital and truly saving action in each part of the Body" (798). *Charisms* are recognized as being special "graces" (from the Greek *charis* meaning grace, the gratuitous gift of redeeming love) of the Holy Spirit that are for the good of the Church and the world. Charisms should have a valued place, but they are not always welcome — partly because they disturb us and partly because they can be imitated by man and so are not always easily discernible as genuine. This is why the Catechism speaks of the necessity of the "discernment of charisms" to ensure that they are genuine gifts of the Spirit (801).

CCC 811-822
The Church Is One

There is a sense in which this section is *the* center of the *entire* divine plan, the center of Christ's mission, and therefore the central purpose of the Church. At the same time, the claim that the Church is one (as also the claim that the Church is holy) seems to run against the evidence around us every day, where there are many baptized Christians not in communion with the Catholic Church or with each other.

It is important, therefore, that we understand the Church's teaching and her logic on this, a logic which we see in the letters of Saint Paul and in the earliest writings of the Church Fathers. Notice the footnotes to Saint Paul's Letters to the Ephesians and Colossians (814-815) pleading for unity by the "bonds" of peace and charity. The Catechism is reminding us of the Church's *real bonds* — bonds that are invisible, as well as visible.

The Catechism also reminds us of the "divine source" of these properties. The Church "does not possess them of herself" (811). "The Church is one because of her source [the Blessed Trinity] ... her founder [Christ] ... and her soul [the Holy Spirit]" (813). Do not miss reading the quotation from Clement of Alexandria who, from as early as the third century, described this "astonishing mystery" (813).

Notice the other *visible bonds* that exist in the Catholic Church: one creed, one form of celebrating the sacraments, and one priesthood (815). To some extent these can also exist beyond her borders, especially the creed and the form of celebrating the sacrament of Baptism.

The two sections on the "wounds to unity" and "toward unity" offer us ways both of understanding the wounded nature of the Church's unity and also valuable guidance so that we might "respond adequately" to the call of the Holy Spirit and "gift of Christ" in desiring and working for the recovery of "the unity of all Christians" (820-821).

CCC 823-829
The Church Is Holy

That the Church is "unfailingly holy" (823) sounds exaggerated to many people. We need, therefore, to understand carefully what the Church truly believes. Let us remember first that, as we have said already, the Church does not possess these characteristics "of herself," but from her divine source, Jesus Christ.

Christ is holy; Christ endows the Church with *his* holiness; Christ *makes holy* the members of the Church gradually. Then, united to Christ, the Church sanctifies, too; she herself "becomes sanctifying" (824). The Church can claim this because Christ has given her "the fullness of the means of salvation" (824). Our becoming holy follows from our being saved from sin. There is *no sanctification without salvation from sin.*

All the activities of the Church are for the sanctification of each person in the whole world, and the Church cannot sanctify unless she has been given sanctity to pass on. There is abundant evidence of this in the saints and saintly behavior in every age of the Church, in men and women, adults and children, rich and poor. There is nothing in any other religion to compare with this innumerable "cloud of witnesses." In these the holiness of the Church is already "unfailing" in her members and *especially in the Most Blessed Virgin Mary.*

At the same time, "All members of the Church, including her ministers, must acknowledge that they are sinners" (827). This is even more important than it sounds. Many people say that they cannot go to Church because they are not good enough, as though only the good go to Church. People need to know that it is precisely when and *because* they are in a sinful mess that the Church is for them, salvation is for them — and *sanctification is for them, too, from God.*

CCC 830-856
The Church Is Catholic

In CCC 830 you have read that "Catholic" means "according to the totality," the "whole," or "fullness," and that the Church is "Catholic" always with a "double sense."

First, there is the sense of the "whole of Christ" present in the Church. This includes the *whole of Christ's Body* (head and members), and the *whole means of salvation* — that is, the whole, or "correct and complete," profession of Faith and the whole sacramental life of seven sacraments.

Second, there is the sense of being *for* the "whole of humanity." The Church is sent to the *whole of the human race*, to spread throughout the *whole world*, and is for *all ages* and through *all time* "ceaselessly" (831), for the return of *all humanity* and *all its goods* to the everlasting kingdom of the Father.

The implications of this "double sense" are explained under the five subheadings that follow. The first explains how "Each particular Church is 'catholic'" in this double sense. This catholicity depends on the fourth "mark" of the Church, which we have yet to consider — that is, through the *apostolic succession* of the Church (833).

When a local community of faithful Christians does not have this fourth "apostolic" mark, it is not yet fully "catholic," but *called to be such* (836). The Catholic Church "knows that she is joined in many ways to the baptized," who by their baptism are "in a certain, although imperfect, communion" with her (838).

The next three sections belong together, and describe with loving care and truth the Church's relationship with different groups of non-Christians, the unbaptized. The attitude given here is that which the Church asks us to adopt wholeheartedly: since "catholic" includes the meaning "for the whole human race," and since the Church's "missionary motivation ... is from God's *love* for all men" (851), we are all called to follow the Holy Spirit, "who leads the Church on her missionary paths" (852) to all those seeking the truth of salvation.

CCC 857-865
The Church Is Apostolic

We have read how these four marks of the Church are "essential features," inseparable characteristics, providing "inexhaustible fruitfulness" and "invincible stability" (811-812). This fourth indelible mark is equally essential, inseparable, and dependent on the Blessed Trinity for its permanence, fruitfulness, and stability.

We know from Saint Paul that the household of God is "built upon the foundation of the apostles and prophets, Christ Jesus himself being the cornerstone" (Eph 2:20). The Catechism helps us see what this means, that this "foundation of the apostles" has three layers of meaning. The Church is founded on: the *twelve men*, called "apostles" in the Scriptures, who were chosen and sent by Jesus; the *teaching* that these chosen men heard from Jesus; and the *ministry*, or "office," that these men received from Jesus.

The historical lives of *the first twelve men*, chosen by Christ to be the foundation of the Church, can be followed closely in the New Testament. Through these twelve, with a leadership given to Peter by Christ himself, the Church was guided by the Holy Spirit to do and understand many things in order that the Good News continue to the ends of the earth. Thus we can read how successors were elected and instituted by "prophetic utterance" and "laying on of hands" (1 Tm 4:14; 2 Tm 1:6). This is the starting point of "apostolic succession" — that is, of the office of bishops as successors of the apostles throughout the world (Acts 20:28).

The *whole Church is apostolic* by remaining "in communion of faith and life" (863) — that is, by being united in heart, mind, and will to the entire plan of the Blessed Trinity, through this apostolic succession. In practice, for us all, this means a unity of attentive, loving obedience to the successor of the apostle given to us, our bishop, provided that he remains in union with his fellow successors and the Pope, in true "succession" of the teaching from the apostles through the centuries.

CCC 871-896
The Hierarchical Constitution of the Church

We now come to an important section which clarifies the distinctions and functions of the diversity of ministries within the "unity of mission" (873). The Christ-centeredness of this section is striking: everything written here emphasizes "ministers of grace" who are "authorized and empowered by Christ" (875).

The first three paragraphs speak of what is true for all the Christian faithful "in their own manner" and "in accord with the condition proper to each one" (871). An understanding of *analogy* is important here. To illustrate this, look at the word "good" that we use analogously all the time. Thus we speak of a "good child" and a "good meal." A child is good according to the nature of a child (for example, kind, obedient), while a meal is good according to the nature of a meal (tasty, nourishing). We do not describe a good child as "tasty and nourishing" or a good meal as "kind and obedient"! So, "analogy" means simply that the *same term* is used (such as the word "good") with the *same* meaning, *but* for each occasion there is a *difference* because of the nature or condition "proper to each one," *according to what something is.*

Many terms used in this and the following sections — "ministry," "prophet," "priest," "king" — are used *analogously* for both lay people and the hierarchy. Priests share in the priesthood of Christ "in their own manner" through the sacrament of Holy Orders. Lay people — without this sacrament and so without the change that this sacrament confers — share in Christ's priesthood in a different way, in accord with the condition "proper" to them as lay people.

An analogous use of terms is used in this section for the bishops and the pope, and for bishops, priests, and deacons. They are all entrusted with the offices of teaching, sanctifying, and governing, but it is important to remember that it is for them, too, "in accord with the condition proper to each one."

CCC 897-913
The Lay Faithful

There are some interesting points concerning the laity here that can *strengthen people's hope*. The Catechism explains that "it belongs to the laity to seek the Kingdom of God by engaging in temporal affairs and directing them according to God's will" (898). All in the Church seek the Kingdom of God; the lay person does this by "engaging in temporal affairs."

Daily work, worshiping through "holy actions," "hardships of life" patiently born, all become "spiritual sacrifices acceptable to God through Jesus Christ" if "accomplished in the Spirit" (901). These are the lay person's participation in *Christ's priestly office* which in the celebration of the Eucharist may "most fittingly be offered to the Father" (901). Parents share in Christ's priestly office "by leading a conjugal life in the Christian spirit and by seeing to the Christian education of their children" (902). Finally, when, because of necessity, help in certain liturgical ministries is required, lay people participate in the priestly office by offering these services.

Participation in *Christ's prophetic office* is through evangelization and catechesis, and by sharing in the *sensus fidei*, the "sense of faith" of those who adhere to the magisterial teaching of the Church and are nourished regularly by the sacraments. Lay people also have the duty to tell priests and other Christian faithful about things they know to be for the good of the Church if it is in their area of expertise (such as in medicine or the education of children) (904-907).

How do lay people share in *Christ's kingly office*? First, it is about personal freedom, which is called a "royal freedom"; second, it is about governing over oneself (908). It also concerns helping to change secular institutions so that they may be "conformed to the norms of justice" (909) since "no human activity ... can be withdrawn from God's dominion" (912).

CCC 914-933
The Consecrated Life

The Holy Spirit "moves" and Christ "proposes to" a great many people to respond in love with the whole of their lives to God, the *source of all love*. In this response there is great liberty, joy, love of obedience, and a desire to imitate Christ most closely in a rich variety of ways. Though multiple in their forms, they have one single source and so can be called "one great tree, with many branches" (917).

What are the three evangelical counsels? To "counsel" a person is to advise him or her; "evangelical" in this context means "or the sake of the Good News of the Kingdom of God; and the three greatest Gospel values advised by the Scriptures have, through the centuries, been recognized as *chastity, poverty,* and *obedience.* The *profession* of these counsels "within a permanent state of life recognized by the Church ... characterizes the life consecrated to God" (915).

In the subheadings you can begin to see the variety of "calls" recognized by the Church as genuine. Hermits, or the "eremitic life," are the first to be mentioned; then consecrated virgins and widows, who do not normally live in religious communities. Those in religious life, living in community in one of the different "religious orders," make up the vast majority of men and women consecrated to God for the whole of their lives. The Benedictine monastic order, begun by Saint Benedict in the fifth century, would be an example of one of the oldest and most widespread across the world, itself having many branches.

Last to be listed in the Catechism are "secular institutes" and "societies of apostolic life," of which a great number have been established in the last hundred years. The members are a great cloud of witnesses working especially in health care, education, and the Church, *showing the world the love of God, the dignity of the human person, and Christ's love for the poor.*

CCC 946-953
Communion in Spiritual Goods

Today we begin a new section, on the *communion of saints*. As you have read in CCC 946, what we profess here flows with perfect logic from the previous sections. If one believes the previous sections to be true, taking God's word as "God's word and not some human thinking" (1 Thes 2:13), then these paragraphs follow from three key truths: *the Church is one Body*, *Christ* is its *Head*, and the members of the Body *can all receive the "riches of Christ"* the Head, especially through the sacraments.

These "riches of Christ" are also called "goods" here. Note that they are spiritual rather than material goods, even if they come *through* material means such as sharing a meal in kindness. The material good is the meal; the spiritual good is the kindness in the people. The spiritual good *always has priority*, and communion with the spiritual good *can always be full*, regardless of the level at which the material good is given — for example, whether the meal is lavish or just very simple. As you will remember, kindness is one of the fruits of the Spirit: "love, joy, peace, patience, kindness, gentleness, faithfulness, goodness, self-control" (Gal 5:22-23).

The phrases in italics in the following paragraphs (949-953) help us to appreciate the *kinds of spiritual goods* there are: faith, the sacraments, charisms, being willing to hold everything in common, and — the most widespread of all — the communion of charity. This last one includes the communion of *suffering in Christ*. Once suffering in Christ is understood as a spiritual good for the redemption of the world, and one knows that it helps to heal the whole Body, one can understand why people take on certain sufferings, such as fasting, or accept pain "for others" in the Body.

CCC 954-959
The Communion of the Church of Heaven and Earth

Each member of the Body of Christ, with Christ as the Head, is in one of three "states."

There are those in the state commonly known as *the Church "militant"* because of their battle against sin. Here they are called *pilgrims on earth* and *wayfarers*. There are those commonly referred to as *the Church "penitent,"* those who have died and desire penance and purification from their sins. "Purgatory" is the name given to the purging away of sin in a final purification "to achieve the holiness necessary to enter the joy of heaven" (1030). Finally, there are those who are even "more closely united to Christ" (956) and are commonly referred to as the *saints in heaven* and *the Church "triumphant,"* because they triumphed, with their Savior, over sin and death.

All three states are in the one Body with the one Head, Jesus Christ. Spiritual communion between the states takes place, especially through love and prayer. This communion is *spiritual* and thus does not include conversation (except on rare occasions such as Our Lady or a saint appearing to someone). Any other appearance — *via* a séance, for example — is from the devil.

A close look at the Catechism text reveals love and prayer at work. We are in the weakest state of sanctity and *receive* the most help from the others. Those in heaven are in the strongest state of sanctity and *give* the most help to the others. We "wayfarers" on earth seek to grow in faith, hope, and charity, and to battle well against temptation and sin; we undergo purification and pray for those who are undergoing purification in purgatory, and we seek to glorify God by faithful living, by participation in the sacraments, and by our prayers. Those in heaven no longer battle against sin and so intercede for *us* in our battle; they no longer need purification themselves and so intercede for those who do; and they glorify God in complete holiness and love.

CCC 963-970
Mary's Motherhood with Regard to the Church

CCC 963 reveals the way in which Mary is always treated in the Catechism. Her *role* is explained in *relation* to Christ, in *relation* to the Spirit, and now in *relation* to the Church. She is open to everyone. She relates to the divine Persons of the Blessed Trinity, to angelic persons (such as Gabriel) and human persons (such as Saint Joseph).

Mary relates always as an ever-virgin, all-pure mother, "full of grace." To contemplate Mary's motherhood for us, notice the verbs and adverbs relating to her in the quotation from *Lumen Gentium*, text to footnote 503: she *advanced* in her pilgrimage of faith; *faithfully persevered* in her union with Jesus; *stood* at the Cross; *remained* in obedience to the divine plan; *endured* the intensity of Jesus' suffering; *joined* herself in her heart with Jesus' sacrifice; *lovingly consented* to the immolation of Jesus as a victim; and *lovingly consented* to being given as a mother to Jesus' disciple. And, having lived in this way in relation to Jesus, the Son of God the Father, she relates to us, above all, "by her prayers" (965).

In this section we also find the explanation of Mary's *assumption* into heaven as a vital element of her *motherhood with regard to the Church*. The text carefully avoids using the word "death" for Mary. Instead it says, "when the course of her earthly life was finished" (966). The Eastern Church refers to this mystery as *dormition*, or "sleeping," because the only tradition that exists is that she was "taken up body and soul into heavenly glory" (966), and no grave for Mary has ever been mentioned or located.

Finally, she is "a mother to us in the order of grace" (968), in the spiritual necessities of our souls. She relates to us with "faith, hope, and burning charity in the Savior's work" for our salvation (968). "Therefore the Blessed Virgin is invoked in the Church under the titles of Advocate, Helper, Benefactress, and Mediatrix" (969).

CCC 971
Devotion to the Blessed Virgin

This single paragraph gives us the foundational reasons for the devotion to the Blessed Virgin in all its multiple ways and manifestations over two thousand years.

We know from the Scripture passage that when Mary says "all generations will call me blessed," she continues with the reasons why this is the case: "the Lord has done great things for me and Holy is his name." We call her blessed for the *things the Lord has done for her and in her.*

The next point to notice is the important distinction made between the "adoration" which is given to the Persons of the Blessed Trinity and the "special devotion" which is given to Mary. These different phrases are translations of different Greek words. The first is *latria*, which is the adoration due to God alone. We call "idolatry" any *latria* given to idols of some kind rather than to God.

The other Greek word is *dulia,* which indicates a form of devotion for those persons and things that *share* God's holiness but are not God himself, with whom none can compare. The word is often translated "honor" or "veneration"; here it is translated as "special devotion"; elsewhere you will find the phrase "special love."

Another point you will find in this paragraph is that *dulia* "greatly fosters" *latria* — that is, when we give "special devotion" to the Blessed Virgin (and to the saints), this *greatly fosters,* and does not replace or diminish, our *utter adoration of Jesus, the Holy Spirit, and our heavenly Father.* If we want to increase our appreciation of Mary, ever-virgin and mother, and so foster that adoration of God, the Church recommends that we honor her feast days, and she will show us all that we need.

CCC 972
Mary — Eschatological Icon of the Church

The Catechism has already used the term "eschatological" a number of times. It comes from the Greek word meaning "last end" or "destiny." The heading here, then, means that Mary is an "icon," an "image," of the end; she is an *image of our destiny*. In Mary we see what the Church *really* is and what it truly "looks like" in heaven.

The side references to this paragraph help us fill out this teaching very nicely. If you look up the side reference to CCC 829, you will read, "And so they [the faithful] turn their eyes to Mary": in her, the Church is already the "all-holy." If you look up the side reference to CCC 773, you are taken back to the section on the *mystery* of the Church, and to the saying there that "Mary goes before us all." All members of the Church are "awaited" by Mary, the one we venerate as our heavenly Mother.

Finally, the side reference CCC 2853 takes us towards the very end of the fourth part of the Catechism, on prayer. Two things — which you will read more about when you reach this part — are striking here. First, we are reminded that *the victory is entirely won by Jesus*. Mary receives all her graces from God, through her Son. Second, we can notice the hatred for "the woman" by the "prince of this world" who has been "cast out." The prince of this world (also called a dragon) lies behind every hatred of Mary, every hatred for the work of God, for holiness and for purity, and for the Church that, through Christ, provides the means for purification and holiness. This is why we pray "Come, Lord Jesus!" and why Mary "shines forth on earth" for us as "a sign of certain hope and comfort."

CCC 976-983
"I Believe in the Forgiveness of Sins"

This powerful section makes clear that *the forgiveness of sins is intimately associated with the sacraments.* The text and many of the cross-references point us towards the sacraments of Baptism and Penance, and also to the gift of the priesthood.

God's action, of course, is not *limited* to the sacraments; indeed, he might have chosen to forgive us without recourse to Baptism and Penance. Nonetheless, just as it is through his *Incarnate* Son that the Father reaches down to reveal himself to us and speak with us, so it is through the "incarnational realities" of the sacraments that Christ's mission of forgiveness continues among us. God's plan is all of a piece.

The close relationship of Baptism and Penance is a second theme in this section. We find forgiveness in Baptism, since here *Christ unites us to himself,* completely forgiving all original and personal sin. Baptism does not "make us perfect," however. The "laborious" (980) work of sanctification is still ahead. Forgiveness is the embrace of love; now the cleansing work of cooperation with the grace of that embrace begins. It continues in part through an ongoing recourse to the sacrament of Penance where there is *absolution* — the forgiveness of sin and the loosening of its hold on us.

A final section on "the power of the keys" concludes this article. Keys are for opening doors. The doors being referred to here are the "gates of forgiveness" (982) in "the house of God" (553). Christ *announced* God's reconciling work and *made it present* in his own Person: "God was in Christ, reconciling the world to himself" (2 Cor 5:19). God's pedagogy is one of words *and* deeds (see 53). The Church, as Christ's Body, also announces this reconciliation and enacts it through the sacraments. Through the Church, Christ wants to make available *all that he did* while on earth (983), making forgiveness possible for *every person,* in *every time,* for *every sin,* for *all who sincerely repent.*

CCC 988-1004
Christ's Resurrection and Ours

Today's reading makes two key points. First, that *Christ's resurrection is the pattern for our own* (989). Our risen bodies will be like his. He is the Lord in whom we *now live*; therefore, the Catechism explains, he is also the Lord "in whom" we *die* and are *resurrected*. He is the faithful one who *never* lets us go, always keeping us with him. We can only be separated from him by our choice — if we choose to turn away forever and die "in mortal sin without repenting and accepting God's merciful love" (1033). The resurrection of the body, then, flows from the personal relationship Jesus has with each of us. We are attached by faith and through the sacraments to the one who declares, "I am the Resurrection and the life" (Jn 11:25; CCC 994). In Baptism, God the Holy Trinity comes to dwell in us, and Christ feeds us with his own Body and Blood in the Eucharist (1002-1003).

The second point is that *the belief in the resurrection of the body follows closely from a number of other central doctrines* (992). It follows the *goodness* of the whole of creation and from God's desire that, in this good creation, "nothing may be lost" (Jn 6:12). God wants to save what he made "very good" (Gn 1:31). It follows from God's *faithfulness* to his promises, and especially his promise to bring about justice. It follows from the *unity of the human being* as both soul and body. Our immortal souls are the "form" of our bodies (365). In other words, our souls are not "trapped" in the body, needing to escape from this; rather, the body is to be redeemed along with the soul. It is striking that so many find this central teaching incomprehensible (996). But the whole Creed points to this culminating teaching: God, who created all things good, became *incarnate* in his own creation precisely in order to unite it to himself (988).

CCC 1005-1014
Dying in Christ Jesus

The only way to resurrection is through death; not any death, but a death in which we "abide" in him (Jn 15:4), united to him. He will not let go of us as long as we do not tear ourselves away from him. His are the "everlasting arms" (Dt 33:37), the hands through which nothing falls. *We allow him to hold us* at the decisive moment of the separation of the body from the soul, and we pray during our lifetime for the grace to do this (1014). A daily dying to self in him, living out the meaning of our Baptism, allows us to have a "quiet conscience" (1010, 1014).

If we find ourselves struggling with the thought of death, seeing it as an enemy, there is a truth in this, for *God did not intend us for death*. He did not intend this "way" for us. When the Catechism says, "In a sense bodily death is natural" (1006), it means that death is natural for the human person *in his fallen condition*. This is why the text immediately goes on to speak of what death is for faith. Death is also profoundly *unnatural* because our father Adam chose not to live according to his true nature, in God's image and likeness, but chose the way of "unlikeness" instead, to use a phrase from Saint Augustine. We have inherited death, the unnatural result of the way of unlikeness, and indeed *we follow this unnatural path every time we choose sin*. Therefore the divine Son who is *the* Image took our nature and lived out the perfect way of "likeness" in all his words, thoughts, and acts (705). He became the *new Way* for us (Jn 14:6), and Christians became known as the "followers of the Way" (Acts 9:2). Therefore, because of Christ, "Christian death has a positive meaning" (1010). Death, from being the enemy, now becomes the gateway to the Father's house.

CCC 1020-1022
The Particular Judgment

With today's reading we reach the final article of the Creed. It is introduced by a single paragraph, leading us into the essence of the Church's teaching on judgment, heaven, purgatory, and hell, and the transformation of the entire cosmos. The opening sentence sets the focus for the article: it is *deeply personal*. It is the *individual Christian* who is the subject of this paragraph, who is called to unite his death to Christ, who hears the words of pardon spoken over him, who is sealed with a final anointing, receives Christ in viaticum, and hears the words of the Church spoken with "gentle assurance" (1020). The subject matter of this article *concerns each of us intimately*. The prayer spoken over the Christian is like a short Creed, reminding the dying soul of the creative, redemptive, and sanctifying work of God the Holy Trinity in his life and calling him forward, in hope, to the expectation of *heavenly bliss* with all of the blessed.

The "particular" judgment treated here refers to the judgment of the *individual*. The *particular judgment* is being contrasted with the *universal judgment* that takes place at Christ's second coming. Judgment is, in both cases, *Christ's encounter with us* — for each of us there is both a "final encounter with Christ in his second coming" (1021) and also "a particular judgment that refers his life to Christ" (1022). God is love, and in the encounter with Christ, love is the *single criterion* by which our lives are measured, for our calling is to live everlastingly with Love himself.

CCC 1023-1029
Heaven

Our fondest memories of places are often associated with remembrances of persons who bathe the location in a loving light. We remember the place in "the light" of the person. Heaven is a "place" of a different order, of course, for it is the dwelling place of the saints, glorified in resurrected bodies. And in heaven the Personal Presence is above all what is sought and what is found — the presence of the Three-in-One whose *light irradiates all.* You will notice that heaven is described in the Catechism almost entirely in terms of communion with others — with the saints, with the Blessed Virgin, with the glorified Christ, with the divine Persons, with the angels (1024).

"This mystery of blessed communion with God and all who are in Christ is beyond all understanding and description" (1027). We know this heavenly communion only by images, remote analogies, and comparisons with moments of the deepest earthly happiness. All of creation at this point becomes a metaphor for what is awaiting us. The text, then, wants to stress the *transcendent bliss* of heaven.

Finally, the Catechism wants to remind us of *the life here on earth,* which is like a tree whose fruits will be found in heaven, encouraging us thereby to be persevering in such a life: it is a life nourished by God's grace, and lifted by him into a state of friendship (1023) through the redemptive work of Christ (1026); it is a life in which we are attentive to our deepest desires for happiness, and remain faithful to Christ whom we come to know as the *place of final rest for such longings* (1024-1025); it is a life in which we joyfully seek God's will for ourselves and all those around us (1029).

CCC 1030-1032
The Final Purification, or Purgatory

Purgatory is not an "intermediate" state between heaven and hell. It is not a midpoint between them. It is the state of the soul who dies "in God's grace and friendship," assured of salvation and of life with God the Holy Trinity and all the blessed in heaven, but who needs "purification" in order to enter into this life (1030).

The purification of which the Catechism speaks is that of being made able to find unadulterated joy in the presence of perfect Love. All traces of envy, jealousy, discontent in the presence of unlimited mercy, self-pity, self-isolating loathing or pride, comparative judgments vis-à-vis others, vainglory, self-righteous anger, lustfulness, or distrustful possessiveness, all must be burned away in the presence of the fire of Love. We so often identify ourselves with elements of these attitudes, thinking we will lose ourselves if we allow them to be clawed away from us. But through this process, on the contrary, "the elect ... retain, or rather find, their true identity, their own name" (1025).

The undoubted pain of such a purification in the face of Love is real, and so the Catechism emphasizes that it is "entirely different from the punishment of the damned" (1031). The text then reminds us of charity — it is entirely appropriate for us to join ourselves in loving intention for the souls undergoing such purification, for we on earth both seek and offer help to those who are undergoing similar cleansing; we should certainly "help those who have died and ... offer our prayers for them," and especially offer the sacrifice of the Mass (1032).

CCC 1033-1037
Hell

From his heart of love, God the Holy Trinity seeks "to communicate the glory of his blessed life" (257). Out of the perfection of his love, God creates, redeems, and heals what is fallen away, and sanctifies, purifying all that he is drawing to him to share in his life. We recall that the Catechism introduces the whole of its text with the quotation from the First Letter of Paul to Timothy, "God our Savior desires all men to be saved" (1 Tm 2:3). It is a verse cited seven more times in the Catechism. God's only desire is for *our salvation*.

Hell is the ultimate self-exclusion from this drawing motion of Love, the final refusal of "communion with God and the blessed" (1033). God is the fullness of Being and calls us to share in his own abundance (see 301). Hell is therefore a *self-destructive choice* — to be *less* than one might be, to find a *parody* of life in the small world of one's own making, a world from which God is excluded and, because of this, the person is demeaned, spiritual joy is denied, and self-gift is replaced by mutual use and abuse. Rather than participate in the reality of God's creation, in which peace, the "tranquillity of order," reigns (see 2304), hell is the state where one continues to seek to "'be like God', but 'without God, before God, and not in accordance with God'" (CCC 398, quoting Saint Maximus the Confessor).

As in the presentation of heaven, the Catechism reminds us of *the life here on earth* which can lead to such a final destiny and of the need for a *radical conversion* of life each time we become aware of the seeds and shoots beginning to grow in that destructive direction. Hell exists only through the willful *choices* of those who *freely* persist in sin. The Church's teaching is therefore a reminder of the incredible *gift of freedom* and of the importance of using our freedom well.

CCC 1038-1041
The Last Judgment

While on earth we make what is necessarily transient, there is an unseen "building" that is taking place in and through our works. It is this, the *unseen reality* of what we are making of our lives, that is to be revealed at the Last Judgment, when the whole of that "unseen" reality is embodied anew in the heavenly bodies of the resurrection.

Our lives in this world are, through the work of grace with which we are called to cooperate, preparing this new body. In this life our choices and loves are expressed in bodily form, but they can remain hidden. Who knows the depth of the love a mother feels for her child and which she expresses through often unnoticed acts of simple renunciation? But the loving choice made is real and endures. Nothing is lost. It is destined to find expression in the glory of the everlasting Kingdom of Love. "When Christ who is our life appears, then you also will appear with him in glory" (Col 3:4). Then "this perishable nature must put on the imperishable, and this mortal nature must put on immortality" (1 Cor 15:53).

Until that time, God has placed on the earth all that we need for the making of this "heavenly dwelling" (2 Cor 5:1-2). Here the Catechism emphasizes the utter seriousness of our choices and actions (1041). Through Saint Augustine, it offers us the image of a *treasury*: the poor whom we serve take our good works and place them in the heavenly treasury (1039). If we are without love and offer nothing, then we will find nothing in heaven. *Only what is given lasts.* Only the *life of love* endures for eternal life with God.

CCC 1042-1050
The Hope of the New Heaven and the New Earth

The whole world belongs to God. He is the Creator of all that exists; and from our good and gracious God comes nothing that is evil. "For he created all things that they might exist" (Wis 1:14), and "he loves everything that exists" (Wis 11:24). All things were made by the "work of his hands" (Ps 28:5) — that is, by the divine Word and the Holy Spirit (see 703-704); they were made *in* Christ and *for* Christ, "and in him all things hold together" (Col 1:17). *God, then, is the origin and the goal of the whole of creation.*

Christ's redemptive work encompasses all of creation. We have seen that, in assuming human nature, the Lord assumed a *microcosm* of the whole of creation, for in the human body and soul all of visible creation is summed up. "Through his very bodily condition he sums up in himself the elements of the material world. Through him they are thus brought to their highest perfection and can raise their voice in praise freely given to the Creator" (364, quoting the Second Vatican Council document *Gaudium et Spes*). In his resurrection and glorification, therefore, Jesus is raising a *universe*. He redeems a *world*. This, the Church teaches, is the first fruits of the "new heavens and a new earth" (2 Pt 3:13). The world itself is to be "restored to its original state" (1047).

The Church confidently affirms the truth that God's plan of loving kindness encompasses the whole of his creation without trying to define what we should, in practice, expect (1048). Her confidence is grounded in God's revelation of his faithfulness. And the visible creation itself "speaks" eloquently of its capacity for transformation in the "ordinary" wonders we daily experience around us. The English Catholic G. K. Chesterton once wrote, "If seeds in the black earth can turn into such beautiful roses, what might not the heart of man become in its long journey toward the stars?"

CCC 1061-1065
"Amen"

The Creed has God the Holy Trinity as the subject. The "Amen" also concerns God.

It is fitting, therefore, that our reading of the Creed ends with this word. "Amen," as the Catechism says, "expresses solidity, trustworthiness, faithfulness" (1062). It is God's final word. He is the *faithful one*, the God of *reliable love*.

When we end our prayers with "Amen," we are also stamping *our* final affirmation on the prayer. "Yes, Lord, I believe what I have just said." At the end of the Eucharistic Prayer the whole congregation proclaims the "Great Amen." The whole of God's people, assembled there, affirm together all that has been prayed. The whole Body utters its single cry of affirmation (1065).

Not only our words, but our *actions*, also, act as confirmations of what we believe. Indeed, because we are body–soul unities, words and acts belong naturally together. And so Saint James counsels, "But be doers of the word, and not hearers only, deceiving yourselves" (Jas 1:22). If the spoken "Amen" lacks the confirmation in deed, there is a danger of deception. Saint James is echoing Jesus' concluding solemn advice in the Sermon on the Mount: "Every one then who hears these words of mine and does them will be like a wise man who built his house upon the rock" (Mt 7:24).

Our passage from the Catechism concludes by emphasizing the truthfulness of the Lord Jesus in this regard. He is the final "Amen" of God, the *One in whom the Word takes flesh wholly faithfully*.

PART TWO
The Celebration of the
Christian Mystery

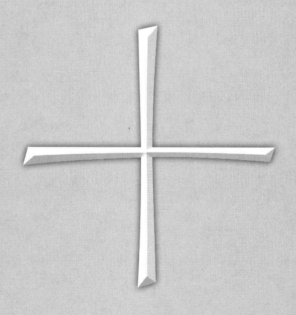

CCC 1066-1068
Introduction to the Liturgy I

Why is the liturgy so *central* to our *ordinary Christian lives*? This is the question that opens Part Two. The brief answer is that through the liturgy Christians can express in their own lives the *mystery of Christ* and can then impart that same mystery to others. The key is found in the opening sentence of CCC 1068: "It is this mystery of Christ that the Church proclaims and celebrates in her liturgy." In the introduction of the *Constitution on the Sacred Liturgy* of Vatican II, the council fathers explain that they sought to "impart an ever-increasing vigor to the Christian life of the faithful." They were confident that this goal would be faithfully achieved *through the renewal of the liturgical life of the Church.*

To understand this better, we are reminded, through the cross-references, to refer to some of the key passages from the first part of the Catechism, especially 50 and 236. There we are introduced to "the mystery" and to God's overall plan of salvation. As we have seen, the "time of the promises" was a preparation for the Incarnation and ministry of Christ whereby, primarily through his Paschal mystery, he redeemed mankind and gave perfect glory to the Father. Through the power of the Holy Spirit, Christ then not only sent his disciples to support his ministry by *preaching the Holy Gospel* to all creatures, but he promised that this *salvific work* would continue unabated down through the centuries, *through the liturgical life of the Church.*

In order that this great work be accomplished, Jesus promised that he would always be present in his Church: in his people when they assembled for prayer; in his word as it is proclaimed in his name; and most especially in the Eucharist wherein he offers himself as he did on the cross — as well as through the ministry of the priest celebrating the Eucharist, who at that moment becomes a living representation of Jesus himself, an *alter Christus.*

CCC 1069-1072
Introduction to the Liturgy II

What exactly is the liturgical life of the Church? CCC 1069 provides us with the answer. Essentially it is *the participation of the Church in the redeeming work of God*. Notice that it is Christ himself who "continues the work of our redemption in, with, and through his Church." It is God's work in which we now participate. Liturgy, then, is the work of the Mystical Body of Christ, through which Christ continues to effect redemption. It is easy to see why the Church teaches that the liturgy is "a sacred action surpassing all others" (1070).

CCC 1070 wants to emphasize *centrality* of the liturgy to our lives by noting how the New Testament term "*leitourgos*" actually has a wider reference point than public worship. We are being "liturgical" when we proclaim the truth of God's revelation and also when we serve our neighbor. The liturgy, as the point of God's active work for our salvation *today*, underpins all that we do and provides the grace we need for our lives.

There is a center to this, however: "The liturgy then is rightly seen as an exercise of the priestly office of Jesus Christ" (1070). Through the liturgy the People of God participate actively *in the exercise of Jesus' priesthood*. With the priest who stands at the altar as a representative of Christ, all the members of Christ's Body can share in the same mystery through public worship and by offering their lives, together with Christ, at the altar to God the Father.

Around this center of God's redemptive work we can place the entire activity of the Church. There must first take place preaching, teaching, evangelization and conversion, which are essential to the liturgical life of the Church. Through these activities one is led to enter the Church through the sacrament of Baptism. From that point, the Christian is empowered to evangelize future Christians and lead them, in turn, into the life of the Church.

CCC 1073-1075
Introduction to the Liturgy III

These final paragraphs from the introduction to Part Two continue to remind us of how the whole of the Christian life is centered upon the liturgy. CCC 1073 explains how our *personal prayer* flows from the liturgy. The ultimate goal of all liturgical prayer is to offer praise and thanksgiving to the Father in, with, and through Christ, in the Holy Spirit. We are led *into* this prayer and praise and "*extend*" it through our personal prayer. Our personal prayer allows us to "internalize" that same work of God that is made present in the liturgy into all the times and events of our daily lives.

The Catechism then turns to the crucial area of *catechesis*. Here we remember that the genre of the Catechism is precisely that of a document assisting in the *handing on of the faith*. Everything in its pages serves that purpose. Central to the Church's work of catechesis is teaching people well *about* the liturgy and the sacraments, and this includes teaching them how to *prepare* for the sacraments and *live from* the redemptive grace of Christ given there.

CCC 1075 provides us with three catechetical "steps," or pedagogical stages (see 53), we can follow to lead people into this awareness of the reality of the liturgy and the sacraments. First, we help people move *from the visible to the invisible*. As we have seen (353), we ourselves have both of these "orders" of creation within us. Then we teach how to understand that words and things can be *signs*, and we point to what is "signified" — as a simple gift can be an expression of love. Finally, we teach how the *sacraments* are signs and instruments that flow from and lead us to the invisible reality of the *mysteries* of the faith, centered on Christ.

CCC 1075 briefly concludes by explaining the structure of Part Two and how it will deal with what is *fundamental* and *common* in the Church's liturgy and sacraments.

CCC 1076
The Sacramental Economy

In today's reading we focus on a single, immensely important paragraph that introduces the whole of Section One of this part.

The Catechism explains that this first section is composed of two chapters: in the first chapter we have the explanation of the "sacramental dispensation," in what the Catechism describes as the "new era" in the "dispensation of the mystery," and this is followed by the nature and essential features of liturgical celebration in the second chapter.

Before Jesus ascended he began to teach his disciples about the way in which he would be with his Church "until the close of the age" (Mt 28:20). We see an example in his appearance to the disciples on the Road to Emmaus (Lk 24:13-49), where he is recognized, after he has been with them in the proclamation and explanation of the Scriptures and then in the breaking of the bread. It is, the Catechism later notes, the clear pattern of the Mass (1347). Jesus is teaching his disciples to expect and to recognize him in the liturgy of the Church and in her sacraments.

Before Jesus ascended he also promised the Holy Spirit, who would continue his presence and ministry in this "age of the Church" during which he "manifests, makes present and communicates his work of salvation" until his second coming. Christ makes present for us the fruits of his Paschal mystery now through the sacramental liturgy. It is *Christ* who acts in the sacraments. It is *Christ* who "dispenses" for each of us the medicinal fruits of his saving work.

As the Catechism leads us into an understanding of the communication of Christ's work of salvation, it wants us first of all to be reminded that this is the work of God the Holy Trinity (1077-1109). Just as our creation was the work of the Blessed Trinity (290), and the resurrection of Christ (648), so also our new creation, in which the likeness of God is restored to us.

CCC 1077-1083
The Father — Source and Goal of the Liturgy

The Father is the *Source* and the *Goal* of the whole of creation. *From* him all that exists flows, and to him all are called. God the Father is the "first origin of everything" (239), and the One to whom Christ finally "delivers the kingdom ... that God may be everything to everyone" (1 Cor 15:24, 28).

The Catechism frames its presentation of the Father's overarching work in the liturgy with references to the opening verses from Paul's Letter to the Ephesians. This letter brings out clearly for us what the Catechism explains as a double movement of blessing. *We* bless God the Father as the One who has *first* blessed us. The two blessings are quite different, of course. The Father's blessing is explained as "a divine and life-giving action" (1078). The Father blesses his creatures in many ways ("every spiritual blessing in the heavenly places"), and the Catechism highlights the most profound blessing of all, which it refers to as "word and gift" (1077, 1078). The Father blesses us with *Jesus*, the Word, and with the *Holy Spirit*, the Gift (see 733, 1082), through whose work in our lives we are restored (see 734).

That work of divine creation and re-creation spans the whole of time, and the Catechism gives us a sense of that great cosmic sweep of divine blessings (1079), and then, especially, the blessings that encompassed all living things (1080), and then all human creatures, and then the particular historical events that marked the blessings of the People of Israel (1081). The Church's liturgy fully reveals and communicates these blessings, summed up in Christ (1082).

In response, and also through the liturgy, the Church offers her *blessing, adoration, and thanksgiving* to the Father by her worship and praise, as the Father fills us with the *gifts of his Son* who suffered and died for us, rose from the dead, and pours into our hearts the power of the Holy Spirit.

CCC 1084-1090
Christ's Work in the Liturgy

When, after the Ascension, the risen Christ took his rightful place at the right hand of the Father, he did not leave us orphans but *continues to act and communicate grace* through the sacraments that he had instituted during his earthly ministry. The sacraments are humanly perceptible signs and symbols that *signify* grace and actually *communicate* that grace through the power of the Holy Spirit.

The final climactic event of the life of Christ was that of the Paschal mystery. It is this mystery of our salvation that Christ "principally" makes present (1085). While it was certainly a historical event that took place once and will never be repeated, at the same time it *transcends all time* through the action of the Holy Spirit, and *its power is continually present* in the liturgical life of the Church. Two reasons are given to explain how this can be: first, because it is the unique event that overcame death itself. Christ's saving work has destroyed death and so cannot "pass away" or die. Second, because Christ is God, and so all of his actions, while taking place *in time*, are *for all times* (1085).

The *principal Actor* in the liturgy, then, is *the glorified Christ* (1084) who is at the heart of the "heavenly liturgy" (1090). In our earthly participation in this great cosmic liturgy, this double movement of divine blessing and response of thanksgiving, it is *the glorified Christ* who acts in the sacraments, who speaks when the Sacred Scriptures are read, and who is present in his ministers and in his gathered people (1088-1089).

While Christ is the "real" Actor in the liturgy, this does not make us mere puppets. Christ makes it possible for us to *join him in his saving work*, "entrusting" to his apostles his divine mission of the sanctification of mankind. In turn, down through the ages, their successors continued this sacred mission — and this succession "structures the whole liturgical life" (1087).

CCC 1091-1109
The Holy Spirit and the Church in the Liturgy I

It is the Holy Spirit who is the catalyst effecting this entire sacramental and divine movement. In all of the sacraments and throughout the seasons of the liturgical year it is the Holy Spirit who helps the faithful to understand more readily the rich plan of salvation as the liturgy reveals it, making it more accessible to the living participation of the faithful.

The role of the Holy Spirit is crucial, then, in the overall work of the Blessed Trinity in the liturgy. As we have seen, the Spirit is the *bond of love and communion*, the One who draws together. Take time to notice in the readings today and tomorrow how much of the text is focusing on this work of *creating communion* and *fostering unity*. So, for example, the Holy Spirit "brings about genuine cooperation" in us, so that we can "live from the life of the risen Christ" (1091). The Spirit is described as "the Spirit of communion" who "unites the Church to the life and mission of Christ" (1092) to "form his Body" (1108).

It is, of course, a *specific union* that the Holy Spirit desires to bring about; his work is to lead the Church to "encounter her Lord" (1092) and be united to him. The Catechism expects us to be able now to anticipate which actions the Holy Spirit performs to bring about this union, for in the liturgy and the sacraments "the Holy Spirit acts in the same way as at other times in the economy of salvation." These "typical" actions of the Spirit are given in the subheadings in this portion of the text: the Holy Spirit *prepares* the Church to receive Christ, *reminds* us of Christ, *reveals* Christ, making him *present* to us, and then finally *brings us into communion* with Christ.

CCC 1091-1109
The Holy Spirit and the Church in the Liturgy II

Because there is a good deal to take in from this treatment of the Holy Spirit in the liturgy, today we invite you to a second reading of this portion of the text.

We noted yesterday that the Catechism was drawing our attention to the *pattern* by which the Holy Spirit "typically" works (1092). The Holy Spirit works "typologically" so that many different figures and events prefigure Christ (1094). We understand the unity of God's plan and how all things come together in Christ when we truly appreciate this "typical" action of the Holy Spirit. Then we see how there is a "harmony" between the Old and New Testaments and why the Church constantly recalls the marvelous works of God, as she sees all of salvation history coming together into a *glorious unity* in Christ.

So, for example, we can recall that Mary was described as the "masterwork" of the mission of the Son and the Spirit (721) and that the Spirit's work in her was to *prepare* her, *fulfill* God's plan in her, *manifest* the Lord in her, and *bring others into communion* with her Son through her. She was presented as the "type" of the Church, and the Church was described in terms similar to Mary (737). As we see here, the liturgy and sacraments are presented in a similar way again, and the sacraments are called "God's masterpieces" (1091), for God is One and his plan of salvation is one.

Finally, note that the work of the Holy Spirit is both *external and objective* and also *interior*. He "gathers" us into the Body of Christ (1097) and then "seeks to awaken faith" in our hearts (1098). He inspires the Sacred Scriptures, and also opens hearts to "a spiritual understanding of the Word" (1101). He makes the bread and wine into the Body and Blood of Christ and works in the hearts of those who are to receive Christ that they may become living offerings to God (1104-1105).

CCC 1113-1116
The Sacraments of Christ

The paragraph that introduces this next article reminds us that we are looking here at what is "common" to the Church's understanding of the sacraments across all of her rites and traditions. We look first at what is *common* in terms of her *doctrine*, her teaching on the sacraments. We then turn to look at what is *common* in terms of the *celebration* of the sacraments.

It then reminds us that the Eucharist lies at the heart of the entire sacramental life of the Church. All the other sacraments flow from it and are effective instruments of grace because of it.

In the short first section on what is common to the sacraments, we begin with the fact that they are "of Christ." The sacraments were founded upon the mysteries of Christ's life and now disperse their distinctive graces through the action of the Holy Spirit. They are "of Christ" in that they were "all instituted by Jesus Christ our Lord" (1114). This "institution" is seen as being more than discovering one particular saying or event in Jesus' ministry. It is in the "mysteries of Christ's life" (1115) as a whole that we see the sacraments instituted. The cross-reference takes us to CCC 512-560 and to the whole of Jesus' life — his infancy, his hidden life, and his public ministry. All that was "visible" in the life of the Word who became flesh has "passed over into his mysteries."

The sacraments are "of Christ" in a second sense. They are "of" the *whole* Christ, the *Christus Totus* (795). The healing and saving powers that flowed from Christ's earthly body during his time on earth now flow from his Body, the Church. Christ, the Head of the Body, dispenses his grace through his Church.

CCC 1117-1121
The Sacraments of the Church

Today we consider the ways in which the sacraments are "of the Church." The Catechism begins by noting one of those "patterns" that mark the economy of salvation, helping us discern what is of the Holy Spirit. God's pedagogy of revelation, we remember, is in gradual stages (53). God reveals himself and his will in steps so that his children can grasp who he is in a measured way. When the Holy Spirit guides the Church, he does so in a similar way; in the unfolding of doctrine (94), in the identification of the canon of Scripture (120), and in the identification of the seven sacraments, we see this same pattern of an unhurried recognition. God the Holy Trinity *accommodates himself to our way of learning* by small degrees.

CCC 1118 then explains the two ways in which the sacraments are "of" the Church: *they flow from her*, as Christ's Body, and *they are for her*, building her as Christ's Body. It is *by* Baptism that Christ makes us into his Body and *by* Penance that he forgives and renews us. It is *by* the Holy Eucharist that he saves and feeds us. The sacraments not only flow from the Church but "make" the Church.

The Catechism then explains how the baptismal and ministerial priesthood act as an "organically structured priestly community," as one living Body with Christ as the Head (1119-1120). Through Baptism and Confirmation the people of God are enabled to celebrate the liturgy through the power of the ministerial priesthood. This ministerial priesthood forms a sacramental bond with the actions of the apostles and with Christ, the source and foundation of all the sacraments.

Baptism, Confirmation and Holy Orders also confer upon the recipients an indelible character, or "seal," which sets one apart for divine worship and the service of the Church in a variety of states and functions. Since this seal is *indelible*, the sacraments that impress it on the soul are never repeated.

CCC 1122-1126
The Sacraments of Faith

Today we read the ways in which the sacraments are "of faith." In the first place, preaching and evangelization, which bring about faith, accompany the sacrament. God "speaks" to his people by both word and act (53), and it is both Jesus' "wisdom" and his "mighty works" (Mt 13:54) that communicate his saving power. Inseparable from the sacraments, then, is the teaching that arouses faith. Jesus' commission to his apostles was to make disciples of all the nations by *baptizing* and by *teaching* (Mt 28:19-20).

The sacraments are "of faith" in a second sense — that *they are themselves a form of teaching*: "because they are signs they also instruct" (1123). Just as Jesus' miracles were described as a "new *teaching*" (Mk 1:27), so the sacraments themselves teach us. As signs and symbols that are full of meaning, they not only presuppose faith, but they also "nourish, strengthen, and express it."

The Catechism then echoes for us an earlier *distinction between personal faith and the faith of the Church* (see 166-168). The objective "faith" of the Church — *that which* the Church believes — *precedes* my faith and so, "whoever says 'I believe' says 'I pledge myself to what *we* believe'" (185). The *act of faith* also belongs first to the Church herself, and I am invited to enter into the believing community: "It is the Church that believes first, and so bears, nourishes, and sustains my faith" (168). And so at Mass we pray, "Lord, look not on my sins, but on *the faith of your Church* ... "

Notice also the Latin phrase that is given in CCC 1124: *lex orandi, lex credendi*. This means that the liturgy and sacraments express the objective faith of the Church. Her beliefs are encapsulated in her official worship. Modifications of a sacrament or of the liturgy may thus only be undertaken by "the supreme authority in the Church," and then only in "the obedience of faith" (1125).

CCC 1127-1129
The Sacraments of Salvation

Over the centuries and under the guidance of the Holy Spirit, the Church has developed visible rites for the celebration of the sacraments which, when properly celebrated, make present the graces that are proper to each sacrament.

The sacraments are said here to be "efficacious" (1127). In other words, they make a difference to our lives; they have actual effects in us. They *make us* more united with each other; they *strengthen* Christ's life in us; they *loosen* our bondage to sin; they *heal* our bodies; and so on. Each sacrament has a different grace. They have these effects *because it is Christ himself who acts in and through them.*

CCC 1128 explains that the sacraments act *ex opere operato*. This is because they are not impersonal "things" but the saving actions of God the Son. We cannot bring such effects about in our lives by ourselves and by our sheer willpower; neither can any human being. Only God himself can do this. This means that their efficaciousness is not dependent upon the personal holiness of the minister. Whether a bishop, priest, or deacon acts in morally good or bad ways is vitally important for many reasons, of course, but the personal moral quality of the minister is irrelevant to the effectiveness of the sacraments. The Church's faith in their effectiveness is placed in Christ, not in the minister's personal goodness.

However, what the Church calls the *fruits* of the sacrament *do* depend on the *genuine faith of the recipient*. The sacramental grace is *present independently of us*, but *it will not work without us*. As we will later read, there must be "cooperation between God's grace and man's freedom" (1993). If faith is present, the grace will flow into the recipient, forging a living bond with Christ the Lord. If faith is not present, the recipient cannot benefit from the grace. God completely respects our freedom. He wants a fully human, personal response to his invitation to us.

CCC 1130
The Sacraments of Eternal Life

Today we contemplate the *purpose* of the sacraments: to bring us to share in God's eternal life. The sacraments of the Church not only produce wonderful fruits of God's gifts to us in our daily lives, but also guarantee *eternal* life. They are a promise of our future glory and a glimpse into the wonder that God has prepared for those who love him.

CCC 1129 has already spoken of the importance of the sacraments for salvation. The Church teaches that, for believers, they are "necessary for salvation." Notice the careful way in which the text is written here. The Catechism is *not* teaching that only those who receive the sacraments can attain to the Kingdom of God. We have already seen that, in the case of those who have no possibility of hearing the Gospel, their response to the actual graces God gives in their lives, following their consciences, is the path on which God will lead them to himself. God leaves *no one* without the possibility of reaching the supreme happiness to which he calls each person made in his image (see 846-848). Nonetheless, the sacraments mark out the *sure path to salvation* that God has prepared. Through the sacraments, Christ, the faithful Shepherd, reaches out to us to draw us to himself and to carry us to our everlasting home.

In today's reading we also see again the role of the Holy Spirit highlighted. The Holy Spirit *unites* the Church to himself so that both the Spirit and the Bride can cry out to Jesus *together*, "Come!" The Spirit is the *Spirit of communion*, the one who makes possible communion with each other and also that final nuptial union with the Bridegroom. Our prayer in the Church is "carried" by God himself in the Holy Spirit. Nothing can impress upon us further the way in which the liturgy is a *divine* work into which we are, by God's good grace, "caught up."

CCC 1135-1139
Who Celebrates? I

We now begin the consideration of what is *common* to the universal Church in the *celebration* of the liturgy. The Catechism proceeds by addressing four questions on the liturgy. The responses to these questions, taken together, address all of the key areas of liturgical celebration.

In today's and tomorrow's reading we look at the question of *who* celebrates the liturgy. An introductory paragraph, CCC 1136, reminds us of the Church's teaching on the "whole Christ," the *Christus Totus*. It is *Christ* who celebrates the liturgy, and "Christ" here means Christ the head and all of his members. It means *Christ and his Church*.

After this introduction, the text is divided into two, into the "heavenly" celebrants (1137-1139) and the "earthly" (1140-1144). Notice here another of those "patterns" — the catechism is following the division we found in the opening of the Creed, that of the visible and the invisible spheres.

The section on the heavenly liturgy draws extensively from the final book of the Bible, the Book of Revelation. This tells of the visions which Saint John had on "the Lord's Day" (1:10). What he saw was the *celebration in the heavens* — the adoration of the Lamb of God, the heavenly sanctuary, the worship of the angels, and so on. Take time to follow the many references to this vision in the Book of Revelation given in CCC 1137-1138.

CCC 1139 tells us that it is "in this eternal liturgy that the Spirit and the Church enable us to participate" when we celebrate the sacraments on earth. This "heavenly liturgy" is what is present but unseen. The heavenly liturgy no longer uses signs (1136) because all that the sacramental signs point to is realized in heaven. When we reach the destination, we no longer need the signs pointing the way. In heaven all is "communion," all is "feast" — in other words, *all desire comes to its point of rest and fulfillment here.*

CCC 1140-1144
Who Celebrates? II

A major theme in this section on the celebrants of the sacramental liturgy is the importance of appreciating that in sacramental celebrations, as in the Church in general, different members work together to form one organic whole. Liturgical services involve the entire Mystical Body of the Church, and the unity of the Mystical Body is realized not by making everyone perform the same functions but precisely through the *cooperation* of each within the whole. *Unity* in the Church does not mean *uniformity*. The Catechism quotes from the *Constitution on the Sacred Liturgy* in order to remind us that "liturgical services are not private functions, but are celebrations of the Church which is the 'sacrament of unity'" (1140).

All the baptized share in the common priesthood of the Lord; but not all of them have the same function. Certain servants within the community are chosen and consecrated by the sacrament of Holy Orders through the power of the Holy Spirit, enabling them to act in the person of Christ the head, for the service of the entire community of the Church. The ordained minister is an *alter Christus*, an "icon" of Christ the head (1142), because he presides in the name of the Lord at the Eucharistic sacrifice.

There are other ministries within the Church, not consecrated by the sacrament of Holy Orders, where specific functions are determined by the bishop in accord with "liturgical traditions" and the "pastoral needs" of the Church (1143). For example, many liturgical traditions have a rich musical heritage and especially value the place of the choir.

CCC 1144 concludes by saying that in the celebration of the sacraments, then, an essential point to remember is the importance of the *separation of roles*, and their *interrelation for the good of the whole*, wherein each person with an office to perform carries out "all" and "only" those parts which pertain to his particular office according to the nature of the rite and the norms of the liturgy.

CCC 1145-1152
How Is the Liturgy Celebrated? I

Over the coming days we will be reading the Catechism's response to the question, "*How* is the liturgy celebrated?" There are four areas of consideration. Liturgy is celebrated through the use of *signs and symbols* (1145-1152), through *words and actions* (1153-1155), through *singing and music* (1156-1158) and through *holy images* (1159-1162). In each of these areas an introductory paragraph sums up that portion of our text (1145, 1153, 1156, and 1159). Our attention, then, will be focused especially on these introductory paragraphs which draw together the key points.

We saw that God's pedagogy involves moving from the visible to the invisible and from the sign to that which is signified (1075). This pedagogy is entirely "fitting" for our nature because we live in a world of signs and symbols. A sacramental celebration simply involves a *particular* set of signs and symbols that seek to convey, in the clearest way possible, the *mystery of salvation and its meaning*. Therefore, these signs must translate, in the most effective manner, the inner meanings of the sacraments which are otherwise hidden from our human understanding. As man needs signs and symbols to ˙ be able to communicate in everyday social activity, so also signs and symbols become indispensable as means by which man can penetrate the veil that separates him from the transcendent in all our sacramental activity.

The Catechism communicates the complex levels of meaning that can be attached to particular signs: there can be significations that belong to the *natural level*, others that are *culturally derived,* and others again that emerge from the *relationship to salvation history* and to *the life of Christ.* (1145). You will notice that the Catechism's structuring of its presentation of the individual sacraments follows this movement from nature, culture, and salvation history to the person of Christ, ensuring always that the fulfillment of signs in Christ is made clear, together with the ways in which the Church relates these signs-fulfilled-in-Christ to specific liturgical celebrations.

CCC 1153-1155
How Is the Liturgy Celebrated? II

Signs can consist of *words* or of *actions*, or a combination. As signs, *words* can signal something visible or can communicate an invisible reality to which we need to be attentive. If I want you to notice a great oak tree, I can say, "I mean that tree that is on the hilltop in front of us." If I wish you to take account of something not immediately visible to the naked eye, I can explain that the oak tree is one I used to climb as a child. My words about the tree now also "carry" the significance of my own relation to it, with my memories and affection. Pointing to the tree, running up to it, and so on, are *actions* that can accompany and reinforce the "sign."

Sacramental celebrations build on this natural foundation of how words and actions signify reality. Yet they are so much more! Every sacramental celebration is a personal encounter with the Lord, a "meeting of God's children with their Father, in Christ and the Holy Spirit" (1153). God takes the initiative in this encounter, and we are called to respond. Every sacramental celebration is a dialogue between God and his children. In this dialogue, Christ and the Holy Spirit assist us so that we can both "hear" what our Father says and respond to his loving voice with faith. The Holy Spirit "awakens faith" in us and also "makes present" the wonders of grace which the sacraments carry (1155).

On our part, the intimate connection between the proclaimed word and the liturgical action should always be made as apparent as possible. We seek to ensure that the words and actions of the sacraments are performed and communicated in appropriate ways to enable a fruitful dialogue and engagement with God's saving work in his Church. Therefore, for example, the Word of God must always be clearly audible and its message effectively delivered.

CCC 1156-1158
How Is the Liturgy Celebrated? III

When the Word of God is put to music and the liturgical assembly sings together the praises of the Lord it makes all the more apparent the *sacramental presence* of God to his people. The Catechism notes that song and music have been strongly connected with liturgical actions throughout the history of the Church and, precisely because of their intrinsic power to move us and to communicate the divine, they must always reflect fidelity to the Word of God, and be of the highest quality and beauty. Why is it that we can "weep, deeply moved" by music, as Saint Augustine witnesses in his *Confessions*? It is perhaps because music engages us at each level of our being and thus can move us easily from the sense level, through the intelligence, to the spiritual level of our being. When accompanied by words and actions, there is a "harmony of signs" (1158) that is deeply satisfying because of its integrative power in our lives.

For this reason, then, the Church gives *criteria for the use of music in the liturgy*. Its power can foster prayer and adoration or else distract us or hinder us from hearing the Father's voice. Any texts to be sung, precisely because of the power of music to move us, must therefore reflect Catholic doctrine, the "*lex credendi*" of the Church (1158). Above all, music should always be *beautiful* and *expressive of prayer*. It also needs to be able to incorporate the *participation of the assembly* at the "designated moments" (1157), according to the actual liturgical celebration. Indeed, this participation is to be "intelligently fostered" (1158). Music and singing should also reflect the "solemn character" of liturgy — that is, it should be selected in view of the fact that it is part of a *sacred celebration*, and in order to highlight key points of the celebration and of the dialogue of our heavenly Father with us.

CCC 1159-1162
How Is the Liturgy Celebrated? IV

Finally, we come to a consideration of holy images. While music and song address the sense of hearing, images address the sense of sight. In the paragraphs we read today you may have noticed that the phrase "the harmony of the signs" is used once more (1162). The Church wants there to be a drawing together, in a liturgical celebration, of the different signs and symbols used, so that our whole being — our body, senses, emotions, mind, and will — are united in one integrated *attitude of receptivity*, alert to the divine action taking place so that we can make a *full-hearted response*.

The place of sacred images has been a disputed one in Christian history, and the Catechism quotes from the Second Council of Nicaea which gave the Church's definitive response to the debates taking place (1161). The third part of the Catechism will discuss the relation of the use of images to the first commandment (see 2129-2132). Here, the Catechism simply points out that the rationale for using such images is deeply Christ-centered and follows from the fact that, in him, the eternal Word became *visible to our sight* (1159).

Related to the image of Christ are all the other holy images such as the representation of Our Lady and the angels and the saints. All are a *reflection of the glory of Christ*. As the Gospels proclaim the message of faith in word, the sacred images do so in their varied mediums, helping to awaken and nourish the faith of believers. In order to reinforce the importance of holy images for the life of faith, and to demonstrate the unity of image and text, the authors of the Catechism placed four pieces of art from the first millennium to lead us into each of the four parts of the work.

CCC 1163-1167
When Is the Liturgy Celebrated? I

We live in time in different ways. Our lives have a *beginning*, and for each of us there is an *end* to earthly life. This is linear time, unrepeated, progressing from one point to another, from conception to death. *Within* that linear time we experience *different kinds of repeated time*, in cycles of differing length. These cycles pertain not only to our own nature and its character, such as how long we are awake and asleep, but also to the wider universe and its lunar and solar cycles.

God reaches us in and through our nature and through the universe that he created. It all belongs to him as Creator. He set its patterns and bounds, "the structure of the world and the activity of the elements" (Wis 7:17). God created all things "by the eternal Word, his beloved Son" (291), and so at the Easter Vigil the Church proclaims, "Christ yesterday and today, the beginning and the end ... all time belongs to him and all the ages."

The "when" of liturgy reflects these truths — about ourselves and how we live in time, on the one hand, and about the meaning of all time being summed up in "the mystery of Christ" on the other (see 280).

In its simplest form, we have "today" (1165). Every *moment* is an occasion when God reaches out to us in Christ and in which we can celebrate his mystery. We can enter into Jesus' "hour" at any point in time. Jesus' "hour" is his Passover from death to eternal life, and every *week* we solemnly enter into this fundamental reality, through celebrating Jesus' day, "the Lord's Day" (1166). At the head of the Church's liturgical season is Sunday, the day of the resurrection of our Lord. This is the fundamental celebration because this is when Jesus conquered the "passing away" of time, establishing the "day that knows no evening" (1166).

CCC 1168-1178
When Is the Liturgy Celebrated? II

The celebration of the Resurrection on the Lord's Day is not only the culmination of the week, but it is also the culmination of the Church *year* in the annual celebration of Easter, the Feast of feasts. Easter is "Great Sunday" (1169).

Over the centuries, the Church has developed around the feast of Easter a series of celebrations representing the *entire mystery of Christ* from the Incarnation to his resurrection, as well as special days for the veneration of the Blessed Virgin Mary, the mother of God, and the memorial of saints. In these memorials the Church proclaims the Paschal mystery of Christ "in" them, offering them to the whole Body of Christ as faithful examples for Christians to follow and as intercessors who bring us closer to Christ (1173).

The Church understands only too well that *the Eucharist lies at the heart of the liturgical life of the Church* through which Christ, together with the faith-filled community — that is, both clergy and faithful — offers to the Father an unending sacrifice of praise. However, the Church not only satisfies this precept by celebrating the Eucharist, but also in other different ways, especially through the Liturgy of the Hours. Flowing from the Eucharist, the Liturgy of the Hours is able to sanctify and transform different *hours* and thus the whole of each *day*.

The "Liturgy of the Hours" is also called the "prayer of the Church" (1174), and the Second Vatican Council taught that this prayer is intended to be a public and common prayer for "the whole People of God" (1175). Through this celebration of hymns, psalms, canticles, litanies, and the Word of God, this public prayer offered to the Father at different hours of the day allows us to enter into the dialogue between the Son and the Father (1174), just as it can form in us a deeper understanding of God's plan (see 1176).

CCC 1179-1186
Where Is the Liturgy Celebrated?

Just as all *time* belongs to Christ, so all *space* also. The worship of the Church is therefore "not tied exclusively to any one place" (1179). We can, and should, pray *anywhere*. But our Mother the Church is wise. We live in time and space: if we do not pray at *specific times*, we are unlikely to pray "at all times" (see 2697); if we do not pray in *specific places*, we are unlikely to pray "anywhere." While the Spirit of the Lord is present everywhere, in our earthly condition we need some physical space in which the community can gather to celebrate the liturgy.

The Church, in her celebration of the sacraments, has "sacred places," churches, and these are also to be signs contributing to that overall "harmony of the signs" (1181) which is present in the liturgy. Churches are to be signs of the Father's house (1186), the saving presence and activity of Christ (1181), and the rescued community that by God's grace has entered into a new Life and into which all God's children are called (1186).

These brick and mortar churches symbolize the Body of the Risen Christ, the community of God's people who are together, the "temple" of the Holy Spirit. The "where" of liturgical celebrations, then, participates in the pedagogy of God with which we are familiar: through all that is visible and that is a "sign," the Father *draws close to us and lifts us up to himself*, from the visible to the invisible, from the sign to that which is signified, and from the sacraments, into the mystery of Christ.

CCC 1200-1206
Liturgical Unity and Diversity

The final set of paragraphs from Section One of Part Two of the Catechism returns to the important question of how to value both unity and diversity.

There are *many* rites in the Church, many variations in celebration, many cultures being expressed, many languages and local traditions from which the liturgy flows and which the liturgy in turn transforms. This rich variety follows from the fact that the Church is for all peoples and nations for all time. She is *catholic* (perhaps you can remind yourself of the meaning of this term, see 830-831). As the Church spread from its birthplace in Jerusalem to all of the Greco-Roman world, it settled in many different geographical locations which represented many different cultures and customs. Liturgical diversity also follows from the *intrinsic depth and breadth of the work of salvation itself.* The Paschal mystery is so unfathomably rich that it cannot be exhausted in all of its aspects by one single liturgical tradition.

The Church is also a unity. From the beginning of the Church until the end of time it is the same Paschal mystery that is celebrated by all the local churches of God. Thus there are *immutable*, unchanging, elements in the liturgy, as well as elements that *can be changed* (1205). The Catechism presents us with the general guidance given by Saint John Paul II in these matters, so that diversity does not "damage unity" (1206). First, the liturgy must express "only fidelity to the common faith." The principle of *lex orandi, lex credendi* must be followed. Second, the different traditions must be faithful to the "sacramental signs that the Church has received from Christ." Oil must be used for anointing, not vinegar; bread for the Eucharist, not rice; water for baptism, not syrup. Finally, there must be faithfulness to "hierarchical communion": in the last resort it is the practice of the bishops in communion with the successor of Saint Peter that determines the legitimate boundaries of diversity.

CCC 1210-1211
The Seven Sacraments of the Church

Today we read the introduction to the second section of this part of the Catechism. Having considered what is common to the doctrine on the sacraments and to the celebration of the liturgy, we now turn to discover the riches of each of the sacraments in turn.

The Church has affirmed that during his earthly ministry *Christ instituted seven sacraments of the new law.* They are Baptism, Confirmation, Holy Eucharist, Penance, Anointing of the Sick, Holy Orders, and Matrimony. As we have seen, these sacraments are signs to the senses that both indicate and actually effect grace.

This introduction also seeks to give us a sense of how the sacraments as a whole relate to our lives. They are said to "form an organic whole" (1211). In other words, they are interconnected with each other in one living whole. We know that, in the first place, the connectedness of the sacraments follows from their being *actions of the glorified Christ.* The text here gives us a second reason: they are also *intimately connected with all the important stages of the Christian life.* They give birth and spiritual growth, they promote healing, mission, and fraternity to the Christian's life of faith. Earlier, the Catechism explained how the divine Son assumed human nature in order to bring every "stage" of human life into communion with him, and so he "experienced all the stages of life" (518). We, in our turn, were then to "accomplish in ourselves the stages of Jesus' life and his mysteries and often to beg him to perfect and realize them in us" (521). This is what is made possible in the sacraments.

From this analogy with the stages of human life the Catechism has structured this section into three groupings. We can note, however, the *unique* place of the Eucharist. It is the "Sacrament of sacraments," the center of the entire sacramental life of the Church, with all the other sacraments flowing from it as from their source.

CCC 1212-1213
The Sacrament of Baptism

Today we read two more introductions. The Catechism, leading us into an understanding of the sacraments by unfolding the analogy it is using to the stages of human life, explains the first group of sacraments, the "Sacraments of Christian Initiation" — namely, Baptism, Confirmation, and the Eucharist. These lie at the "foundation" of every Christian life. Born into the life of Christ through Baptism, strengthened by a fuller outpouring of the Holy Spirit in Confirmation, the Christian receives the Eucharist as the Bread of Life and the food of eternal life.

CCC 1213 then provides us with the introductory paragraph to the sacrament of Baptism. This is described as "the gateway to life in the Spirit." The Catechism takes the trouble to provide us with the Latin phrase for this as well. Why is this such an important phrase to give us? You will see the answer if you look ahead to the title of the first section of Part Three of the Catechism. This is the part that unpacks how we live out our faith in Christ. You will notice that it is precisely *life in the Spirit*.

It is Baptism, in other words, that is the gateway to the *Christian life*, that allows us to enter into it. The Christian life is one lived by *God's grace*. It is the call to share in the very *life of God*, and it is the *sacramental grace* we receive that makes this possible. Baptism provides access to all the other sacraments, enabling a full sharing in this sacramental grace, for our growth in Christ, our daily food, our healing, and calling us out to share in Christ's mission of redeeming love. Through the power of this sacrament of Baptism we set out on the Christian journey. We are delivered from all sin, become children of God and members of Christ, of the Body the Church, and become active sharers in her mission.

CCC 1214-1216
What Is This Sacrament Called?

You will find in the Catechism's treatments of the sacraments an initial discussion of what the sacrament is called. The Church believes that *naming* something correctly is vital. Names communicate to us the *nature* of a thing, its *essence*, what it *is*. The names of things in the faith are not arbitrary labels, but allow us to understand what they truly are.

When we name a sacrament, we are always forging a link between the *sign* and *that which is signified*. Something that we can sense is united to the spiritual reality which is present. The names we give can truly make this link, bringing the material and spiritual realms together, because they *are* so related in reality. God made the heaven and the earth as one single *unified cosmos*. The universe has levels of being, in which the lower levels participate in the higher.

When we consider the sacraments, we are looking at a naming that is truly remarkable, because in this case the *created world* is linked to the *world of uncreated grace*, the life of God. The names of the sacraments are to help us, then, to "move" from the created sign to that which is signified in the realm of uncreated grace.

Look at the text from Saint Gregory of Nazianzus on the sacrament of Baptism (1216). The names and images here capture our imagination and excite desire, drawing us upwards towards the spiritual realities, pointing us to that level where God's grace is at work. Because sacramental grace is invisible, we need a strong grasp of these names in order to lift us to the truth of what is divinely taking place so that we can begin to "see" the action of God the Blessed Trinity in his creation.

CCC 1217-1228
Baptism in the Economy of Salvation

After the naming of the sacrament, the Catechism usually presents the particular sacrament to us within the whole of God's plan of salvation. By doing so it is reminding us that the individual sacraments are not arbitrary. They are precisely *the way God has planned to reach out to us with his grace*. We have seen, from the introduction (1210-1211), that they "fit" human nature, touching each of the stages of our lives. This section on how each particular sacrament can be found in God's "economy," or plan, reinforces this. The sacraments "fit" the whole of *creation* and *history*.

You will see that the unfolding of the sacrament follows the pattern which we found in CCC 1145. We move from its "prefiguration" in *creation* and human culture, and in the events of the *Old Covenant*, to its "institution" in the person and work of *Christ*, and conclude with how the sacrament is lived in *the Church*. This portion of the presentation of the sacrament is usually divided into three, as it is here, to remind us of the gradual unfolding of God's plan in relation to the revelation of the three divine Persons. You will notice, therefore, that what prefigured Baptism is especially related to the Person of the *Father* (1217-1222), the institution of the sacrament related to Christ, the *Son* (1223-1225), and the sacrament in the life of the Church related to the *Holy Spirit* (1226-1228).

All of those find their fulfillment in Jesus Christ (1223). This is also the heart and focus of our reading, for it is *his life* which is handed on to us in the sacrament. In Baptism we are given a share in *his* death and resurrection. The beautiful imagery of Saint Paul explains how the newly baptized enters into communion with the death of Christ, is buried with him in the saving waters, and rises with him in newness of life (Rom 6:3-4).

CCC 1229-1245
How Is the Sacrament of Baptism Celebrated?

Now that the essence of the sacrament has been *named*, with the links forged between the signs of the sacrament and the sacramental grace it communicates, and now that the sacrament in question has been *placed within God's loving plan* for his creation, the Catechism turns to outline how the celebration of this aspect of Christ's mystery takes place. The words and actions, symbols and signs are laid out for us.

The text here (the use of small type is explained in CCC 20) explains important elements about the *historical developments of the sacrament* over the time of the history of the Church. It also begins to note some of the more important variations between rites. Some account is given, then, of the diversity that enriches the sacrament. The main focus, however, remains on establishing what is *stable* and *common* in the celebration of the sacrament. Although the celebration of Baptism has varied greatly over the centuries, certain elements have always remained consistent. These elements have included the proclamation of the Word with catechetical instruction, acceptance of the Gospel, conversion, and a profession of faith. There is the immersion of the candidate in water, or pouring of the water on the head, while invoking the name of the Father and the Son and the Holy Spirit.

CCC 1234 is an important paragraph, which explains that the rites, with their signs and words, are "mystagogy." The term means *learning about the mysteries*. By carefully following the elements of the rites we learn how to "enter" into the mystery of the sacrament. Most of us will have received the sacrament of Baptism as a child, and our reading of this text in the Catechism now is mystagogy — we are learning anew how to enter into what was *given to us* once and for all when we were baptized. Through this learning, the Holy Spirit can teach us how to conform our lives more and more deeply to that of Christ.

CCC 1246-1256
Who Can Receive and Confer Baptism?

The simple answer to these questions of who can receive and confer Baptism is that *any person not yet baptized* is eligible to receive Baptism, including infants, while the *ordinary ministers* of Baptism are the bishop and the priest, together with, in the Latin Church, the deacon. However, in the case of necessity *any person* can baptize as long as they do so by pouring water over the head of the recipient while reciting the Trinitarian formula. The *universality* of these answers — "any person" — reflects the *foundational* importance of Baptism (1256). Baptism, we recall, is the gateway to sacramental grace, and it is this grace that enables us to live a Christian life. God calls everyone to share in his life, therefore Baptism is for every person. Baptism needs to be as available to people as the air we breathe, and so any person (even a nonbeliever) can baptize.

Notice a simple point regarding the sacraments that is contained in these questions about conferring a sacrament and receiving it — that they are *given* by another. No one ordains himself; no one anoints or baptizes himself; a sacrament is always given by another. This fact reflects the life of the Church in which "no one can bestow grace on himself; it must be given and offered" (875), and of creation itself: "Creatures exist only in dependence on each other, to complete each other, in the service of each other" (340).

This principle can help us appreciate why the Church in both the East and the West baptizes infants. In CCC 1253-1255 we find an important piece on faith and Baptism, and this connection might seem to counter infant Baptism. However, the Church from the beginning baptized *households*, whole *families*, and not just individuals (see Acts 16:31-33). We support each other in the faith, and infants can be supported by the faith of their parents, their family and the local church.

CCC 1257-1261
The Necessity of Baptism

The "necessity" of Baptism is related to salvation. If there was no *need* for salvation, or if there was no *offer* of salvation, then Baptism would not be necessary. But there is such a need and such an offer. Therefore Baptism is necessary.

Building off this fact of the necessity for redemption and of God's saving act in Christ, today's reading develops two key principles: first, that God *desires all to be saved*; second, that Christ himself "affirms that Baptism is necessary for salvation" (1257). Baptism is not optional. We have already begun to appreciate how Baptism lays the foundation for all else in the Christian life. Baptism is necessary, then, similar to how the letter "A" is necessary in the recitation of the alphabet. It is necessary to begin with "A" in order to reach the other letters.

Given the necessity of Baptism, which the Church derives in faithfulness to Christ himself, what of those cases where it would seem impossible for Baptism to take place? The Catechism looks at four such situations:

- Those who are martyred for the faith before being baptized (1258). In this case their sharing bodily in the death of Christ is described as a *"Baptism of Blood."*
- Those who die before being baptized who were "catechumens" — that is, actively preparing for Baptism. Their *desire for Baptism*, together with their love and repentance, is held to assure them of salvation.
- Those who never learned of Christ but seek the will of God according to their understanding and conscience are held to be those who, because of their openness to truth, *would have sought Baptism had they known of God's gracious offer.*
- Finally, infants who died without being baptized. The Church here has the overarching knowledge that it is God's will that all be saved. God *wants each particular infant to find salvation*, and so this allows us "to hope that there is a way of salvation for children who have died without Baptism" (1261).

CCC 1262-1274
The Grace of Baptism

To conclude its teaching on each sacrament, the Catechism has an extended section on the "effects," or "grace," that Jesus extends to us in the particular sacrament to make us into new creatures who are able to share in God the Holy Trinity's eternal life of happiness.

This consideration of the grace of Baptism is divided into five areas. Each element of the grace of Baptism is indicated by a bold subheading and by italicized phrases under that heading.

The overall point here is that *Baptism begins our restoration*. God intends to restore to us all that we lost through the Fall (see 385-409). Baptism sets us on this path of restoration, forgiving our sins and restoring us to communion with God. Baptism is the *foundation* of this new life with the Father, the Son, and the Holy Spirit. It is the beginning of a journey. Because it is salvific, *Baptism begins the reversal of what sin shattered*. "Sin destroyed the communion of men with God, and that of men among themselves" (761). Baptism restores communion: it means that we now *belong* to God (1265-1266) and that we *belong* to the Church, to his People (1267-1271).

Baptism is also described as placing a "seal" upon us. Baptism sets God's indelible mark of favor and faithfulness on us even as he calls us to our new life of hope, faith, and love. He promises to be faithful to us with his grace until the end, when all that he has promised us in Christ will be completely given. Each of us is, in turn, called to be a "faithful Christian who has 'kept the seal' until the end" (1274).

As the Catechism concludes this consideration of Baptism, it very appropriately turns to Confirmation, to God's "Yes!" to his choice of us and to his further outpouring of the Holy Spirit so that we can be more and more conformed to the likeness of his beloved Son.

CCC 1285-1292
Confirmation in the Economy of Salvation

We often think of Confirmation as something that is primarily about our commitment to God, whereas it principally concerns *his* unshakeable commitment to us. The introductory paragraph explains that this sacrament is the occasion for "the completion of baptismal grace" (1285). It is the occasion for a *further outpouring of God's own life into our own*, to make the path on which Baptism started us more secure and well-marked, to enable us to have an increased sensitivity to the relationships which sustain us on the path, and to strengthen us with additional grace for the rigors of the journey. The phrases used in this paragraph each emphasize this notion of God's further gifting of us — thus we are "*more perfectly bound* to the Church," are "enriched with a *special strength* of the Holy Spirit," and are "*more strictly obliged* to spread and defend the faith."

In this way, the sacrament of Confirmation is a witness to the *unity* of the sacraments. God does not intend them to stand alone. It is not enough for us to be born — we must grow up and develop, and be well-nourished; so also it is not enough to be baptized: we must receive the further grace of Confirmation to strengthen us, and both of these together are oriented towards the ongoing divine nourishment we receive in the Eucharist. "Baptism, the Eucharist, and the sacrament of Confirmation together constitute the 'sacraments of Christian initiation', whose unity must be safeguarded" (1285). God cares for our integral *growth*.

The paragraphs on this sacrament in God's plan of salvation (1286-1292) further impress upon us that Confirmation is concerned with deepening and unifying our lives in communion with others. The gift of the Holy Spirit is promised to the King of Israel (1286), and he reveals that this promise is, in reality, for sharing with the whole Body of the People (1287). The One anointed by the Holy Spirit, the Christ, makes the anointing available to all people.

CCC 1293-1301
The Signs and the Rite of Confirmation

Today's beautiful presentation on the signs in Confirmation and on the celebration of the rite is in two sections. CCC 1297-1301 take us through the main points of the celebration of Confirmation. In the East, Confirmation has been celebrated from the earliest times as one single rite with Baptism, whereas in the West a temporal separation has occurred between the two sacraments. In the East the priest who baptizes usually confers the sacrament, while in the West the reservation of the completion of Baptism to the bishop has caused this separation. However, in both East and West, the emphasis remains on the *unity* of these sacraments.

In the earlier section (1293-1296) the Catechism discusses the *anointing* that is given in Confirmation. Related to this anointing is the significance of being *sealed* — "Be sealed with the gift of the Holy Spirit" (see 1300). As we have already seen from Catechism texts (1121, 1216, 1274), this is a deeply scriptural notion. In his Letter to the Ephesians, Saint Paul writes of Christians being "sealed with the promised Holy Spirit" (1:13). In a way that is similar to Baptism, Confirmation signifies and imprints a spiritual sign or "character." This seal of the Holy Spirit marks "our total belonging to Christ" (1296) as well as his promise of divine protection throughout our pilgrim journey. There were a number of occasions when a "sealing" took place in the ancient world, and perhaps the clearest one for our understanding of this sacrament is the practice of shepherds using an iron *sphragis* (the Greek word for *seal*) to imprint their right of ownership on their sheep, to mark those sheep as belonging to their flock. So Christ, in sealing us with the Holy Spirit, identifies us as belonging to him. At the same time, that gift of the Holy Spirit (see the prayer of the bishop in 1299) enables us better to know and hear the voice of the Shepherd.

CCC 1302-1305
The Effects of Confirmation

This passage is an extraordinary one: the opening paragraph draws our attention to the relation of the sacrament of Confirmation to *the coming of the Holy Spirit at Pentecost* (1302). The Pentecost reference is then echoed again later in the section, where the one who is confirmed is described as having been clothed "with power from on high" that he might be a witness to Christ (see Acts 1:8). Pentecost is the launching of the Church into *evangelization and mission*, and it is significant that the Western Church has maintained the link strongly with the bishop as minister of the sacrament (1313), for bishops are the successors of the apostles, of those who were originally "sent" to proclaim the Gospel by Christ. Confirmation makes the one being confirmed *apostolic*, sent on mission.

The coming of the Holy Spirit at Pentecost is also the moment of the *public manifestation of the Church*, and we see here that Confirmation brings Baptism to maturity so as to enable a *public witness* to Christ to be made (1304-1305). Confirmation is thus related to the power to give witness to Christ — "to confess the name of Christ boldly, and never to be ashamed of the Cross" (1303). The word we translate as "witness" is *martyria* in the original Greek, and we have already seen that Baptism is closely associated with martyrdom and with dying "in" and with Christ. Confirmation brings about an "increase and deepening of baptismal grace" (1303). It brings about a deeper union with Christ in his death and resurrection.

Above all, the sacrament of Confirmation "unites us more firmly to Christ" in his identity as the beloved Son of the Father. It "roots us more deeply in the divine filiation which makes us cry, 'Abba! Father!'" (1303). The sacrament is the *Father's confirmation of us as his beloved sons and daughters "in Christ."* The Holy Spirit is given to us so that this might be the *secure identity* from which we live.

CCC 1306-1314
Who Can Receive and Confer This Sacrament?

The Catechism's presentation here helps us to appreciate the distinction between the "immutable" aspects of a sacrament and those that can change (see 1205). The age at which one is confirmed, the minister of the sacrament, the ordering of the sacraments of initiation — these have differed over the centuries and between traditions and rites.

There are many immutable points, however, and the opening paragraph regarding the *reception* of this sacrament (1306-1311) underscores three points. First, that Confirmation can be received *only by those who are already baptized*; second, that both sacraments *can be received only once*; and third, that the baptized *should* receive this sacrament. The permanent character of the sacrament is thus emphasized, together with the ordering and unity of the sacraments of Baptism and Confirmation. God does not want to leave us "incomplete" (1306). We need *all* that the Father *wants* to confer on us. The exceptions noted in CCC 1307 and 1314 reinforce the importance of the strengthening God wants us to have, and especially "at the hour of death," that time of frailty that is rightly the focus of many of our prayers.

Regarding the *minister* of the sacrament (1312-1314), the Catechism draws our attention to the legitimate differences in the traditions of East and West. In the West the usual reservation of this sacrament to the bishop underlies the way in which Confirmation strengthens the bond with the Church in her "apostolic origins" and in her "mission of bearing witness to Christ" (1313), for the bishop is the successor to the apostles. When explaining the circumstances when it is a priest who is the minister, the Catechism takes care to note the ways in which the role of the bishop is still central (1312).

The final words in the treatment remind us once again that Confirmation is a *gift*, is grace. It is *the Father's gift of the Holy Spirit*, of the conferral of the fullness of anointing that Christ himself received.

CCC 1322-1327
The Sacrament of the Eucharist

The Eucharist is the culminating point of the "sacraments of initiation." The sacraments of initiation, both Baptism and Confirmation, find their ultimate completion within the celebration of the Eucharist. This is the point made in CCC 1322.

But the Eucharist does not tidily fit within a sequence, even as the culminating point of a group, for "the Eucharist is the source and summit of the Christian life" (1324). It is the "Sacrament of sacraments" (1211). In and through the Eucharist we find the springs of grace for the *entire Christian life* and are able to experience here on earth a *foretaste of the heavenly liturgy and of eternal life*. CCC 1324 leads us into a consideration of how the Eucharist stands apart since "the whole spiritual good of the Church" is contained in this sacrament.

The whole of the Catechism's treatment of the Eucharist will make clear why this sacrament is so significant, and today's reading draws our attention to its unique place in the Church. As you will have seen, these paragraphs we are reading here are made up almost entirely of quotations from documents of the Second Vatican Council, documents approved at the most recent worldwide council of bishops. In addition, reference is made back to Saint Paul's First Letter to the Corinthians, a letter containing some of the earliest extended teachings on the Eucharist. Finally, there is a striking quotation from Saint Irenaeus (c. AD 130-200): "Our way of thinking is attuned to the Eucharist, and the Eucharist in turn confirms our way of thinking" (1327). Irenaeus' statement echoes the musical image we found presented on the cover line drawing, with the Shepherd holding the sheep attentive through playing the "melodious symphony of the truth." The Eucharist is this symphony in abbreviated form, for CCC 1327 also teaches, "In brief, the Eucharist is the sum and summary of our faith." Here in the Eucharist we find the *whole of the Christian faith*.

CCC 1328-1332
What Is This Sacrament Called?

As always, the naming of the sacrament is deeply significant in identifying its essential nature. CCC 1328 warns us of the challenge with which naming presents us in the case of the Eucharist, for there is an "inexhaustible richness" here and any name will only be able to evoke "certain aspects." The text of the Catechism conveys a sense of awe and reverence before this task of naming.

We can notice how many of the names given have to do with a meal: the Lord's Supper; the wedding feast; the Breaking of Bread. At the Eucharist, the Lord *feeds us with himself*, and it is through this that the Lord makes us know our *hunger* for him. It is always this way: through the experience of the good we become aware of our deep longing for it and of the ache of emptiness. It is through the experience of beauty that we realize how often we have been content with mediocrity. It is through meeting a person of real holiness that we find ourselves longing for the grace to live in that same way. So it is that *God causes us to long for him* through giving himself to us in the Eucharist.

This act of feeding us, then, finds its fulfillment in the *communion* that is brought about, with God and with our neighbor. Our hunger is intensified and ultimately satisfied through the deepened unity brought about by the Eucharist. Many of the other names have to do with this movement towards a restoration of communion and overcoming the isolation of sin and rupture: *Holy Sacrifice, Thanksgiving, Communion*. The names given to the Eucharist express both the divine source of the sacrament, as in *the Divine Liturgy* and *the Sacred Mysteries*, and also the call to draw all people into this restored communion around the action of Christ and the Holy Spirit through mission (*Holy Mass*).

CCC 1333-1336
The Eucharist in the Economy of Salvation I

As we begin to explore how the signs and symbols, words and gestures which we find in the Eucharist have their origin in the very heart of God's plan for our salvation, we can note how the Catechism traces this background to the simple elements of creation and ancient Near Eastern culture before moving on to events in the history of the Jewish people (see 1145). We begin with bread and wine representing "the goodness of creation" and "the gesture of the king-priest Melchizedek" (1333).

We then move on to events around the Exodus (1334). Most significantly, of course, is the foreshadowing of the Eucharist within the Old Covenant in the meal celebrated each year by the Jews on Passover. With the use of unleavened bread, they celebrated this meal as a commemoration of their hasty departure from the slavery of Egypt through the liberating power of God. Each year they would recall these saving events within the context of a sacred meal.

CCC 1335 brings us to the ministry of Jesus himself who reflects, in his feeding of the crowds and in his multiplication of wine, some of the great "themes" from the history of the People of Israel, and also, through these actions, looks forward, prefiguring the Cross and the institution of the Eucharist itself.

In an important reference, the Catechism then draws our attention to how the Cross and the Eucharist are inseparable. "It is the same mystery and it never ceases to be an occasion of division" (1336). The Church teaches that the Eucharist is indeed the "same mystery," for the Eucharist was instituted to "perpetuate the sacrifice of the cross throughout the ages" (1323). And from the beginning both the Cross and the Eucharist were the causes of division. These are the two areas where the disciples "stumbled." Just as they protested at Jesus' announcement of his coming passion, so they rebelled at his offering them himself as their food.

CCC 1337-1344
The Eucharist in the Economy of Salvation II

So we come to Jesus' institution of the "Sacrament of sacraments." Note the phrase "New Testament" in CCC 1337. We are used to thinking of this as a reference to the corpus of inspired writings from the period of the apostles. In fact, *the "New Testament" writings were given that name from its use here at the Last Supper.* This is the only time the phrase is used. Jesus speaks of the "New Testament," or "New Covenant," in his blood (Lk 22:20; Mt 26:28; Mk 14:24). The "Old Covenant" was made with the People of Israel at Sinai, and Jesus, by celebrating the Last Supper within the Passover meal, "gave the Jewish Passover its definitive meaning" (1340). This central act of making a new covenant lies at the heart of the redemptive plan of the Father.

What was formerly, under the Old Covenant, a representation of the saving actions of God for his people now becomes a true and living memorial of *Jesus' death and resurrection*, making Christ's sacrifice on the cross offered to the Father truly present and its power available to all mankind.

Jesus gave a command to "Do this," and this "sacrament of love" (1323), this "pledge" of the love Jesus has for us that signifies that he loves us "to the end" (1337), until he returns to bring us to our home of everlasting Love, has been faithfully celebrated and made "the center of the Church's life" (1343). In a famous passage from his history of liturgy, Dom Gregory Dix asks: "Was ever another command so obeyed? For century after century, spreading slowly to every continent and country and among every race on earth, this action has been done, in every conceivable human circumstance, for every conceivable human need from infancy and before it to extreme old age and after it, from the pinnacles of earthly greatness to the refuge of fugitives in the caves and dens of the earth" (*The Shape of the Liturgy*).

CCC 1345-1347
The Liturgical Celebration of the Eucharist I

The subheading of today's reading is "The Mass of all ages." The text explains that it is that *same* Mass with the *same* "basic lines of the order of the Eucharistic celebration" that is celebrated today in common with what has been celebrated in "all ages" and across "all the great liturgical families" — that is, all of the different families of Eucharistic rites (1345). We are fortunate indeed to have an extended account of the Mass from the second century — just a little more than one hundred years after Pentecost. A reading of this account easily allows us to recognize this as the *same Mass* as that which we experience every Sunday. We can see that throughout the ages the Church has continued to celebrate the Eucharist. While it has evolved in some aspects, the celebration of the Eucharist has always included the *proclamation of the Word of God*, a fervent *prayer of thanksgiving* to God the Father for all his many graces, and above all, at the culmination of the celebration, the *consecration* of bread and wine into the Body and Blood of the Lord. This was followed by the reception of the Body and Blood of the Lord.

CCC 1346 then offers us a way of "summing up" what this order is. The Mass can be thought of as having two basic parts: the Liturgy of the Word and the Liturgy of the Eucharist. The *unity* of the two parts is emphasized: they form "one single act of worship," and the cross-reference, CCC 103, speaks of the veneration of the Lord in the two together and explains how the "bread of life" is served from the "one table" of God's Word and Christ's Body.

Finally, the Catechism reminds us, very simply, that we can trace back the "Mass of all ages" in this "basic" order to Jesus himself and to his "celebration" on the road to Emmaus (1347).

CCC 1348-1355
The Liturgical Celebration of the Eucharist II

The Catechism now walks us through the main parts of the Mass in the "movement of the celebration." The text continues to pick up phrases from the account by Saint Justin Martyr, as though to remind us that this is the Mass, not only as it is celebrated now, but as it has always been. Indeed, two further references to this same account from the second century are included, on the meaning of the "collection" (1351) and on the basic Eucharistic "discipline" that was practiced concerning who might receive communion (1355).

To remind us that when we celebrate Mass we are celebrating the Mass that *Jesus* himself celebrated — in the flesh at the Last Supper and in his resurrected body with his disciples — and that Jesus is "the principal agent of the Eucharist" (1348), the account opens with a strong restatement of the Church's central teaching that it is *Christ* who acts in the sacraments.

This emphasis on Christ does not exclude *us*. In fact, the teaching on the headship of Christ in the celebration appears in the paragraph that is focused on the first "movement" of the Mass, that "All gather together" (1348). Christ, *as* the principal agent, *gathers* us. He gives "all" their "own active parts," just as he takes "all human attempts to offer sacrifices" and unites them to his own sacrifice (1350).

The longest explanation in this account of the "movement of the celebration" naturally concerns the Eucharistic Prayer, since this is the "heart and summit" of the Mass (1352). The parts of this prayer are helpfully identified, and we are given the original Greek title for this prayer: *anaphora*, "offering up," was used in the Greek translation of the Old Testament (the Septuagint) for the priest's offering of the sacrifice. The whole of this prayer is directed to the Father. It is he who blessed us with his Son and Holy Spirit and whose blessing we seek at every Mass.

CCC 1356-1358
The Sacramental Sacrifice

These three paragraphs lead us into the heart of the weighty teaching on the meaning of the Eucharist. They provide an orientation so that we are not later lost in the detail but can always return to this overview.

The first point made underscores *the sacredness of the Mass.* All that we have read of the faithfulness of the Church across the ages to the "basic lines of the order of the Eucharistic celebration" (1345) has followed from the recognition that this is simply the call to act in obedience to Jesus' command — "we know ourselves to be bound" (1356).

The next paragraph introduces the *three main aspects* under which the Eucharist will be considered: as *thanksgiving* (1359-1361), as *sacrifice* (1362-1372), and as *presence* (1373-1381).

Finally, *these three themes are related to the Persons of the Blessed Trinity.* We know that the redemptive activity of God the Blessed Trinity is always a "work at once common and personal" in which each divine Person acts in "what is proper" to them and always does so in a way that also expresses and reveals "their one divine nature" (259). In specifying the Persons in relation to each of these aspects of the Eucharistic mystery, then, the Catechism is not dividing the Persons from one another, but is simply allowing a certain focus to illuminate the heart of what is taking place.

CCC 1359-1361
Thanksgiving and Praise to the Father

We call the Mass "Eucharist," which means "thanksgiving." When Jesus commands his Church, "Do this in remembrance of me," he is commanding her first of all to thank and praise the Father. It is a "sacrifice" of praise (1359) and a "sacrifice" of thanksgiving that we offer. When we use the word "sacrifice" today, we often associate it with negative connotations — something is a "sacrifice" for us because it is difficult or unpleasant. In this case the phrase "sacrifice of thanksgiving" would mean that we are commanded to give thanks even though it is uncongenial to us! When the Church uses the term, though, she is thinking of the original meaning as "making sacred" (from the Latin *sacer*, "sacred," and *facere*, "to make"). When we offer a *sacrifice* of praise, or thanksgiving, we *make our praise sacred*.

How do we do this? In part it is by directing our thanks and praise not to any human being but *to the Father*, to the one who is holy. In part it is through the Church's thanks and praise being *united to Christ*. "Through Christ the Church can offer the sacrifice of praise" (1359). "This sacrifice of praise is possible only through Christ" (1361). It is because of the holiness, the sacredness, of Christ, who "unites the faithful to his person, to his praise," that we can make this "sacrifice."

In making this sacrifice of praise we discover who we are. We offer it "in the name of all creation" (1361). We discover our true identity as the priests of the whole of creation whom we can represent in this "making sacred," this bringing to the Father. We are the "little worlds," the microcosms of the created order who can sum up in our own being "all that God has made good, beautiful and just" (1359).

CCC 1362-1372
The Sacrificial Memorial

When I "remember" something, I "call it to mind," I bring it forth into the present. What was past is now here with me "in my mind." We also use the word "recollection" — we "collect" things from the past and bring them into the present. When you or I remember things, however, we do not make the *actual* past events come into the present, but only mental images of those events. With God it is different. In God what we think of as past, present, and future are all equally present. God's name is "I Am." He is "the God who is always there, present to his people in order to save them" (207).

There is one unique event in history that participates in God's "remembering" in this way, that is always "made present": "the sacrifice Christ offered once for all on the cross remains ever present" (1364). A cross-reference to CCC 1085 reminds us of the reasons for this — that the Paschal mystery is Christ's overcoming of death, so the event does not "die" or "pass away." "His Passover 'once for all' remains ever present in the liturgy of his Church" (2746). Christ establishes his triumph over death as the *living event* that is made present to us whenever the Church celebrates the Eucharist.

The "sacrifice of the Mass," then, is not a different or a new sacrifice. It is the *one* sacrifice of Christ that is "re-presented" (made present again) (1366). The form in which the sacrifice is offered *is* different — it is made in an "unbloody manner" (1367), but it is *one and the same sacrifice.*

Why this re-presentation? It is so that the *fruits*, the *effects*, of Christ's redemptive sacrifice might be applied to us. This application can take place only through the Church's free participation "in the offering." The Bridegroom offers salvation. The Bride must receive it. "The wholly redeemed city" (1372) thus unites itself with "Christ and with his total offering" (1368).

CCC 1373-1381
The Presence of Christ

The "real presence" of Christ in the consecrated Body and Blood flows from the *logic* of his love. The real presence is "highly fitting" once we appreciate the *depths* of Christ's love. He wanted to give us the sign of the love with which he loved us to the end and to remain "mysteriously in our midst as the one who loved us and gave himself up for us" (1380).

The real presence is *more* than his presence in other ways. Jesus is present to us in many different and "real" ways — in other Christians, in his word, in the sick, in the other sacraments "of which he is the author," in the ordained minister, and so on. All of these, the Catechism confirms, are ways in which he is present (1373). But the "mode of Christ's presence under the Eucharistic species is unique" (1374). Here Jesus himself meets us, "the *whole Christ ... truly, really, and substantially.*" The term "substance" here is a way of saying "what this really is." "Substance" refers to identity. "Transubstantiation" means that the identity has changed. In the Body and Blood Christ gives himself to us. It is as simple as that.

It does not "look" as though it is Christ; it does not "taste" like Christ; it does not "feel" like Christ. We believe that this is Christ, not only because it is "fitting" but because he has assured us that this is so. We rely on "divine authority" (1381), on the words of Christ himself (see also 1338). When the priest presents us with the Body of Christ we reply, "Amen," "Yes, it is true!" Every Eucharist is an invitation to share in the *fiat* of Mary, whose assent of faith enabled the Son to take flesh in her.

CCC 1382-1390
The Paschal Banquet

In the Mass a delicate movement takes place. Christ invites and gathers us together *as his guests* at the great wedding feast, speaks to us in his word, joins us to his offering to the Father in a great act of love and sacrifice of praise, unites us to himself in this offering on the altar.

All of this, the "celebration of the Eucharistic sacrifice," is "wholly directed toward the intimate union of the faithful with Christ through communion" (1382). And so Jesus offers himself for us and then addresses us, saying, "I must stay at your house today" (Lk 19:5). *Jesus wants to be our guest.* He wants us to invite him into our homes, to say, as the disciples did on the road to Emmaus, "Stay with us, for it is toward evening and the day is now far spent" (Lk 24:29).

The Church offers us the heartfelt response of the centurion to Jesus on hearing Jesus' desire to be with us: "*Domine, non sum dingus.*" We reply humbly and seek the Lord's cleansing power. In the face of such an invitation and with such a Guest, I seek his forgiveness in the sacrament of Reconciliation for any grave sin (1385) and also prepare in every way I can to receive him well "under my roof" (1386-1387).

As is clear, those who do not receive Christ still benefit from his saving work through participation in the Mass (see also 1651), but accompanying the marvelous privilege of participation in the Mass is the recommendation, with the right disposition, to receive the Eucharist each time one participates in the celebration. The Church also obliges the faithful to "take part in the Divine Liturgy" on Sundays and holy days of obligation, and to receive the Eucharist at least once a year, most appropriately during the Easter season.

CCC 1391-1395
The Fruits of Holy Communion I

Christ calls us and unites us to himself *so that he can be the source of our lives.* "Life in Christ has its foundation in the Eucharistic banquet" (1391). "Life in Christ" is the title for Part Three of the Catechism: the Christian life is "fed" by the Eucharist. Jesus feeds us with himself so that we can enjoy health and strength.

The "fruits" of Holy Communion concern deeper kinds of unity, with Christ himself and with others. The "principal" fruit of Holy Communion is the simple fact of our *union with Jesus.* Union with Christ is an end in itself. We read a good book precisely for the sake of enjoying a good book. We *might* also be hoping to "improve our mind," but this is normally a secondary consideration. The good act is itself the "end" we seek. Christ, of course, is our "whole spiritual good" (1324). He is always and everywhere *the* Good that we seek.

With this deeper union with Christ comes a natural *separation from all that keeps us from him.* Sin is a lack of what should be present, a discord in the harmony that we should enjoy, a disorder disrupting the "tranquillity of order" for which God intends us. Sin keeps us in a lackluster life, in a state of partial being, in ways of life that do not satisfy. The fruit of Holy Communion in this case, then, is a healing and mending of what is damaged, a reinstating of proper order in our lives, a providing us with the fullness that God wants to give us in Jesus. The Catechism points out that Christ provides this specific grace of forgiveness and spiritual healing in the sacrament of Penance, and we should turn to that sacrament as the *natural preparation* for the Eucharist. Nonetheless, we should not underestimate how the Eucharist "strengthens our charity" and helps us to "break our disordered attachments" (1394).

CCC 1396-1401
The Fruits of Holy Communion II

From the union with Christ the head, the Catechism moves on to a further fruit of Holy Communion, the unity of Christ's Mystical Body — the unity of the members of Christ. The Catechism uses the striking phrase, "the Eucharist makes the Church" (1396). Communion, it teaches, "renews, strengthens, and deepens" our incorporation into the Church. It brings to fulfillment what is begun in us at Baptism.

It is *from* the union that the Church has with Christ the Head that her own unity in the Body is strengthened. After the Sacrifice has been offered to the Father, the priest offers us, from the altar, the "peace of Christ." It is Christ who reconciled "to himself all things," "making peace by the blood of his cross" (Col 1:20). The members "take" this peace and share it among themselves. There is a movement out from the Eucharist also to "take" this peace, this fruit of the redeeming Cross, to the poor. The "logic" of Christ's love, of Christ who "died for all men without exception" (605), "commits us to the poor" (1397).

CCC 1398-1401 treat of the Eucharist as the great *sacrament of unity* uniting all true members of the Church in the *bond of love*. As the Catechism has already noted, it is ironically also a constant source of division. "The first announcement of the Eucharist divided the disciples" (1336), and the disciples of Christ in many different ecclesial bodies today are divided over this central teaching of Jesus. Consequently, intercommunion is not permitted with those ecclesial communities derived from the Reformation who deny the sacrament of Holy Orders and true fidelity to our Holy Father the Pope. However, for those churches separated from us, which yet possess the true sacraments and apostolic succession, intercommunion is permitted. Above all, a fruit of the Eucharist is to commit us to "urgent" prayers for a time of "complete unity" (1398).

CCC 1402-1405
The Eucharist — "Pledge of the Glory to Come"

In heaven, "celebration is wholly communion and feast" (1136). Participation in the Eucharist here on earth is the "source and summit" of our Christian lives since we live in the world of signs and symbols. We receive Christ, in his fullness, but in a "veiled" presence (1404). Our eyes cannot yet bear the light of the glorified Christ. Nonetheless, that is our destiny, and the Eucharist is already an anticipation of the heavenly banquet. So it becomes for us a pledge of future glory uniting us in the Holy Spirit to Christ, not only in his Body and Blood, but also to Christ who is now seated at the right hand of the Father in heaven. Thus it becomes a "bridge over the troubled water" of our pilgrim journey here on earth, strengthening us and supporting us along the way.

The Catechism's treatment of the Eucharist concludes by reminding us again of the way in which Christ's redemptive work affects the *whole of creation* (1405). The Eucharist, it teaches, is the clearest sign of the renewal of the heavens and the earth. In the Eucharist, the material elements of bread and wine are taken and transubstantiated into the Body and Blood of Christ. We ourselves are taken up into the offering that Christ makes and "made" into his new Body. In the Eucharist, at each celebration, there is a pledge and sign of the *work of redemption* which the Father is undertaking through his two "hands," the Son and the Holy Spirit.

CCC 1420-1421
The Sacraments of Healing

During his earthly ministry the Lord Jesus restored many to physical healing as well as spiritual healing through the forgiveness of sins. But knowing that his days were limited here on earth he willed that his Church continue his healing ministry through the power of the Holy Spirit. The Church has done so through the two sacraments of healing, the sacrament of Penance and the sacrament of the Anointing of the Sick. The first "group" of sacraments, of Baptism, Confirmation and the Eucharist, concerned our new birth, our growth and our healthy nourishment. This second pair is concerned with the ways in which Christ acts in the sacraments to restore what is damaged, when our bodies or souls suffer injury or neglect, or when we deliberately act without due care for the good of our lives with which God has entrusted us.

The Catechism notes that Jesus *cares for the whole person*. He seeks the healing of both our souls and our bodies. The text describes him as the "physician of our souls and bodies" (1421). The close relationship between the two reflects our nature — we are body and soul forming a "single nature" (365). Because we are soul–body unities we find that Christ's mission of healing uses the same word for both spiritual and bodily healing. For example, it is the same word in the Greek New Testament that is used to speak of Jesus bringing "salvation" to the house of Zacchaeus (Lk 19:9) and of his "making well" those who touched the fringe of his garment (Mk 6:56).

The pairing of these two sacraments under the single heading of "healing" reminds us that *sin is a form of sickness*, analogous to bodily sickness, though more serious since it concerns the health of the whole person, and not just the bodily aspect. The first of these two sacraments to be considered is therefore the sacrament of Penance, for the healing of the soul.

CCC 1422-1424
What Is This Sacrament Called?

With the knowledge that the new life that Christians have received through the Sacraments of Initiation can be weakened and even destroyed by sin, the Lord, through his Church, has provided for the means by which one can be reconciled once again to the new life in Christ.

When we sin, we injure our communion with God and with others. Yet notice how the text reveals the most powerful activity flowing *from* the injured parties. It is from *God* that pardon is given, and it is the *Church* that has been laboring for the conversion of those in a state of sin, "by charity, by example, and by prayer" (1422). We depend upon the grace of God and upon others for our continual conversion.

Five names are given here for the sacrament, each one drawing our attention to a particular aspect of its reality. The first, *conversion*, uses the image of the journey and of our "straying" from the path by sin. The literal meaning of the word we use for sin is "missing the mark" in the original Greek. When we sin we step in the wrong direction. The sacrament calls us to take "the first step in returning to the Father." The second name, *penance*, draws attention to our "consecrating" — that is, dedicating for God — the "steps" we take. We "offer" to God the challenges and hardships of the journey back to him.

The third name, *confession*, is used to describe the actual disclosure of sins to a priest but also has a more ancient meaning. The "confessors" in the Church are the saints who suffer persecution for the sake of their profession of the faith. In the sacrament, in this sense, we are willing to undergo hardship for the sake of the "confession" of God's goodness and mercy. *Forgiveness* and *Reconciliation* both express fruits of the sacrament, and the Catechism again calls attention to the restoration to communion with both God and man through God's action.

CCC 1425-1429
Baptism and Ongoing Conversion

The Church, as we know is one, holy, catholic, and apostolic — but she is also sinful, made up of men and women who are in need of constant conversion. CCC 1426 refers us back to the effects of the Fall. Some of these are removed by Baptism, which gives us a new status as God's children (see 1265-1266). Baptism also confers a permanent "character." God places his "seal" of belonging on us (1121). He *never* lets us go. "If we are faithless, he remains faithful — for he cannot deny himself" (2 Tm 2:13).

But we *often* let *him* go. Baptism removes sin, but not weakness. Look at CCC 1426 and the cross-reference to 1264. God leaves us in our weakness, and the Christian path is therefore a "way of weakness," of constant dependence upon God's grace.

In our weakness we often fall into sin. The Church does not accept the idea of a rebaptism after sin, for this would be to deny God's faithfulness, as though his seal on us could be eradicated. But the truth is that we *have* still turned away from him. There is the need for a return, for a genuine conversion, a change in us so that baptismal grace can work in us. The Catechism, in a striking phrase, calls this "second conversion" an "uninterrupted task" (1428). It also affirms the primacy of grace in the ongoing work of conversion: it is the heart that is "drawn and moved by grace to respond" that begins to tread the way of return to the merciful Father.

CCC 1430-1433
Interior Penance

The *order* of the next two sections is significant. The Catechism first treats of interior penance (1430-1433) before then examining the "many forms of penance in the Christian life" (1434-1439). The "many forms" are *the different expressions of interior penance.* CCC 1430 insists that Jesus' call to conversion does not aim "first" at "outward works." He calls *first* for *the conversion of the heart.* Without this, the Catechism teaches, any penances remain "sterile and false." "Sterile" means without life; "false" means without truth. The "way" of penance needs the presence of Jesus as the life and the truth. The Christian life and its truth *must* arise from the heart. "Heart" here does not mean the seat of emotion, but rather the "depths of one's being, where the person decides for or against God" (368). When Christ meets us, he puts out "into the deep" to catch us (see Lk 5:4). It is the *heart* Jesus wants.

Through his Church, then, the Lord calls all the baptized to an ongoing conversion, primarily by an interior conversion of the heart which in turn must be expressed through visible signs, gestures, and works of penance. Interior conversion calls for sincere sorrow for our sins accompanied by a firm purpose of amendment to do our reasonable best to correct and avoid sin in the future.

Another point that is stressed in this section is that conversion *must* be a work of *God* in us. God makes a new heart for us and "makes" our hearts return to him. What comes first in this movement is the love of God for us. Our conversion is always a response to this. It is we who turned away from God, but the turning back is not our doing alone. It is through *his unshakeable* love for us that "*our* heart is *shaken* by the horror and weight of sin." It is the "Consoler" who gives grace for repentance.

CCC 1434-1439
The Many Forms of Penance in Christian Life

The Catechism is intensely practical and reminds us of the numerous ways in which we can express the movement of returning love that God has awoken in our hearts. Such ways both *express* the interior conversion and also *support* it through action.

The *three classic forms of expression* on which Jesus teaches in the Sermon on the Mount are fasting, prayer, and almsgiving (see Mt 6:1-18). The Catechism explains how three fundamental "relations" in our lives, which the Fall damaged, are gradually restored through these practices as our relationship to God (prayer), others (almsgiving), and ourselves in the unity of our body and soul (fasting) are strengthened (see 400).

With these relationships as the focus for our expression, so that the Holy Spirit can gradually nourish our communion with God and draw out sincere love towards others, we can begin to examine *each concrete aspect of our daily lives.* "Conversion is accomplished in daily life" (1435). The Catechism assists us by identifying in some detail a range of ways in which we can reflect on our social and personal relations with others, our sacramental life, our habits of Bible reading, practice of prayer, and engagement with the sacramental grace that God makes available to us throughout the liturgical year and its feasts and seasons. Little by little our lives are conformed to the "stages" of Christ's life as we invite him more and more to live out his virtues in us.

CCC 1440-1449
The Sacrament of Penance and Reconciliation

Today's reading directly addresses question many ask: "Why cannot I simply confess my sins to God, without the intervention or involvement of the Church?"

It is true that sin is "before all else an offense against God" (1440) since we belong to him as our Lord and Creator. It is also true that, because of this, "Only God forgives sins" (1441). At the end of this section the Catechism provides the prayer of absolution and explains that this prayer "expresses the essential elements of the sacrament" (1449). These essential elements have to do with the saving and forgiving work of *God*: "The *Father of mercies* is the source of all forgiveness. He effects the reconciliation of sinners through the *Passover of his Son* and the *gift of his Spirit.*" Indeed, the penitent's interior conversion is "through the action of the Holy Spirit" (1448). It would appear that penance and forgiveness are essentially actions that take place between the individual and God.

In fact, the text is at pains not to let us forget that there is another dimension. While sin is above all an offense against God, at "the same time" it ruptures communion with the Church. This is why conversion entails *both* God's forgiveness *and* reconciliation with the Church (1440).

A recurring theme in the Catechism is the intrinsic relationality of the human person. "The human race forms a unity" (360). Relationships with others, and life in society, is not "an extraneous addition" but a "requirement" of our nature (1879). The Mystical Body of the Church, founded on union with the New Adam, builds on this natural reality of our unity in the Old Adam. The notion of our living "separate" lives is a turning away from our true nature and a denial of our true selves. Our restoration to the likeness in which we were created requires a profound *turning towards others.* The ministry of the Church is essential to this sacrament.

CCC 1450-1460
The Acts of the Penitent

This passage movingly expresses the *deeply challenging* nature of participation in the sacrament. The acts of the penitent can be identified very simply: any person seeking reconciliation with the Lord through the Church must first make a careful examination of conscience and have a full repentance for their sins, must make a truthful confession of those sins to a bishop or priest, and must then perform some form of satisfaction. The acts are summarized in the subheadings: contrition, the confession of sins, and satisfaction.

The quotation from the Roman Catechism in CCC 1450 notes that, in all of this, the sinner must be able to "endure all things willingly." The three acts are *acts of "willing endurance."*

First, the sinner must be able to endure *sorrow of the soul* as he contemplates sins committed. The greater the love one contemplates, the more perfect will be one's contrition, for the corresponding distance established by sin will be more clearly seen. The great saints see themselves as the greatest of sinners precisely because of their deep awareness of the love of God.

Second, one must endure looking "squarely" at one's sins and *take responsibility* for them. One must have the courage to show all of one's wounds to the doctor, to endure the light being shed in areas one prefers to keep "most secret," even to oneself (1456). The rewards are great: disclosure frees us and makes a new future possible (1455), allows divine medicine to work (1456), and forms our consciences and enables us to move on in the spiritual life (1458).

Finally, one must endure the challenges of *repairing harm* to others, to ourselves, and to our relationship with God. We are forgiven and strengthened through the sacrament, but the disorders remain. I lashed out through anger and am forgiven. Now comes the long work of cooperating with grace to heal the unreasonable anger in me. The Catechism reminds us that we "can do all things in him" who strengthens us (Phil 4:13)!

CCC 1461-1467
The Minister of This Sacrament

In the Catechism's discussion of God's almighty power (268-374) it is explained that God's power is in no way arbitrary, for he is the *Father* almighty. The Catechism lists ways in which God's fatherly omnipotence is expressed: through caring for our needs; by adopting us as his sons and daughters; and "finally by his infinite mercy, for he displays his power at its height by freely forgiving sins" (270). Because he utterly transcends us, God can display his power without overwhelming us. He does not need to "win." He shows this on the cross, where he apparently "loses" to human violence. God's almighty power of transcendent love cannot be defeated.

Alongside CCC 270 is a cross-reference to this sacrament. The "power" of God is displayed "at its height" in the forgiveness of sins. *It is of this "infinite mercy," this "almighty power," that the bishops and priests are the ministers.* "Indeed bishops and priests, by virtue of the sacrament of Holy Orders, have the power to forgive all sins 'in the name of the Father, and of the Son, and of the Holy Spirit'" (1461). The ministry is so crucial that, while certain grave sins are reserved to the Apostolic See or to the local bishop, in danger of death any priest can absolve a person from any sin whether he is authorized or not (1463).

The Catechism then paints a "picture" of the confessor: "not the master of God's forgiveness, but its servant" (1466); the image of the Good Shepherd, of the Good Samaritan, of the Father of the runaway son, of the just judge; one who loves the truth, is faithful to the Magisterium and can "lead" well. The one who is the "sign and instrument" of God's almighty power of mercy does penance for the sinner who approaches him and is bound, under very severe penalties, to honor "the sacramental seal" which guarantees absolute secrecy concerning the sins revealed to him in confession (1467).

CCC 1468-1469
The Effects of the Sacrament

There are *three effects* of this sacrament discussed. The main effect and purpose of this sacrament is *reconciliation with God,* which will usually lead to peace and serenity of conscience and a strong impulse of grace to help the penitent in his resolution to avoid sin in the future. This effect of the sacrament is so significant that it is described as a true "spiritual resurrection" (1468). It is a "resurrection" since it anticipates the state of glorious friendship with God at the end of time.

The second effect is also a *healing grace conferred which heals the woundedness of the penitent and also effects a healing upon the Church,* the Mystical Body of Christ, which has suffered from the sin of one of her members. We might think of the healing bestowed in this sacrament as affecting ourselves mainly. We go home at peace, with a clean conscience, renewed in hope. Over and above this effect, however, is a real strengthening of the Church. The English poet, John Donne, wrote, "Any man's death diminishes me, / Because I am involved in mankind, / And therefore never send to know for whom the bell tolls; / It tolls for thee." This is true of our relation to human beings in general. The Catechism is reminding us how *much more* this is the case in the Body of Christ. Therefore, "one restored to ecclesial communion" has a "revitalizing effect on the life of the Church" (1469).

The third effect is in the habit we form, through frequenting the sacrament, of *allowing the merciful judge, Christ, to shed his light on us.* At the end of our earthly life we will be judged, but then there will be no further opportunity for conversion. Here and now we can receive in ourselves Christ's judgment and, by his sustaining grace, enter onto the road of conversion (1470).

CCC 1471-1479
Indulgences

The forgiveness of sins and the restoration of communion with God effects *the remission of the eternal punishment* due to sin (this would be hell), but the *temporal punishment* due to sin remains. This temporal punishment must be "satisfied" while here on earth through the sufferings of everyday Christian living or after death in a state of deprivation of the Beatific Vision in purgatory.

We need to understand this point in the light of the nature of sin. Sin is its own punishment. When we sin, we are ultimately choosing against God, and so we lose our friendship with him. When we sin, we "break faith" with God, with ourselves and others. For example, the sin of lying leads, amongst other things, to the *loss of the truth* and to *becoming a liar*. And "he who does not believe God has made him a liar" (1 Jn 5:10). These losses to ourselves that sin causes are the "punishments of sin."

The path of penance and "uninterrupted" conversion involves "enduring" these losses, this "punishment," as our healing takes place, and we are called to patience in this process (1473). But God our Father "indulges" us — he longs to hasten the healing process. And he does so in accord with our nature as members of each other in the Mystical Body of his Son. In this Body we can "bear one another's burdens, and so fulfill the law of Christ" (Gal 6:2). We can pray for each other and "offer up" our own sufferings and difficulties. The Church herself also has a great "treasury," the *true* treasures of goodness and holiness, the "spiritual goods of the communion of saints" (1476) — and, above all, the infinite merits of Christ himself. Christ has given to his ministers authority to distribute these spiritual treasures among "the poor," those suffering the temporal effects of sin, whether on earth or in purgatory.

CCC 1480-1484
The Celebration of the Sacrament of Penance

As with all of the sacraments, the Catechism explains that while this sacrament has developed in form over the centuries, certain fundamental elements have always remained constant.

A good deal of this section is placed *in small print*, which, we can remember, normally "indicates observations of an historical or apologetic nature, or supplementary doctrinal explanations" (20). There is also one other reason for the use of small print in the Catechism: these are "quotations ... from patristic, liturgical, magisterial, or hagiographical sources" which are "intended to enrich the doctrinal presentations" (21).

In the paragraphs we are considering today, CCC 1481 falls into the category of a liturgical text intended to enrich the presentation. It is a beautiful example of a "formula of absolution" which draws on many familiar figures from the Scriptures and reminds the penitent of the fact that the sacrament of Penance is an "anticipation" of the Day of Judgment. CCC 1482-1483 carefully explain how to think about the communal and personal elements in the celebration of the sacrament, given that Penance has both dimensions in it and that the effects of the sacrament are necessarily both of a personal and also of a social kind. You will see that some elements, listed in 1482, "express more clearly the ecclesial character of penance," while certain elements are usually to be expressed individually.

CCC 1483 also warns against certain abuses of the sacrament in over-casual interpretations of "grave necessity," and the reasons for this insistence on individual confession are given in CCC 1484. The Shepherd knows his sheep personally and calls them by name, one by one. Jesus wants each one to hear his voice speaking *personally* to them.

CCC 1499-1513
The Anointing of the Sick

Today we have a lengthy reading introducing the second of the sacraments of healing. It is placed, as usual, within the framework of the "economy of salvation," moving from illness in *the created order* and human society (1500-1501), to how illness was viewed in the time of *the Old Covenant* (1502), then to Christ's "actions and words" and to how *the Mystery of Christ* applies to the area of suffering and sickness (1503-1505), and finally to the apostolic mission and the sacrament in *the age of the Church* (1506-1513).

Sickness in the Old Testament was always *mysteriously linked to sin and evil* and the knowledge that fidelity to God and his law could lead to the restoration of health and life. However, it was the prophets who began to prophesy concerning the redemptive meaning of suffering for the sins of others.

This *redemptive* quality of suffering came to full fruition in Jesus' ministry of healing. Jesus is the great *healer*. Throughout his life Jesus cured every kind of infirmity including that of sin. Constantly he displayed his great love and compassion for the sick — those who were sick physically as well as those who were sick spiritually. Through his passion, death and resurrection the Lord invites all to follow his example by accepting our crosses daily.

The healing ministry of Jesus *continues* to reach out to the sick and suffering through the Church and its sacramental life. Throughout the ages the Church has practiced an anointing of the sick person with sacred oil. This anointing was intended to heal and to encourage the sick not to give in to despair or discouragement, but to follow Christ in his acceptance of the Cross. The Catechism explains that through a gradual development this anointing was eventually being conferred more exclusively to those at the point of death. Because of this it became identified as Extreme Unction. Its broader use, however, is now recovered.

CCC 1514-1516
Who Receives and Who Administers This Sacrament?

We saw in yesterday's reading that there was a gradual move towards reserving this sacrament for those who were at the point of death. This was perhaps a natural evolution since the need for a special strengthening for the final journey of the Christian has always been recognized. Today, however, the Church identifies this anointing as the sacrament of the sick, a sacrament that should be available to every one of the faithful who may begin to be in danger of death from sickness or old age. It is for those who suffer from a "grave illness," those who are undergoing a serious operation, and also those who are simply elderly "whose frailty becomes more pronounced." At the time of our weakness the Lord comes alongside us in this sacrament to reassure us, comfort and strengthen us.

CCC 1516 addresses the question of preparation for the sacrament. It mentions the "whole ecclesial community" being involved in this since illness tends to isolate us. The "prayers and fraternal attention" of the members of Christ is therefore an important element in assisting the development of "good dispositions," especially hope and trust. Readings from the extensive scriptural references underpinning the whole previous section would also be most suitable as preparatory supports: the ability to hear of the "preferential love for the sick" (1503) on the part of Christ the Physician is a powerful antidote to isolation and fear.

CCC 1516 asks that the faithful be instructed in the meaning and "benefits of this sacrament," encouraging the sick to call upon a priest or bishop in case of necessity. Since the priest and bishop are the only ministers of this sacrament, they must always be at the service of the sick who are in their midst.

CCC 1517-1519
How Is This Sacrament Celebrated?

In CCC 1517 the Catechism notes that it is very "fitting" that the celebration of the sacrament be within the Eucharist. "Fitting" is a word that is often used in the Catechism when speaking of the sacraments and how they are celebrated. Like a well-measured suit of clothes that "fit" the body, a celebration is to be conducted in such a way as "fit" the Trinitarian action and cooperative works of Christ's Body suitably (see for example, 1207, 1293, 1380). Thus it is "fitting" that the Eucharist be celebrated daily because it is an anticipation of the Eternal Day of the Kingdom (2837). Paying attention to what is "fitting" helps us to see how doctrine, celebration and life come together coherently in the Mystery of Christ (see 90). The reason why it is "fitting" that the celebration of this sacrament be within the Eucharist is because the latter is the "memorial of the Lord's Passover." The Eucharist is Christ's definitive redemptive act, healing the bonds of communion between God and man. The healing that is celebrated and brought about in this sacrament by the action of Christ flows from that great act of healing in creation that Jesus brought about "once and for all" by his offering of himself in obedience to the Father.

You will see that the description of the sacrament in CCC 1518-1519 is a simple one. The celebration of the sacrament of Anointing of the Sick includes the following principal elements — the priest or bishop lays his hands on the sick person in silence, praying for the outpouring of the Holy Spirit. This follows the anointing with the oil of the sick on the head and on the hands of the recipient in the Roman rite, and on other parts of the body as well in the other rites. This is accompanied by special prayers asking for the grace of strength and of healing attached to this sacrament.

CCC 1520-1525
The Effects of the Sacrament and Viaticum

We now reach the end of our catechesis on this beautiful sacrament of the Church. When we celebrate a sacrament alone with the minister or with just a few friends or family members, and also when it is being celebrated in an unusual setting, such as a hospital or nursing home, it is easy to forget the point which the Catechism made in CCC 1517: "it is a liturgical and communal celebration." As we know, *no sacrament is "private."* In the case of *every* sacrament, God the Blessed Trinity and the Body of the Church establish *bonds of communion* with us.

The effects of this sacrament concern these bonds — bonds with the Holy Spirit, with Christ, with the Church, and with our heavenly Father who is expecting us home. The effects which detail these bonds are set out very clearly in four paragraphs. If received with faith, the sacrament unites the individual more closely to the redemptive sufferings of Jesus (1521), and to the gifts of the Holy Spirit of strength, peace, courage in the face of suffering, and even the forgiveness of sins (1520). This in turn adds to the benefit of *all* the People of God as the sick person, and Christ, by his acceptance of the Cross, contributes to the sanctification of the Church (1522). Finally, by this last anointing, one is fortified for that final struggle leading to the *end* of our *earthly life* and the *beginning* of our *heavenly life* (1523).

In CCC 1517 you will have seen that the Catechism explains that the sacrament can be celebrated outside of Mass, preceded by the sacrament of Penance and followed by the Eucharist. In this circumstance, as the last sacrament received on our earthly journey, the Eucharist is referred to as "viaticum," providing the final grace for the passage over to eternal life. This is treated in CCC 1524-1525. Notice the beautiful summary of these healing sacraments as those which "complete the earthly pilgrimage."

CCC 1533-1535
The Sacraments at the Service of Communion

As the sacraments of Baptism, Confirmation, and Eucharist confer through the Holy Spirit a new life in Christ, and as the sacraments of Penance and the Anointing of the Sick provide healing and strength, including that special grace needed for the completion of our earthly pilgrimage, the sacraments of Holy Orders and Matrimony confer *special graces for serving and building up the People of God.*

These two sacraments, then, are *uniquely other-directed.* "If they contribute as well to personal salvation, it is through service to others that they do so" (1543). The sacraments *do* contribute to our own salvation, for the Lord does indeed save us "through" love of others, but this way of expressing it reminds us that the service of others is never to be considered as a "means" to my salvation. Rather we are to "let love be genuine" (Rom 12:9).

The term "communion" is used in the title here. Holy Orders *serves the communion of the Church*, the members of the ecclesial Body. The sacrament of Matrimony *serves the communion of the domestic church*, the members of the family. The other word used here is *consecration*, which indicates a setting apart. The "general" consecration through Baptism and Confirmation to the common priesthood, to be a "kingdom of priests" (784) set apart for God, is here specified into "particular" consecrations of service.

CCC 1536-1538
Why Is This Sacrament Called "Orders"?

Christ instituted the sacrament of Holy Orders at the Last Supper. He entrusted his sacred mission to his apostles, who were commanded to continue to exercise this mission in the Church until the end of time. Today, the Church confers this sacrament upon a man, by which he is integrated into the "order" of bishops, priests, and deacons. By a special gift of the Holy Spirit he is sealed with an indelible, spiritual character configuring him to Christ and enabling him to act in the name of Christ the Lord.

This short section reminds us that we should understand what is presented here in relation to the earlier treatment on the hierarchical and apostolic nature of the Church (874-896). The text specifies that in *this* part of the Catechism we will focus solely on the "sacramental means by which this ministry is handed on" (1536).

We first of all look in these paragraphs at the single "name" that is given to this sacrament, "Holy Orders." "Holy" means "set apart" and "Orders" designates a particular group or body of people. The word "Orders" also reminds us of those who "give orders," those who are in command. The term thus also signifies a "governing body" (1535). And as well as thinking of "giving orders" we can also think of the value of an "ordered" society. This is not just a society that receives "orders," but one which has a harmony, a structure, a coherence. The sacrament of Holy Orders, then, *provides a structure and ordering for the whole of the People of God*, serving the common priesthood in this way.

From "Order" the Catechism moves on to the term "ordination." This is the word used for the rite of "integration" into an "order." While it earlier had a more general meaning of "blessing" or "consecration," and could refer to a number of "orders" in the Church, the use of the term has evolved to specify the distinct sacramental meaning attached to Holy Orders.

CCC 1539-1553
The Sacrament of Holy Orders
in the Economy of Salvation

As always, the Catechism wants to show us the beauty and coherence of God's plan for our salvation and how each element in the plan serves the overarching purpose of making available to us all of the graces needed for life with him.

The section begins with an account of the two priesthoods that we find in *the period of the Old Covenant,* the "time of the promises." The whole of the "chosen people" were consecrated as a "kingdom of priests" (1539). The Catechism refers us to Isaiah 61:6: "you shall be called the priests of the Lord." They were set apart ("holy") for the service of God for the sake of his mission to the whole world, to be a holy people in all the nations. God also chose *one* of the tribes from the "kingdom of priests" to serve this nation — the order of Levites, who were appointed to offer gifts and sacrifices to the Lord "on behalf of men" (1539).

All that is contained in the Old Covenant *finds its fulfillment in the Lord Jesus* (1544). During his own ministry, he taught the crowds and *called everyone to follow him.* From this *general call* we see the New Testament teaching on the "holy priesthood" of all believers (1 Pt 2:5). In addition, Jesus called the Twelve Apostles (Mt 10:1-4). From this *particular call* we see the ministerial priesthood of the New Covenant.

In this section, the Catechism also explains the *relation of the two priesthoods:* the *ministerial* priesthood is a service to the *common* priesthood. The former exists for "the good of men and the communion of the Church" (1551). Our text also details how the priest is a *representative figure.* He represents *Christ* who is the head of the Church (in Latin, *in persona Christi Capitis*). His authority flows from this. Precisely *as* the representative of *Christ* the priest can also "represent" the Church, for the Church is Christ's Body.

CCC 1554-1571
The Three Degrees of the Sacrament of Holy Orders

God provides for the grace-filled "order" of his Church through three "degrees" of the sacrament: bishops, priests, and deacons. All three degrees are entered through "ordination," although only the first two share in Christ's priesthood.

In the first degree, *the bishop receives the fullness of this sacrament of Holy Orders* (1557), making him a legitimate successor to the apostles sharing with the pope and the college of bishops the care, not only of his own Church, but of all the Churches (1559-1561). He assumes the roles of teaching, sanctifying, and ruling.

In the second degree, *priests are joined to the episcopal order as "coworkers,"* sharing in the authority of Christ. Configured to the Lord through the conferral of a special character by the Holy Spirit the priest can act in the person of Christ himself. While depending on the bishop for the exercise of his ministry he is nonetheless empowered to *preach the Gospel,* to be a *pastor to his flock,* and to *celebrate divine worship* as a priest of the New Covenant. Every priest pursues his ministerial functions in a sacramental bond with other priests, forming the "presbyterate." While having responsibility for a particular church as a coworker of the bishop, he has truly been ordained for a universal mission. *It is from the Mass that the priestly ministry draws all of its power.* The ministerial function of the priest is carried out to a "supreme degree" when, acting in the person of Christ, he unites the offerings of the faithful to the sacrifice of Christ in the holy sacrifice of the Mass.

In the third degree of the sacrament of Holy Orders, *the deacon is also configured to Christ and ordained specifically for service.* Deacons, like priests, receive the imposition of the hands of the bishop. Their specific tasks are to assist the bishop and priests in the ministry of the word, in aspects of divine worship, in pastoral care, and in various ministries of charity.

CCC 1572-1574
The Celebration of This Sacrament

The "sacred order" of the Body of Christ depends upon this sacrament, and it is noteworthy that the Catechism emphasizes the importance of as many members of the Body as possible taking part in the celebration of this sacrament that concerns the good of each member so intimately. The celebration should take place if possible at the *cathedral*, the place from which the bishop exercises the authority given to him by Christ to teach, sanctify, and govern. If possible it should take place on a *Sunday*, the day of Resurrection, because this is the sacrament of the new order, bestowing all of the graces that flow from Christ's Paschal mystery. Finally, it is "proper" to celebrate this sacrament "within the *Eucharistic* liturgy," for the particular sacred "power" conferred is derived from the Last Supper and is intimately related to the Sacrament of sacraments.

As with other accounts of the sacraments, the Catechism distinguishes between the essential elements of the rite and varying practices between the three degrees and also among the "different liturgical traditions." The rich symbolism of the three degrees as signs of the many ways in which the Holy Spirit makes each fruitful for the Church is deeply instructive for us (see 1574).

The essential sign is the laying on of hands by the bishop (1573). A cross-reference to CCC 699 takes us to the hand as a *symbol of the Holy Spirit's action*. There we read, "It is by the apostles' imposition of hands that the Holy Spirit is given." In the Acts of the Apostles we can see examples of the apostles laying their hands on the first deacons (6:6; see also 13:3).

CCC 1575-1580
Who Can Confer and Receive This Sacrament?

In the paragraphs on the *conferring of the sacrament* (1575-1576), notice the way in which the Catechism reminds us of the action of the Blessed Trinity. It is *Christ's* flock that needs care, and the Shepherd does not run away or abandon his sheep. He always provides for his flock. It is from the *Father's* right hand — that is, with his authority — that Christ "gifts" the Church with apostles and pastors. It is by the "gift of the *Spirit*" that apostolic succession is maintained. This Trinitarian focus provides us with an appropriate understanding of the divine overshadowing which enables "validly ordained bishops" to, in turn, "validly confer" the sacrament.

Regarding *the reception of the sacrament* (1577-1580), while in the Western Church only celibate, baptized men may be ordained to the priesthood, the Eastern Churches follow a different discipline. While bishops must be celibate when chosen, a married man can be ordained as a priest or deacon. However, a man who has already received the sacrament of Holy Orders as a celibate can no longer marry.

The fact of a male priesthood has been hotly debated and the Catechism dedicates one paragraph to this question, referring us to two documents of the Magisterium, a declaration of the Congregation for the Faith, *Inter Insigniores* (1976), and Saint John Paul II's apostolic letter *Mulieris Dignitatem* (1988). The Church is clear: "The ordination of women is not possible" (1577). The reason is the example of Jesus himself. He chose men alone. The New Testament witnesses to a significant place of women in Jesus' ministry, and notes that they were the first witnesses of the Resurrection. But Jesus did not choose them as his priests.

With regard to celibacy, the Catechism clearly wishes to articulate its value and to note that in both the Eastern and Western traditions celibacy is attached to the sacrament in some way. At the same time, it expresses the variations as differences in the "discipline" of the Churches.

CCC 1581-1589
The Effects of the Sacrament of Holy Orders

The two points treated here are the "indelible character" conferred and the grace of the Holy Spirit. With regard to the first, we have seen that Baptism and Confirmation both confer this permanent "mark." The mark is the sign of Christ's permanent choice of us. It is his unbreakable "seal" set upon us. What about priesthood? Baptism and Confirmation are sacraments intended for *all* members of Christ's faithful. Why would the permanent "seal" be set upon just some of the members of his Body? What is the significance of this? The Catechism makes clear that it is precisely the importance of the ordained person *for the sake of the whole Body* that is being "sealed" here. The ordained person is given this special grace "so that he may serve as Christ's instrument for his Church" (1581). The character imprinted is "for ever" for that reason (1583). The sacrament of Holy Orders makes present for us and confirms Christ's choice and "sealing" of each person by placing in our midst the person of Christ himself in the person of the minister.

With regard to the grace of the Holy Spirit given in this sacrament, the Catechism, which has been discussing the different liturgical traditions and disciplines of East and West, selects an ordination prayer from the liturgies of the West (1586) and the East (1587) to provide us with beautiful examples of *lex orandi, lex credendi*. This is then followed by a "call to holiness" from two saints of the Church, reminding us that, although the unworthiness of the ordained minister does not impede the action of Christ in the sacraments, nonetheless the calling of the ordained is to holiness. Again, the first saint is from the Eastern tradition, the second from the Western. The Catechism, to use a phrase of Saint John Paul II, breathes with the "two lungs" of the Church.

CCC 1601-1608
Marriage in God's Plan I

We have seen that the sacrament of Holy Orders provides the sacred "ordering" to the Church as the Body of Christ. The final quotation from the Catechism's presentation of this sacrament, from Saint John Vianney, spoke of the priesthood as "the love of the heart of Jesus" (1589). It is a striking connection with the other sacrament "at the service of communion," for the sacrament of Matrimony might be said to provide the Church with her sacred "heart" as the Bride of Christ. *Marriage signifies and makes present the spousal love between the divine Bridegroom and his Bride.*

The Catechism dedicates an extended consideration to the place of marriage in God's plan since it plays *such* a significant role there. The Scriptures *open* with a marriage, that of our first parents, and they close with the account of the wedding of the Bride, the Church, with her divine Spouse, the Lamb. Marriage "frames" the divine plan. It provides the entry point and the goal of the whole of creation.

The vocation of the intimate union between a man and a woman in marriage is inherent in their very nature as creatures in the image and likeness of God. The Catechism, then, explains that although marriage has experienced variations through the centuries in different cultures, social structures and spiritual attitudes, it has never been purely a human institution. It is grounded in our nature.

Since man and woman have been created in the image of God who is love, their principal call is to love. In turn that love is intended to be fruitful. This bountiful union, however, is constantly threatened by the disorder of sin which can cause a rupture of the original blessed union between a man and a woman. Nevertheless, these disturbances can be overcome with the help of God's grace which is ever available to them.

CCC 1609-1620
Marriage in God's Plan II

The heart of today's reading can be found in CCC 1617: "The entire Christian life bears the mark of the spousal love of Christ and the Church." That is the climax towards which we move in the text.

We begin with the place of marriage in the Old Covenant, under the "pedagogy of the law" — God's gradual teaching of us, leading us to understand his plan in due course in its fullness. This short section (1609-1611) identifies some of those advancing "markers" of growing understanding which we find in the law and the prophets concerning the unity and indissolubility of marriage.

The central section, "Marriage in the Lord," manifests the newness of Christ's coming for our understanding of marriage. The Son of God, through the Incarnation and the Paschal mystery, unites himself to all mankind in a bond of everlasting love. This incredible fact becomes the *center* of the Church's understanding for the sacrament.

At the very beginning of his public ministry Jesus performs his first miracle at a wedding banquet. The Church sees the presence of Jesus at this wedding feast in Cana as a significant confirmation by Jesus of the goodness of marriage and of the ultimate efficacious significance of the presence of God. Thus, raised to the dignity of a sacrament, marriage now becomes a rich symbol of Christ's love for his Church.

CCC 1618-1620 explain that, although Christ, through his Church, has affirmed the sacramental beauty and value of marriage, it is not obligatory for everyone. There are those who are called upon to renounce the great good of Matrimony to more exclusively concentrate on the things of the Lord. They become "a powerful sign of the supremacy" of a singular bond with the Lord whereby an individual forsakes the pleasures of this world in order to embrace more faithfully the pleasures of the kingdom to come.

CCC 1621-1624
The Celebration of Marriage

Celebrations of this sacrament are deeply valued in all cultures. In the discussion of the Latin rite we once again find the importance of the Mass being highlighted. It is said to be most "fitting" that the spouses should seal their consent to each other through the mutual offering of their own lives *united to the offering of Christ for his Church* present in the Eucharistic sacrifice.

In order that the sacrament be "valid, worthy, and fruitful" the bride and groom must prepare themselves well under the direction of the Church. We see here another example of how *the sacraments are intrinsically linked to one another and provide particular graces* as the couple, as part of their preparation, are encouraged to receive the sacrament of Penance. Christ wants a newly married couple to have benefited from his strengthening and healing as they set out on the new journey of life together.

In the Latin Church, the *spouses* are also the *ministers* of this sacrament as they express their consent before the Church. In this consent the spouses commit themselves to each other irrevocably in order to live out a covenant of faithful and fruitful love. The priest is there as a *witness* of the Church to receive this consent. In the Eastern Church, however, it is the *priest or bishop* who is the *minister* of this sacrament, emphasizing in this particular way the *ecclesial* nature of the sacrament.

CCC 1625-1637
Matrimonial Consent

Today's reading contains some foundational principles for our understanding of marriage. The section begins by stating what might seem obvious (though it is now sometimes contested), that the parties to marriage are a *man* and a *woman*. There are two sexes in creation and marriage involves the union of the two. For a *sacramental* marriage they are also *baptized*: the man and woman are "entering" marriage through the "gateway" of Baptism.

The next point is also crucial, that they must each "freely express their consent" (1625). Without a *free consent* the "marriage" would be "null and void" (1629). Marriage concerns the gift of oneself to another person. Only a free choice allows this to be a fully human act. No one else can substitute for me in this act of self-gift (1627).

CCC 1625 gives us one other condition that is needed for the marriage to be truly "free": it must not be "impeded by any natural or ecclesiastical law." The criterion of "ecclesiastical law," or "form," is treated in CCC 1631. The "natural law" is *the moral law which obliges everyone*, which is valid for all. If I am already validly married, for example, I am not "free" to give my consent to another. The "natural law" "impedes" this.

CCC 1633-1637 express important points about *the marriages of Catholics with those who are not Catholic*. A marriage between a Catholic and a baptized non-Catholic ("mixed marriages") may be validated, but only with the permission of the proper ecclesiastical authority. However, for a valid marriage between a Catholic and a non-baptized person ("disparity of cult") a dispensation is required. In both cases, sincere married love, humble and faithful practice of family virtues, and perseverance in prayer can help the spouses to overcome all and every obstacle that may exist in such a union. The Church is realistic, however, in requiring potential spouses to recognize the difficulties often present in these unions.

CCC 1638-1642
The Effects of the Sacrament of Matrimony

In our society there is a considerable focus on the subjective dimension of relationships. The place of the personal will in maintaining a relationship and its reality is often at the forefront of our thinking. When we experience love powerfully, we might speak of a strong relationship; when love or interest weakens, we might think that there is less "substance" to the relationship.

We do not think of blood relationships in this way, of course. I may not have a strong love for my sibling, but he or she is still my brother and sister. I may have fallen out with my child, but I know that this is still my daughter or son. There is an objective "belonging" in each case that is independent of the ebb and flow of my feelings. When it comes to marriage, however, many in our society have a tendency to think differently. "Less love" seems to indicate "less of a marriage."

The Church thinks differently: *the sacrament of Matrimony establishes an objective bond between the couple.* "From a valid marriage arises a bond between the spouses which by its very nature is perpetual and exclusive" (1638). This bond is "sealed by God himself" (1639) and "gives rise to a covenant guaranteed by God's fidelity" (1640). Once a marriage has been ratified and consummated it is *indissoluble.* "The Church does not have the power to contravene this disposition of divine wisdom" (1640).

After the presentation of the marriage bond, the Catechism discusses the special graces that flow from the sacrament. Through this sacrament the spouses are blessed with the gift of *all the graces* necessary both to attain holiness and also to carry out faithfully the duties and other responsibilities associated with marriage, especially that of "welcoming and educating their children" (1641). A powerful and beautiful restatement of *Christ as the living source of this grace*, as the one who accompanies the couple day by day, concludes this section.

CCC 1643-1654
The Goods and Requirements of Conjugal Love

The sacrament of Matrimony presupposes a conjugal love which aspires to the growth of a deeply personal unity which will lead to the formation of the couple as "one heart and soul." For this kind of growth in a unity of love to be possible, one can understand why marriage "demands" indissolubility and faithfulness in a state characterized by the generous self-giving of the couple, and always open to the great good of fertility.

Still, "it can seem difficult, even impossible, to bind oneself for life to another human being" (1648). The sins of which we are only too aware threaten the stability of the marriage bond — especially adultery and polygamy, contradicting, as they do, the equal dignity of man and woman and the unity and fidelity of married love. Also opposed to the grace of marriage are acts that deliberately attack one's procreative potential, and divorce, which attacks the indissolubility of marriage. Spouses who faithfully witness to God's grace in often very difficult situations "deserve the gratitude and support" of Christ's Body (1648).

There are occasions when the Church will permit the physical separation of spouses when their living together becomes practically impossible. This separation does not dissolve the marriage bond and the spouses are not free to enter a new union. The best solution to this difficult situation would be eventual reconciliation, or else an ecclesiastical annulment.

Unfortunately, many Catholics today have had recourse to *civil* divorce and entered into a new *civil* union. With regard to these members of Christ's Body, the Church seeks to *actively care* for them so that they do not feel abandoned, encourages them to live a life of *sincere faith*, to persevere in a *deep life of prayer*, to undertake *works of charity*, and to see to the *Christian education* of their children. However, they are not permitted to receive sacramental absolution or Holy Communion as long as their situation persists, unless there is a willingness to live "as brother and sister."

CCC 1655-1658
The Domestic Church

This section, which concludes the treatment of the sacrament of Matrimony, is a ringing call to families to be centers of faith, love, and hope for the sake of a new evangelization of the culture around them. An implicit parallel is drawn between the position of Christian families in the early centuries of the Church, who were "islands of Christian life in an unbelieving world" (1655), and families in our own day who live "in a world often alien and even hostile to faith" (1656).

There is a clear challenge here to families not to be passive recipients of this alien culture but to be centers of "living, radiant faith." The family is the "basic" Christian community, the most fundamental "cell" of both society and of the Church. For this reason the family has the title "the domestic church." In the family parents and children can live out in a communal and familial fashion *the very nature of the Church*. The father and mother and all the other members of a family exercise the priesthood of the laity through the reception of the sacraments, prayer and thanksgiving, self-denial, active charity, and the witness of a holy life. All of this contributes towards making the family a community of grace and prayer and truly a "domestic church."

The domestic church can also mirror and accompany the "great family which is the Church" in the active hospitality it shows to those who are without families, whose family lives are threatened and under stress, to single people and to the poor, helping to witness to the fact that "the Church is a home and family for everyone," as Saint John Paul II expressed it (1658).

CCC 1667-1676
Sacramentals

Alongside the sacraments, the Church has *instituted certain sacred signs* which are meant to better *dispose one to receive the sacraments* by sanctifying various circumstances in life. These sacred signs include blessings and the dedication of persons and things meant for the praise and worship of God.

While "sacramentals," as they are called, do not *confer* the grace of the Holy Spirit as the sacraments do, *they do prepare us to sanctify almost every event of life*. The sacramentals "draw their power" from the grace of the Paschal mystery of Christ. "There is scarcely any proper use of material things which cannot be thus directed toward the sanctification of men and the praise of God" (1670).

Sacramentals, then, can assume many different forms. The Catechism discusses one significant form at some length, which is when the Church authoritatively *calls upon the name of our Lord Jesus* to protect a person or object from the power of Satan. This is called an "exorcism" and it is normally performed within the rite of Baptism. There are also occasions when an exorcism may be undertaken in a more "solemn" or prolonged manner. Only a priest authorized by the bishop may confer this solemn exorcism.

The Catechism notes that the sacramental liturgy and sacramentals themselves are surrounded by a plethora of various forms of *piety and popular devotion*. These include practices such as the veneration of relics, pilgrimages, the Stations of the Cross, the Rosary, and many others. While strictly speaking these practices may not be considered liturgical, nevertheless, ultimately they are derived from it — they can be seen as "extending" the liturgical life of the Church — and can lead back to it, back to the sources of sacramental grace God has provided for his people.

CCC 1680-1690
Christian Funerals

We conclude the Part Two of the Catechism on the note of *Christian death*. As we saw, when reading about the teaching on death at the end of Part One, this is another way of speaking about the entry into *everlasting life*. This is the "last Passover of the child of God ... into the life of the Kingdom" (1680).

At the *moment* of death the Christian *enters* into his new birth begun at Baptism, strengthened in Confirmation, and nourished in the Eucharist. The death of a Christian finds its fullest meaning in light of the death and resurrection of Jesus.

Throughout his pilgrim journey here on earth the Christian has been accompanied and nourished by his mother, the Church. Brought into the life of grace at birth through the gift of the Holy Spirit, at the end of life's journey the Church commits to the earth the body that is now destined for glory.

The Church celebrates this entrance of a soul into "the Father's hands" with the rite of Christian burial. Within this rite, which may differ in the many regions and situations in which it is celebrated, the Paschal mystery of Christ is the principal theme. However, the order of celebration is common to all the liturgical traditions and includes the greeting of the Christian community, the liturgy of the word by which the mystery of Christian death is explained in the belief of the Risen Christ, the celebration of the Eucharistic Sacrifice, and finally the last "farewell," commending the soul of the departed to the mercy of God, to the source of eternal life. The entire funeral ceremony leads to the final hope of the resurrection and union with God for eternity.

PART THREE
Life in Christ

CCC 1691-1696
Introduction to Moral Catechesis I

Part Three of the Catechism offers an extensive and systematic catechesis of the Christian moral life, which it succinctly calls our *life in Christ*. This moral catechesis begins by inviting us to recognize that the Christian moral life is not merely holding a Christian position on certain moral issues or making choices that correspond to a Christian sense of right and wrong, but rather leading a life "worthy of the Gospel" (1692) in accord with the dignity we receive through redemption in Jesus Christ.

The text clearly indicates that *we are only capable of such a life by faith in Jesus Christ and by the grace of the sacraments*, and in this way it signals the deep connection between this part of the Catechism and all that has come before it. An authentic Christian moral life proclaims the truths of the faith described in Part One of the Catechism and develops the power of the grace of the sacramental life outlined in Part Two, with our incorporation into Christ at Baptism representing the original meeting point of faith and grace in our lives.

By concentrating on how we are "incorporated into Christ by Baptism" (1694), the Catechism links the Christian moral life to our adoption as the children of God and the way in which "the Holy Spirit renews us interiorly through a spiritual transformation" (1695). This adoption and spiritual transformation confers on us a new dignity, rescues us from the power of sin and darkness, and calls us into the light of the Kingdom of God.

All of these truths converge to become the measure of our moral lives. In other words, the good Christian will be the one who imitates Christ, acts like a child of God, appears transformed by the Holy Spirit and shows true human dignity while turning from sin and seeking the Kingdom of God.

CCC 1697-1698
Introduction to Moral Catechesis II

Having linked the essence of the Christian moral life with our incorporation into Christ through Baptism, the Catechism now provides us with the fundamental reference points for a sound catechesis of the Christian moral life. At the same time, this section of the text offers a quick overview of the major themes that we will encounter in this part of the Catechism.

A sound catechesis of the Christian moral life will "reveal in all clarity the joy and the demands of the way of Christ" (1697) and will both emphasize the action of God in our lives and spell out the proper response we should make to him. This focus on the interplay between God's initiative through Christ and our response shapes our entire moral lives and frees us from the idea that we somehow make ourselves good by sheer effort or skillful decision-making. The fundamental principles of this catechesis help us recognize that *the good Christian is the one who is ready to renounce sin and allow God to work in his or her life.*

The major themes of this moral catechesis will include how God works through the Holy Spirit that guides us and the grace that transforms us, which leads into the beatitudes and the theme of sin and forgiveness. They will also include an account of the virtues and the law of charity by which we adequately respond to God's grace on a daily basis, as well as the theme of the ecclesial community where we encounter God and encourage each other.

However, throughout all these themes, we must take *Jesus Christ himself* as the fundamental reference point for this catechesis. By "looking to him in faith" (1698), we find a summary of the entire Christian moral life, from both the side of God and that of man, and find in him hope that what has been fulfilled in him can take place in us.

CCC 1701-1709
Man: The Image of God

The Catechism begins to unfold the content of its moral catechesis by grounding morality in the fundamental teaching that "Christ ... makes man fully manifest to himself and brings to light his exalted vocation" (1701). At the same time, the text draws our attention to the core truth that *our dignity rests in being the image of God*, the image received from the mystery of creation, disfigured by the first sin, and restored and ennobled by the grace of God. This approach sets our morality within the Gospel's basic dynamic of creation, sin, and redemption and makes our identity as the image of God the focal point for observing this dynamic in our own lives.

The text continues by briefly sketching key terms by which the divine image is present in every human person. The divine image is present in us insofar as we are each endowed with a spiritual and immortal soul, willed for our own sake, and destined for eternal beatitude. We manifest the divine image by the powers of the human soul, especially human reason, by which we can understand "the order of things established by the Creator," and free will, by which we can direct ourselves to the "true good" (1704).

In other words, *we are like God because we are capable of seeking and loving what is true and good*, and we live up to this identity when, by our daily choices, we follow the voice of God in our hearts that urges us to do good and avoid evil.

Although our souls are now wounded by sin, we can be healed by the merits of Christ, allowing us to become the children of God with the ability to "follow the example of Christ" and attain "the perfection of charity which is holiness" (1709). Healed by the grace of God, each of us can live a Christian moral life that blossoms into beatitude in the glory of heaven.

CCC 1716-1724
Our Vocation to Beatitude

The Catechism continues its moral catechesis with a consideration of the *vocation to eternal beatitude* that fulfills the potential of the human soul by bringing us into the Trinitarian life of God in heaven.

The Beatitudes stand "at the heart of Jesus' preaching" (1716), and they recall the promises of God's covenants with his chosen people and fulfill them by ordering them to the Kingdom of Heaven. The Catechism presents the Beatitudes as "promises that sustain hope in the midst of tribulation" (1717) and a portrait of Jesus that serves as a guiding light to all of us who seek to follow Christ. We should think of the Beatitudes as an expression of our vocation as believers, a depiction of the basic actions and attitudes that characterize the Christian moral life.

The New Testament call to eternal beatitude fulfills our natural desire for happiness, which serves to make us seek God, "the One who alone can fulfill it" (1718). Although our desire for happiness in God can be called natural in its origin, it is supernatural in its fulfillment and uniquely Christian in meaning. The New Testament describes our beatitude in various ways, but Christian beatitude essentially means *sharing in the divine nature and the joy of the Trinitarian life in heaven.* Such beatitude can only be received as a free gift from God, making it the supernatural fruit of God's grace.

The Catechism links this beatitude back to the Christian moral life by speaking of how God's offer of this supernatural beatitude "confronts us with decisive moral choices" and "invites us to purify our hearts of bad instincts" (1723). The teachings of the Gospel — especially the Decalogue and the Sermon on the Mount — and the catechesis of the Church should be understood as the *paths that lead to happiness,* to which God calls us. From this perspective, the Christian moral life means following these paths "step by step, by everyday acts," by the grace of the Holy Spirit (1724).

CCC 1730-1733
Freedom and Responsibility I

The power to seek beatitude in God by our everyday acts is called *human freedom*, and here the Catechism turns our attention to the *dignity and responsibility* that accompany freedom. God has given us the dignity of free persons so that, of our own accord, we can seek him and find our happiness in him; in order to do this, however, we must develop and exercise our freedom with the help of God's grace.

In the most basic sense, freedom means "the power rooted in reason and will, to act or not to act" (1731). However, freedom not only means doing things but also *shaping ourselves by our choices*. In speaking of freedom in these terms, the text highlights the *deep connection in Christian morality between the kind of choices we make and the kind of persons we become through the exercise of freedom*. Human freedom "attains its perfection when directed toward God, our beatitude" (1731), because the very meaning of freedom revolves around the ability to make the choices that will make each of us the sort of person who finds happiness in God alone.

The perfection of freedom will be reached in heaven, where the power of freedom will definitively be joined to its ultimate good: God. In this life, though, we experience freedom as "the possibility of choosing between good and evil, and thus of growing in perfection or of falling and sinning" (1732). Despite this common experience, the true meaning of freedom can be found only in its essential relationship to truth about what is good, and for this reason the text clarifies that "there is no true freedom except in the service of what is good and just" so that "the more one does what is good, the freer one becomes" (1733). Conversely, we only abuse our freedom when we choose to do evil, and this abuse of freedom can even lead us to "the slavery of sin" (1733; Rom 6:17).

CCC 1734-1737
Freedom and Responsibility II

The deep connection between the good or evil of the choices we make and the type of person we become is called *moral responsibility*, which the Catechism here addresses.

The power of freedom makes us responsible for our actions "to the extent that they are voluntary" (1734). In Catholic morality, this means that the more clearly we understand the effects of our choices and the more freely we will those effects, the more moral responsibility we have for the goodness or evil of our choices. Moral responsibility can be enhanced by progress in virtue, clearer knowledge of the good, and greater self-control, but it can also be diminished by factors that impede our use of reason and will.

As the Catechism indicates, there are factors that can diminish a person's use of reason and will in certain cases, thereby lessening or eliminating the guilt of that person. For this reason, we cannot evaluate the moral responsibility of someone until we consider possible extenuating circumstances, even in cases where we can clearly judge and speak of the evil of the choice made by that person. We can, in other words, employ the concept of responsibility to distinguish the sin from the sinner and see that moral blame is a separate question from the objective evil of a choice.

The text also briefly mentions those cases where the effects of a choice can be "tolerated" without being properly willed by a person (1737). This enables us to evaluate those cases in which some good choice leads to negative side effects in order to see whether the choice remains morally acceptable despite these negative effects. However, as the text points out, we are not responsible for a bad effect only if it is not willed either as an end or as a means.

In all cases, then, we must be doing a good action with a good intention, and it will never be acceptable to choose to do evil, even with the best of intentions.

CCC 1739-1742
Human Freedom in the Economy of Salvation

Like our inherent dignity itself, the power of human freedom has been marred by human sinfulness, and the Catechism continues its moral catechesis by considering the effects of sin on human freedom and *our need for the healing power of God's grace.*

Salvation history clearly demonstrates the various threats to human freedom and the ways in which the abuse of freedom through sin has led to a multitude of problems. The most fundamental threat to freedom is the allure of a defective understanding of it as "the right to say or do everything" we wish or the idea that freedom amounts to seeking the satisfaction of our interests in earthly things. However, our freedom is also threatened by economic, social, political, and cultural conditions that tempt us to sin in order to find practical solutions to problems and unjust situations. We are tempted to violate, and ultimately diminish, our freedom when sinful situations make further sin seem like the only practical solution to our problems.

Having sketched the threats to our freedom, the Catechism turns our attention to Christ and his saving grace in order to indicate the *source of true freedom* amidst these temptations and trials. Jesus has set us free from the bondage of sin, has given us the truth that makes us free, and has empowered us with the Holy Spirit in order to give us the freedom of the children of God. We will find that *true freedom grows the more we cooperate with God's grace,* because "the more docile we are to the promptings of grace, the more we grow in inner freedom and confidence during trials, such as those we face in the pressure and constraints of the outer world" (1742).

As our freedom grows through this healing power of God's grace, we will not only improve our own personal lives, but *we will also be better able to help others by serving God in the Church and in the world.*

CCC 1749-1753
The Morality of Human Acts I

This very brief section of the Catechism sketches the proper way in which we should understand the "human acts" by which we exercise our freedom in everyday life. Human acts are the *deliberate choices we make with some awareness of what we are doing*, which, no matter how small, have moral significance: "they are either good or evil" (1749).

As the text explains, the morality of a human act derives from the *object, end, and circumstances* — the three "constitutive elements" of the act (1750). In real life, these components are woven together into one seamless act, but for the sake of moral analysis, we break them down, one by one, beginning with the object of the act.

The *object of choice* is often called the "means" and indicates "what" we are doing when we make a deliberate choice. However, as the text clarifies, the object of choice "morally specifies" the human act rather than providing a merely physical description of what a person is doing (1751). In other words, the object enables us to name a person's behavior in morally significant terms, using words such as idolatry, adultery, or theft to describe certain kinds of evil choices, for example.

Of course, every object or means is chosen for the sake of some *intention or end*, so the moral analysis of a human act considers this component next. Whereas the object exists in the behavior of a person, the end resides in the mind and heart and explains why we are doing what we are doing. The Catechism recalls the famous maxim "the end does not justify the means" in order to clarify that some objects of choice are "intrinsically disordered" and cannot be justified by any good intentions (1753).

Here we see the text highlighting the recurring theme that there are some choices that we simply must never make, no matter what great good we hope to gain, or what great evil we hope to prevent.

CCC 1754-1756
The Morality of Human Acts II

The Catechism continues its teachings on human acts by presenting the notion of "circumstances" or the "secondary elements" of the human act, which provide further details, such as when, where, how much, how long, and the further "consequences" of the act (1754).

The *circumstances* help us evaluate the morality of human acts, providing some insight into the degree of the moral goodness or evil found in an act by virtue of its *object* and *end*. For example, the goodness of giving alms to help the poor can, at times, be more clearly seen in how much was given or the sacrifice that was made to give a certain amount. The circumstances can also provide some insight into the moral responsibility of the person, because the factors that lessen moral responsibility would be found in the circumstances. However, while circumstances can diminish a person's personal guilt, even extreme circumstances cannot make "good nor right an action that is in itself evil" (1754).

The Catechism concludes its teaching on the human act with one of the most important hallmarks of biblical and Catholic morality, by addressing what we call *moral absolutes* and so-called *intrinsically evil acts*, and by also addressing the temptation to justify evil choices with good intentions or extreme circumstances.

The text recalls the basic principle by which a "morally good act requires the goodness of the object, of the end, and of the circumstances together" (1755), which means simply that for an act to be good, all of its elements must be good because one bad component spoils the whole act.

Specifically, we recognize that *an evil object of choice can of itself make a human act evil*, regardless of any good intentions of the person or extenuating circumstances. In other words, the Catechism reminds us once again that there are some choices that are "always gravely illicit by reason of their object," and that we "may not do evil so that good may result from it" (1756).

CCC 1762-1770
The Morality of the Passions

Although we live out our moral lives by human acts, deliberate choices made through reason and will, *our passions play a fundamental role* because they can incline us to make certain choices and in this way indirectly shape our moral development. This section of the Catechism summarizes the Catholic understanding of human passions and their relevance for the Christian moral life.

In describing our passions as "movements of the sensitive appetite" (1763), the text locates our passions in the soul's response to our sensory experiences, both through the five senses of the body and through the imagination, and in how these movements "incline us to act or not act" (1763) according to what we feel or imagine. Since our passions cannot produce choices directly, *the moral relevance of our passions will be found in how they influence our use of reason and will in making choices.*

We experience a great variety of passions in the inner life of the soul, but the Catechism concentrates on love, or the basic attraction to, desire for, and enjoyment of the good, and hatred, which stands in opposition to love, as aversion to, fear of, and sadness and anger in the face of evil. The passions can play a positive role in our moral lives when our desire for the good leads us to make good choices, but we need well-ordered passions for this to take place.

The Catechism clarifies that *having certain feelings cannot make you a morally good or evil person*, because "in themselves passions are neither good nor evil" (1767), and "strong feelings are not decisive for the morality or the holiness of persons" (1768). Nonetheless, the Catechism reminds us that "moral perfection consists in man's being moved to the good not by his will alone" (1770), but by passions as well. For this reason, *the genuine Christian moral life is a life of passion, passion that is perfected by the virtues and stirred by the Holy Spirit.*

CCC 1776-1782
The Judgment of Conscience

The genuine meaning of human freedom requires each of us to do what is good and true, but *this meaning cannot be fulfilled unless we can discern good from evil and truth from falsehood*; this brings us to the vital importance of the *human conscience*. The Catechism's teachings on conscience offer a typically Catholic, balanced understanding that blends together three meanings of the word "conscience" in order to explain how the human conscience serves as a source of both personal conviction and objective moral truths.

The text presents the first meaning of conscience in terms of an *inner "sanctuary" where we encounter the voice of God and discover in our heart "a law inscribed by God"* (1776). This meaning grounds the function of conscience in objective moral truths and ultimately enables the human conscience to carry with it a sense of divine authority.

When we hear the voice of God in our consciences, we do not receive from God step by step instructions as to how we should act in each moment. Rather, we receive from him "perception of the principles of morality" (1780), especially the primary principle that enjoins us to do good and avoid evil. Our *awareness of the universal principles of morality* is the second meaning of the word "conscience."

Of course, these principles need to be applied to concrete cases in order to have practical value for us, and the *judgment of reason by which we make this application* is the third meaning of conscience. At this point in the process, conscience becomes a judgment of reason by which we recognize "the moral quality of a concrete act" (1778).

Instead of being merely a private opinion about the morality of a given act, this threefold meaning of conscience allows us to understand the judgment of conscience as the *obligatory recognition of the requirements of the principles of morality expressed by the divine law, written by God, in our hearts.*

CCC 1783-1785
The Formation of Conscience

The *dignity of the human conscience* rests in how it enables us to use our reasoning powers to apply the divine law, written in our hearts, in recognizing the good to be done here and now. However, due to the limits of human reason, our judgments of conscience are not infallible, and *we need to form our consciences well in order to discern the truth about the good to be done.* This section of the Catechism describes both our need for the formation of conscience as well as the basic shape this formation should take in the Christian moral life.

Our need to form our consciences corresponds to both the *need for natural moral education* and the *need to counteract the negative influences of sin* (1783). Beginning in early childhood, we need moral formation that awakens in us an understanding of the requirements of the divine law and that develops the virtues that dispose the conscience to formulate "its judgments according to reason, in conformity with the true good willed by the wisdom of the Creator" (1783).

However, the text clearly indicates that "the education of conscience is indispensable for human beings who are subjected to negative influences and tempted by sin" (1783). Here we see the Catechism striking a familiar tone by affirming the natural goodness of the human heart while also acknowledging the way human sinfulness has marred our natural tendency to what is good.

Following a well-established pattern, the Catechism restates our need for divine revelation to overcome the effects of human sinfulness, which means that the *formation of conscience must be grounded in Sacred Scripture and the authoritative teachings of the Church.* This means that we should admit the defects in our own judgments of conscience if they conflict with the clear teachings of divine revelation; the Catechism, though, never suggests that we can become lazy and neglect our own personal formation. These teachings are meant to serve, rather than replace, our consciences.

CCC 1786-1794
Choice, Conscience, and Erroneous Judgment

Whenever we have a breakdown in the function of conscience, we are *susceptible to doubt and prone to error*, and the Catechism concludes its teaching on conscience by addressing these two issues.

If we find ourselves in situations "that make moral judgments less assured and decision difficult" (1787), we are morally obliged to try to resolve this doubt and "seriously seek what is right and good and discern the will of God expressed in divine law" (1787). To help resolve any doubts we may have about our choices, the Catechism suggests interpreting the situation by the virtue of prudence, listening to the wisdom of others, reflecting on the teachings of the Bible and the Church, and seeking the help of the Holy Spirit. In all cases, we should remember that we must never do evil so that good may result from it and that we must follow the Golden Rule — to do unto others what we would want done to us.

In cases of an *erroneous judgment of conscience*, we call some action good when it is, in truth, evil, and are thus led to commit evil by following our conscience. The Catechism describes how the issue of personal guilt in such cases becomes a question of whether error has resulted from our own laziness or sinfulness, from the influence of others, or from some insurmountable ignorance. However, even though personal guilt can be diminished in some of these cases, an erroneous judgment of conscience still leads us to commit evil, so we "must therefore work to correct the errors of moral conscience" (1793).

These possibilities of doubt and error can create serious problems in our moral lives, but they do not lessen the basic dignity of our consciences. Instead, they serve as potent reminders of our responsibility to diligently form our consciences, which "guarantees freedom and engenders peace" (1784).

CCC 1803-1804
The Human Virtues

While we certainly must have *knowledge of the good* in order to do the good, we also need the *inner strength to do what we know to be good*, and for this reason the Catechism now turns to the theme of the virtues and their role in the Christian moral life.

We should not underestimate the importance of this catechesis on virtue, because it carefully draws together so many of the central ideas that have already been expressed in Part Three of the Catechism. The theme of virtue brings us back to the "spiritual powers" of the soul and our call "to become like God" (1803), to the way we shape ourselves by our choices, to the need to act "according to reason and faith" and to "order our passions" (1804), and to the way the Christian moral life should "dispose all the powers of the human being for communion with divine love" (1804).

Beginning here with the human virtues, the text defines virtue as "a habitual and firm disposition to do the good" (1803) that makes it "possible" for us to live out the demands of law and conscience with "ease, self-mastery, and joy" (1804). This understanding of virtue roots the moral life in the *good inner tendencies of our hearts* rather than in some burdensome external conformity to demands imposed on us from the outside. However, the virtues do not *force* us to choose what is good, thus *perfecting our freedom* rather than eliminating it.

At the same time, as the text points out, it is by our freedom that we develop these virtues, since they "are acquired by human effort" as "the fruit and seed of morally good acts" (1804). In this way, the Catechism is designating virtue as one of the main ways to understand how we shape ourselves by our own freedom, while also keeping the focus of our morality on the inner life of the person.

CCC 1805-1811
The Cardinal Virtues and Grace

The traditional and biblical (see Wis 8:7) understanding of the human virtues recognizes four cardinal virtues that "play a pivotal role" (1805) in the moral life, and here the Catechism describes these cardinal virtues.

This traditional understanding of the cardinal virtues adopted by the Catechism helps the text keep the focus of morality on the inner life of the person and reminds us that we should be moved to good not "by the will alone," but also with our whole being (1770). Each of the cardinal virtues is given a specific role to play in our moral lives, but, more importantly, *together they represent how moral perfection extends to all of our spiritual powers*. The four cardinal virtues correspond to the fourfold source of actions in our soul located in the interaction of reason (prudence), will (justice), the irascible passions (fortitude), and the concupiscible passions (temperance). We may need other smaller virtues in various situations, but since the cardinal virtues perfect the four sources of action in us, "all the others are grouped around them" (1805).

Prudence serves as the lead virtue, helping us "apply moral principles to particular cases without error" so that we can make sound judgments of conscience (1806). *Justice* "consists in the constant and firm will to give their due to God and neighbor" (1807) and enhances all our relationships, which is why Scripture often mentions "the just man" as the example of moral goodness in general. *Fortitude* orders the passions of the irascible appetite, helping us have the patience and courage "to resist temptations and to overcome obstacles in the moral life" (1808). *Temperance* orders how our passions respond to pleasant and easy situations, enabling us to keep our desires "within the limits of what is honorable" (1809) and enjoy the legitimate pleasures of this life without overindulging in them.

In these terms it is not difficult to see how four virtues, cooperating with God's grace, can transform our entire lives.

CCC 1812-1832
The Theological Virtues

In our catechesis on the virtues, we now come to the specific Christian practice of the virtues through the theological virtues of faith, hope, and charity. Rather than merely being three additional virtues for us to develop, the theological virtues are "the foundation of Christian moral activity" and "give it its special character" by making us capable of acting as children of God and meriting eternal life (1813).

We call *faith, hope, and charity* the "theological virtues" because they relate directly to our personal relationship with God, but the Catechism wants to highlight how they also integrate our daily choices into our relationship with God. Theological virtues can change our daily lives because they "inform and give life to all the moral virtues" and open us to "the presence and action of the Holy Spirit in the spiritual faculties" of the soul (1813). They set a higher standard for the Christian practice of the virtues but also give the help we need to live up to this higher standard.

The Catechism describes how each of the theological virtues functions, with *faith* giving us the proper acceptance of God's revelation (1814), *hope* ordering our desire for happiness for eternal life in his kingdom (1817), and *charity* making us love God above all things for his own sake and our neighbor out of love for God (1822). However, the text clearly emphasizes the virtue of charity, which corresponds to "the new commandment" of Christ (1823) and becomes the basis and measure of the authentic "Christian practice" of all the virtues (1827).

The theme of virtue leads directly to the sense in which "the moral life of Christians is sustained by the gifts of the Holy Spirit" (1830). The Catechism uses these seven gifts to complete the catechesis on the virtues in order to remind us, once again, that *the Christian moral life finds its fullness in the work that God does in us rather than what we do for him.*

CCC 1846-1851
Mercy and Sin

Most of us fall into the trap of thinking of sin simply in terms of failure and guilt, thereby imagining it to be an entirely negative aspect of the Christian moral life. However, here we see the Catechism striking a different tone by locating the notion of sin within "the revelation in Jesus Christ of God's mercy to sinners" (1846) and the work of forgiveness through the mercy of God and the conversion of our hearts.

In a certain sense, the theme of sin has a positive meaning, because by acknowledging our sins we open ourselves to experience God's love for us through his forgiveness of our sins and in his cleansing of us "from all unrighteousness" (1847). The Catechism is encouraging us to see that *acknowledging our sins means that we believe we are capable of doing better with God's help, which is a positive view of both ourselves and God.*

In order to help us properly recognize sin in our lives, the Catechism speaks of sin not only as an immoral choice, or "an offense against reason" (1849), but more importantly as "an offense against God" (1850) like the first sin revealed in the Book of Genesis. The Catechism lists several essential characteristics found in original sin, but our focus should be on how sin entails "revolting against God" (1850), not only by breaking his rules but by rejecting his dominion over us. Sin is an offense against God in the sense that by sinning we in some way oppose God's authority over us and strike out on our own from "a perverse attachment to certain goods" (1849).

The Catechism wants us to see that the destructive nature of sin will be found in the way we replace God's authority with our pride, which is "diametrically opposed to the obedience of Jesus" (1850) and *contradicts the very essence of our vocation as disciples of Christ.*

CCC 1852-1860
The Different Kinds and the Gravity of Sin

Every sin is an offense against God and in some way bears the essential characteristics found in the original sin, but "there are a great many kinds of sin" (1852), as explained in this section of the Catechism.

We can distinguish among the various kinds of sin according to what they are as human acts, the virtues they oppose or the commandments they violate, but in all cases we are talking about what is "in the heart of man, in his free will" (1853). Here we see the Catechism again striking a balance between the essential meaning of sin, which will *always be found in how our hearts rebel against God,* and the full meaning of our sins, which *extends to the harm we do and to the virtues we corrupt in ourselves.*

The Catechism's treatment of the various kinds of sin concentrates on how we can evaluate sins "according to their gravity" (1854). Based on Scripture, Tradition, and human experience, the Catholic understanding of sin makes a distinction between *mortal sin* and *venial sin* both in terms of how gravely one of God's commandments has been violated and, primarily, how the theological virtue of charity in the heart has been violated, as charity always stands at the center of the Christian moral life.

The Catechism concentrates our attention on the inner life of the heart by stressing how mortal sin "destroys charity in the heart of man" (1855), while venial sin wounds charity by failing to live up to the demands of the moral law. To help clarify this emphasis on the heart, notice how we need "full knowledge and deliberate consent" (1857) to have a mortal sin and how there can be venial sins that have grave matter but lack these two conditions. True to the pattern of this entire catechesis, the text acknowledges what is external but concentrates the meaning of gravity on the *charity within our hearts.*

CCC 1861-1869
The Gravity and Proliferation of Sin

Beyond the traditional distinction between mortal and venial sin, we now see the text seeking to emphasize that mortal sin is a real possibility that could, by lack of repentance, lead to exclusion from Christ's kingdom and eternal death, "for our freedom has the power to make choices forever, with no turning back" (1861).

The fact that mortal sin "is a radical possibility of human freedom" (1861) can be disturbing because of the enormous significance it gives to our choices and the responsibility it places on us. Many in the contemporary Church have actually denied this traditional concept of mortal sin, so the Catechism is trying to leave no room for doubt when it comes to the *massive responsibility that comes with the gift of freedom.* At the same time, the text reminds us that we need only repent to receive mercy and forgiveness from God. We should not fear God's judgment as much as we should recognize that "hardness of heart can lead to final impenitence and eternal loss" (1864).

The text concludes this catechesis on sin by calling attention to the corrosive effects of sin and the way that sin "tends to reproduce itself and reinforce itself" (1865) within the life of each individual and within our communities. The capital sins "engender other sins" (1866) by putting us on the wrong path and by corrupting our sense of good and evil.

Our sin can also cause us to lead each other into sin, and our personal sins can reinforce social situations that create "structures of sin" and somehow make sin the social norm (1869). We can even contribute to the sins of others if we refuse to discourage them "when we have an obligation to do so" (1868).

Above all, then, we need to be aware that neglecting to allow God's grace to convert us from our sinful ways has grave consequences for the world around us in addition to all the harm done to our own lives.

CCC 1877-1885
The Communal Character of the Human Vocation

We now begin Chapter Two of the Catechism's teaching on the Christian moral life, where the text continues to focus on our vocation "to show forth the image of God and to be transformed into the image of the Father's only Son" but begins to consider how this personal vocation "also concerns the human community as a whole" (1877).

While our happiness will be found in God himself, *the love by which we have communion with God extends into a love of neighbor,* and this love of neighbor introduces the theme of society into our moral catechesis. *Living in society with others* helps us develop our spiritual potential, especially the potential for love, and this makes society a fundamental good of the person and vital for the proper development of our Christian moral lives. The "human person needs to live in society" (1879) not just for practical reasons, but rather for spiritual development, and this development is the measure of a good society.

As this teaching on society unfolds, we can see that *the basic relationships of a society must be healthy in order for society to function as it should.* The individual members of society should show "loyalty" to the community and "respect to those in authority" (1880), while participating with others in the pursuit of the society's common purpose. At the same time, the community should implement what the Church calls "the principle of subsidiarity" (1883) and help individuals be successful without depriving its members of their rightful freedom and initiative.

Those who govern within society should "behave as ministers of divine providence" and imitate God in showing "great regard for human freedom" (1884). We should especially be on guard against the dangers of "collectivism" (1885), which violates the notion of human autonomy and subordinates everyone to the practical goals of the larger community. Such collectivism would ultimately defeat the true purpose of human societies and frustrate the development of the human person that society should serve.

CCC 1886-1889
Conversion and Society

As the Catechism continues its teachings on society, it reminds us that *the need for conversion extends beyond each of us as individuals to the societies we create together.* From the outset of this moral catechesis, the Catechism has been working with the premise that we need *grace and conversion of heart* in order to be restored from the effects of human sinfulness. Now the text is simply applying the need for conversion to our social lives as well.

The relationship between the person and society goes in both directions, in that we create our societies, and are then influenced by them. In order to create just and dignified societies, we need to draw upon our "spiritual and moral capacities" (1888) and commit ourselves to inner conversion. Because human society primarily belongs to the spiritual order rather than the technical or practical level, *our own spiritual well-being will determine the kind of societies we are able to create.* At the same time, poorly formed societies create institutions and conditions that are "an inducement to sin" (1888). For this reason, the Catechism presents personal conversion as both the basis and the fruit of social justice.

The text also gives us some key points to keep in mind in this pursuit of personal conversion and social justice. Both need to be rooted in a "just hierarchy of values" (1886), where spiritual and interior values are given priority over material and exterior values.

Additionally, components of social justice, such as decent living conditions, should not become ends in themselves, but should, rather, be highly valued as an important part of our personal and spiritual development. Above all, we should maintain the primacy of charity in the pursuit of social justice, recognizing that *our love of God and neighbor requires social justice and that social justice requires us to love one another with the help of God's grace.* Like the rest of our moral lives, social justice is primarily a matter of the heart.

CCC 1897-1904
Authority

Well-ordered human societies can help us show forth our dignity and fulfill our personal vocations, but our societies cannot function in this way unless they have "some people invested with legitimate authority" (1897). In this section of the Catechism, we get a sense of how Christians should view authority and how we might judge whether or not we are dealing with a legitimate authority.

Since we are social by our human nature, and "every human community needs an authority to govern it" (1898), the Catechism connects the concept of authority with the human nature given to us by God. Authority within human societies is *part of God's plan for us and not just some practical need of our social lives*. Likewise, God's plan asks us to be obedient, respectful and even grateful to those who exercise legitimate authority within our communities. Herein lies the moral significance of our relationships to those in authority.

Catholic social teaching allows for various forms of government within the natural order established by God, and "the choice of the political regime and the appointment of rulers are left to the free decision of the citizens" (1901). However, any political regime is morally legitimate *only to the extent that it serves the common good* of the community and *upholds the fundamental dignity of all the members of the community*.

This service of the common good and promotion of human dignity becomes the measure of legitimate authority and just laws, thus giving us the criteria by which we would choose to obey and respect those in authority over us. Since authority "is exercised legitimately only when it seeks the common good of the group concerned and if it employs morally licit means to attain it" (1903), unjust laws that violate these criteria are not binding on us in conscience; those who enact such laws, therefore, would be morally blameworthy for their abuse of their role within the community.

CCC 1905-1917
The Common Good, Responsibility, and Participation

Because we are social by nature, the perfection of the human person cannot be found merely in the good of each individual, but rather includes some participation in the common good shared with others. Here the Catechism provides us with the basic meaning of the term "common good" in Catholic teaching and explains how the common good factors into the Christian moral life.

The term "common good" refers to "the sum total of social conditions" (1906) that promote the fulfillment of the human person, both as an individual and as a social being. The human person is a bodily and spiritual being, with an emphasis on the spiritual, so *the common good of a society must promote both the material, and especially the spiritual, development of the person.*

The text offers us three focal points for our understanding of the common good. First, the common good should be grounded in respect for the dignity, rights, and vocation of each person, all of which converge in our ability to love God and neighbor. Second, it should foster the well-being and development of each person by making accessible to each "what is needed to lead a truly human life" (1908). Third, the common good includes the stability and security needed to live our lives in peace. This understanding applies to both the local and international levels.

The Catechism concludes its teachings on the common good by describing the *moral responsibility that we each have towards the common good.* We rightly participate in the common good when we use the conditions of our society to better ourselves and live out our personal vocations. At the same time, we need to build up the common good by promoting it directly or indirectly by our respect for authority. Above all, we need to recognize that the Christian moral life obliges us to take account of how our actions better the lives of those around us.

CCC 1928-1933
Respect for the Human Person

We have already seen how all the social teachings of the Church are centered on the dignity and personal vocation of the human person. The core value of society, and the measure of a good society, will always be found in how society respects the *dignity of the human person* and enables each of us to fulfill our *personal vocation to love*. The Catechism now presents this larger theme through the concept of "social justice," understood in its personal, moral, and spiritual senses.

As Christians, we should not think of social justice primarily in terms of political or legal rights to be protected by legislation and social institutions, even though these are important in their own right. Instead, we should focus on the connection between the inherent dignity of the human person and the Gospel call to love one another, making this connection the *basis of our commitment to social justice*.

Social justice means promoting and protecting the inherent dignity and inalienable rights of the human person, which "are prior to society and must be recognized by it" (1930). This means that true social justice promotes both the right and the obligation to do what is truly befitting of the dignity of the human person, but it also means that no one can claim the right to do what is immoral or contrary to human dignity.

However, in promoting social justice, we will find that it is not quite enough to view each other just in generic terms of human persons with dignity. *Social justice requires an attitude in which we view each other as neighbors, and even brothers and sisters, rather than merely fellow citizens.* For this reason, legislation alone cannot bring about social justice. As the text points out, only through the virtue of charity can we fulfill the Gospel command to love our neighbors and overcome the pride, selfishness, fears, and prejudices that erode social justice.

CCC 1934-1942
Equality, Differences, and Human Solidarity

As an extension of its teaching on how social justice can only be achieved through the virtue of charity, by which we recognize the other as a neighbor whom God calls us to love, the Catechism now describes the Christian sense of equality and solidarity among all men.

To properly love our neighbors and give them their due, we need to believe that all men are created in the image of God with rational souls, have been redeemed by the sacrifice of Christ, and are called to the same divine beatitude in heaven. These core truths of the human person ensure that we all have the same inherent dignity despite the differences (such as age, race, physical and mental abilities, or social conditions) there may be among us.

Some of these differences "belong to God's plan" and encourage us to develop virtues as we learn to work together in sharing our various talents (1937). Social justice requires us to *affirm the equality of every person whenever we encounter these legitimate differences*. However, some social inequalities result from human sinfulness, and in these cases, social justice requires us to work to overcome or eliminate the causes of such inequalities.

The dynamic of social justice finds its completion in the concept of *human solidarity*, which fulfills the "demand of human and Christian brotherhood" (1939). Human solidarity surpasses simply a sense of equality among people by lessening competition between us and our neighbors and by encouraging everyone to work together for the common good. We express our solidarity by sharing our material and spiritual goods with each other and by working for social conditions that lessen tensions and conflicts among various groups and individuals.

The Catechism recognizes that solidarity will need to take various forms, but it reminds us that solidarity should always mean *working together to make everybody's life better while avoiding the temptation to focus on the success of a few select people in our lives.*

CCC 1949-1953
The Moral Law

We now begin Chapter Three of Part Three, where the Catechism examines the life of the believer in terms of "the law that guides him and the grace that sustains him" (1949). This section of the Catechism explains the proper meaning of the moral law and the various forms of law by which God guides us.

The Catechism's description of the moral law intends to dispel a false notion of law that describes it as an arbitrary code imposed on us by an external authority. The proper understanding of the moral law recognizes it as *a gift given to us* as "the work of divine Wisdom" (1950) by which God shares with us the knowledge of what is truly good and evil. Since the proper meaning of moral goodness corresponds to the divine plan for human happiness, we should receive the moral law as a sure guide to which actions fulfill that meaning and which actions contradict it.

The text summarizes the basic characteristics of a *true and just law* within the Catholic Tradition, defining law as "a rule of conduct enacted by competent authority for the sake of the common good" (1951); but the text primarily seeks to present law as a product of reason tracing its origin back to the divine order established by God. To give law its proper place in our moral lives, we must think of law as *an expression of the demands of human reason and what it ought to know about moral goodness*. However, we must also see that human reason derives its knowledge of moral goodness from a *share in divine wisdom* concerning the plan of God for human existence and happiness, a plan which the text also calls "the eternal law" and "the providence of the living God" (1951).

This sets the foundation for the Catechism's whole catechesis on law by making human reason the measure of human actions while also giving God his rightful authority in our moral lives.

CCC 1954-1959
The Natural Moral Law

The Catechism continues its catechesis on law by devoting considerable space to the *natural moral law*. Maintaining the rightful place of the natural law within the Christian moral life has been a long-standing hallmark of Catholic morality, and many official teachings of the Church will reference the natural law in order to clarify that Christian morality corresponds to the demands of our *inherent human dignity*. Acknowledging the natural law's place in our moral lives helps us avoid thinking of the Christian life as some unnatural way of life imposed on us from the outside by God.

The text describes the natural law both as "the original moral sense which enables man to discern by reason the good and the evil" (1954) and also as "the light of understanding placed in us by God" (1955). We should think of it, then, as divine in its origin but natural to our humanity in the way we experience it within ourselves. God is the one who "writes" this law in our hearts, but we call this law natural precisely because our own human reason expresses the demands of the law. *As divine and human, the natural law represents the special interplay of divinity and humanity that always characterizes authentic Catholic morality.*

The attributes of the natural law include the ways in which this law is "universal" (1956), "immutable" (1958), and indelible, which means that the natural law is known by everyone, is permanent throughout history and across cultures, and is unable to be "destroyed or removed from the heart" of anyone (1958). Because of these attributes, the natural law can serve as the basis of each individual's moral life and as "the indispensable moral foundation for building the human community" (1959).

While the Catechism will later recognize the law of the Gospel as the premier law of the Christian moral life, the natural law will always remain the original moral sense by which we can evaluate our choices and our communities.

CCC 1960-1964
The Old Law

Our catechesis on law now addresses the limitations of the natural moral law in "the present sinful situation of man" and our need for the "revealed law" in order to know moral truths with ease, certitude, and "no admixture of error" (1960). Essentially, the Catechism is showing us how the meaning of law follows the basic pattern of its whole moral catechesis, which acknowledges that our inherent goodness needs God's healing grace because of the effects of sin.

Human reason has an original moral sense in the form of natural law, but since our humanity has been marred by sin "the precepts of natural law are not perceived by everyone clearly and immediately" (1960). As a result, "sinful man needs grace and revelation" (1960), which come to us first as the Old Law and then as the New Law.

The Old Law is the law that God revealed to Israel when he chose them to be his people as revealed in the Old Testament. The Old Law "expresses many truths naturally accessible to reason" but in such a way that these truths are "stated and authenticated within the covenant of salvation" (1961). The Old Law represents an initial stage of the revealed law and can be summarized in the Ten Commandments. The central meaning of the Ten Commandments is found in how "they prohibit what is contrary to the love of God and neighbor and prescribe what is essential to it" (1962).

By expressing the moral demands of love, the Old Law should be viewed as holy and good, yet still imperfect because it shows us what must be done without itself giving us the strength to do it. We call the Old Law "a preparation for the Gospel" (1964) because it helped humanity see how *the full moral demands of love stand beyond the ability of the human heart burdened by sin*, thus signaling our need for something more, *signaling our need for redemption in Jesus Christ.*

CCC 1965-1970
The New Law, or the Law of the Gospel, I

This section of the Catechism turns our attention to the Law of the Gospel, "the perfection here on earth of the divine law, natural and revealed" (1965), also called the "New Law" to express how it completes what was begun in the Old Law of God's covenant with Israel.

The New Law is the perfection of all law because it restates all the moral demands of love contained in the natural law and in the Old Law, but also "releases their hidden potential" by *viewing those demands through the Person of Jesus Christ and the grace of the Holy Spirit*. The "newness" of the Law of the Gospel refers not to the progression of time but to the new way in which this law functions in our lives by virtue of the New Covenant to which it belongs.

Although the New Law is "the grace of the Holy Spirit given to the faithful through faith in Christ" (1966), not a set of rules to follow, the Sermon on the Mount teaches us "what must be done" (1966) through sacramental grace. Our Lord's Sermon on the Mount restates the demands of love expressed in the Ten Commandments and simultaneously shifts the focus of morality to the inner workings of the human heart and away from external actions. The Sermon on the Mount also *more deeply connects our moral life with the Father in heaven*, who sees the inner movements of our hearts and rewards us accordingly, and calls us to imitate the perfection of the heavenly Father. This relationship with our Father orientates our moral lives and all our religious acts to the Kingdom of Heaven and to the eternal life promised in the New Covenant in Christ.

For this reason, the Catechism ultimately concentrates our understanding of the New Law on the way it calls us to "put into practice the words of the Lord" (1970) and his new commandment to love one another as he has loved us.

CCC 1971-1974
The New Law, or the Law of the Gospel, II

As the Catechism presents this catechesis on the New Law, we see how it sets a very high standard for the Christian moral life, with its focus on the purity of the inner movements of our hearts and its call to imitate the love of Jesus. Yet, the Catechism encourages us to take hope in the New Law precisely because it brings to us the good news that by our union with Christ we can rise to such heights in our moral lives.

To highlight the newness of the Law of the Gospel, the Catechism explains that the New Law is one of love, "because it makes us act out of the love infused by the Holy Spirit." It is a law of grace, "because it confers the strength of grace to act, by means of faith and the sacraments," and it is a law of freedom, because it "inclines us to act spontaneously by the prompting of charity" as a friend of Christ (1972). By presenting the New Law in terms of the infusion of the Holy Spirit and the gift of grace and charity we receive through the sacraments, the Catechism calls us to see that what the Gospel demands of us is surpassed by what the Gospel promises to give us through faith in Jesus Christ.

Since the entire Law of the Gospel is contained in the new commandment to love, the Catechism concludes its teaching on the New Law from the perspective of charity and the traditional distinction between "God's commandments and the evangelical counsels" (1973). The commandments of the New Law prohibit anything that is incompatible with charity, while the counsels aim to remove whatever hinders the development of charity, even that which is not sinful in itself. We fulfill the New Law by striving for an ever greater love of God and neighbor, and the counsels of the Gospel point out the more direct ways to greater charity within the limits of each person's vocation.

CCC 1987-1995
Justification

Throughout its entire moral catechesis the Catechism has emphasized our need for God's grace in order to live out an authentic Christian moral life. Now the text focuses directly on the theme of grace and how we should understand the notions of justification, grace, and merit.

Justification is the first fruit of the work of God's grace in our hearts whereby we are *cleansed of our sins and made righteous by the power of the Holy Spirit.* The Catechism wants to emphasize how justification refers not merely to the change brought about in our relationship with God, but to how we ourselves are interiorly transformed when "we take part in Christ's passion by dying to sin, and in his resurrection by being born to a new life" through faith and the sacraments (1988).

Our transformation in Christ is called *conversion*, "the first work of the grace of the Holy Spirit" from which we receive justification by repenting of our sins and "accepting forgiveness and righteousness from on high" (1989). The Catechism rightly calls the process of justification through conversion the "most excellent work of God's love" (1994), surpassing the work of creation. Justification has been merited for us by Christ's passion, but it does not work like magic, because we must assent in faith to this transformation, being careful not to reject it by resisting the working of God's grace in our lives.

Justification makes the Holy Spirit the "master of the interior life" and leads to the sanctification of our "whole being" (1995), which explains why God can expect so much of us in our moral lives. Having transformed us through the power of the Holy Spirit, God simply asks us to show forth this great work of transformation in our daily lives by cooperating with the Holy Spirit, and he even prompts us to this co-operation by the inner workings of his grace. *Truly he gives far more than he asks in return.*

CCC 1996-2005
Grace

The meaning of justification previously sketched by the Catechism enables us to understand the Christian moral life as *a call to show forth in our actions the excellent work of God's grace in our hearts.* Now the Catechism offers a profound and theologically precise treatment of how we should understand the meaning of grace and its role in our lives.

The word *grace* itself derives its meaning from the completely "gratuitous" character of God's work in our hearts (1998, 1999). We should think of grace as "the free and undeserved help that God gives us to respond to his call to become children of God" (1996), and even more so as "a participation in the life of God" that "introduces us into the intimacy of Trinitarian life" (1997). Although grace "demands man's free response" (2002), the readiness "for the reception of grace is already a work of grace" (2001), so the Catechism repeatedly points to the utterly gratuitous character of God's grace, even at the level of our free cooperation.

The Catechism secondarily presents grace in terms of the various gifts and supernatural "dispositions" that transform our souls and enable us to live in intimacy with God and "act by his love" (2000). In other words, grace also refers to the effects of God's presence on the soul, how our souls are healed of sin and sanctified by the infusion of the Holy Spirit stemming from our union with Christ in Baptism.

By combining the primary and secondary meanings of grace, the Catechism concludes that "grace is first and foremost the gift of the Spirit who justifies and sanctifies us" (2003). We are reminded that grace "escapes our experience" such that we cannot "rely on our feelings or our works to conclude that we are justified and saved" (2005). We can in faith, however, rely on the help of the Holy Spirit promised to us by Christ, which is precisely what the Catechism is teaching us to do.

CCC 2006-2011
Merit

This moral catechesis of the Catechism has consistently referred to the *theological virtue of charity* as the primary basis of how our actions can be a genuine imitation of the love of Jesus Christ. Now the Catechism turns our attention to the fruits of acting in charity by giving a theological explanation of "merit" or what the Sermon on the Mount calls the "recompense" we can expect from our heavenly Father.

The Catechism clearly states that merit as a requirement of justice does not exist in our relationship with God the Creator, because "between God and us there is an immeasurable inequality, for we have received everything from him" (2007), which strictly prevents us from claiming that God owes us anything. Nonetheless, we can "merit before God in the Christian life" (2008) in a supernatural way by virtue of God's utterly free gift of grace, which makes us his adopted children.

We have come again to the foundational meaning of the Christian moral life as rooted in our divine adoption through Jesus, and now we are seeing how this adoption "can bestow *true merit* on us as a result of God's gratuitous justice" (2009). It should be simple enough to understand that in calling us to act like his children, God has promised to act like a Father who rewards our good behavior.

However, the Catechism truly solidifies the place of merit in our moral catechesis by highlighting how "the charity of Christ is the source in us of all our merits before God" (2011). *All our good actions have their source in Christ and his Holy Spirit*, and this is precisely what "ensures the supernatural quality of our acts and consequently their merit before God and before men" (2011). *The theme of merit, then, emphasizes not what we can expect to receive from God but rather the supernatural transformation we have already received in Baptism*, which is truly the basis of the Christian moral life.

CCC 2012-2016
Christian Holiness

With its catechesis on grace, the Catechism gives us both a sound understanding of how our daily actions can attain a supernatural quality by the working of God's grace in our hearts and a sense of how striving for holiness is the genuine measure of the Christian moral life. By including the theme of Christian holiness within this moral catechesis, the text is clearly trying to recover an element of Catholic morality that had been neglected for much of the modern period, where the pursuit of holiness was often limited to the sphere of spirituality.

One major catalyst for the kind of renewal of Catholic morality on display here in the Catechism was the Second Vatican Council, so we see the text especially drawing upon the Council's teaching on the *universal call to holiness*. According to the Council, "Christians in any state or walk of life are called to the fullness of Christian life and to the perfection of charity" (2013). This teaching emphasizes that *we are all called to the same holiness no matter what state of life we have in the Church*, recalling the principle of the "true equality" of all the faithful expressed in Part One of the Catechism (see 872 and 873). For this reason, we need not look outside our daily Christian lives in order to find the opportunity for holiness in its fullest measure.

At the same time, the text is reminding us that our Christian moral lives should be understood as our chance to accept God's covenantal love for us, because holiness will be found in an "ever more intimate union with Christ" that we achieve through a participation "in the mystery of Christ through the sacraments" (2014). In other words, the core meaning of holiness and the genuine meaning of the Christian moral life necessarily meet in the *union with God that we have in Christ through his grace and our cooperation with it*.

CCC 2030-2034
Moral Life and the Magisterium of the Church I

With these teachings on the role of the Church in the Christian moral life, the Catechism comes full circle to the starting point of its moral catechesis: *our incorporation into Christ through Baptism*, whereby we also become members of the Church. The "ecclesial catechesis" (1697) offered here shows the fundamental connection between life in the Church and our moral lives.

Participation in the life of the Church reflects, in a supernatural way, the *social nature of the human person*, and here the Catechism applies this basic truth of the human person to the Christian moral life, identifying the Church as the place, "in communion with all the baptized, that the Christian fulfills his vocation" (2030). The Catechism recalls several foundational elements of its entire moral catechesis by linking our life in the Church to "the Word of God," which counteracts the defects of our sinfulness, to "the grace of the sacraments" that heals and sustains us, and to "the example of holiness" found in the Virgin Mary and all the saints that inspires and enlightens us (2030).

However, the relevance of the Church emerges even more clearly when we recognize that "the moral life is spiritual worship" (2031). The text especially highlights how "the moral life finds its source and summit in the Eucharistic sacrifice" (2031), and it is through life in the Church that we can participate in this *unsurpassed form of worship*.

The Church further forms our moral lives by acting as a "mother and teacher" who shares her wisdom concerning "the faith to be believed and put into practice" (2034). The pope and the bishops are "the authentic teachers" of the Church, endowed "with the authority of Christ" through apostolic succession (2034). The teachings of the Church are meant to serve our moral development; we should look with *filial trust to the Church for guidance* in the moral life, but we must also take the *personal responsibility* to grow in our own understanding of God's plan for us.

CCC 2035-2040
Moral Life and the Magisterium of the Church II

Our life in the Church includes the right to be educated in the faith by the pope and the bishops, who together comprise the ordinary *Magisterium of the Church*. This section of the Catechism describes the authority of the Magisterium regarding questions of morality and how we should receive the teachings of the Magisterium in our life in the Church.

By virtue of the authority the pope and bishops have from Christ, the Magisterium can teach with "the charism of *infallibility*" (2035), ensuring the truth of its teachings. This infallibility extends as far as the deposit of divine revelation in Scripture and includes all elements of doctrine "without which the saving truths of the faith cannot be preserved, explained, or observed" (2035). Even the precepts of the natural law, which we should know in our hearts, can be taught in this way because God's revelation shows their observance to be necessary for salvation.

Like divine revelation that they express, the teachings of the Magisterium come to the assistance of "wounded human reason" (2037). We have a right to receive this divine assistance in our moral lives, and this gives the Magisterium both the duty and the right to proclaim these saving truths to us. In other words, the Magisterium owes us the service that it renders us by its teachings and would do us an injustice if it failed to authoritatively teach the truths of the Christian moral life.

Of course, *the Church can serve us only if we receive her teachings in the proper spirit*. We should look upon the teachings of the Magisterium with a "filial spirit" (2040) of trust and gratitude towards our mother who nourishes us with the sacraments and forms us by her wisdom. We should not, however, mindlessly follow the letter of Church teachings. Instead, we have the *personal responsibility to actively receive these teachings in faith and make them our own by forming our consciences in accordance with this wisdom*.

CCC 2041-2046
Precepts, the Moral Life, and Missionary Witness

The Catechism concludes this ecclesial catechesis by considering how the five precepts of the Church *regulate* our participation in the life of the Church and how our missionary witness *completes* our life in the Church.

The five precepts of the Church remind us that the Christian moral life is rooted in and "nourished by liturgical life" (2041), and they set the minimum requirements of our participation in it. By observing the precepts on the participation in the Eucharistic liturgy and the practices of penance and fasting, *we cultivate the work of conversion in our own lives, help maintain our connection with the other members of the Church, and position ourselves to fulfill our roles as individual members of the Body of Christ.*

However, in order to fulfill our diverse roles in the Church, we need to recognize the *deep connection between the Christian moral life and the Church's mission to proclaim the Gospel.* The Catechism is encouraging us to see that just as we can expect to receive much from the Church that fosters our own moral growth, we can give back to the Church by the ways in which our moral lives serve as a witness to the Gospel.

By our fidelity to our baptismal promises, we directly testify to the *power of God's grace* and demonstrate the *real possibility of conversion and righteousness* to those we encounter on a daily basis. We can also indirectly serve as missionaries when our moral lives authenticate the Gospel preached by the official missionaries of the Church. The Catechism's main point is that *we really do play a vital role in building up the Church by the constancy of our convictions and by the uprightness of our moral lives.* With our moral lives, we can help accomplish the mission of the Church not only by helping to grow the ecclesial community but also by ushering in the reign of God, which brings justice and peace to the world.

CCC 2052-2055
"Teacher, What Must I Do … ?"

All that the Church seeks to teach us about life in Christ finds its daily application in the keeping of the Ten Commandments, which, since the earliest days of the Church, "have occupied a predominant place in the catechesis of baptismal candidates and the faithful" (2065). We are first alerted to the importance of the Ten Commandments for our overall moral catechesis by the simple fact that the Catechism devotes almost five hundred articles (2052-2550) to explain their relevance for the Christian life. These opening paragraphs help us better appreciate the Ten Commandments by dispelling the idea that we are simply dealing with ten moral rules regarding a few special issues and by recalling how the commandments are linked to the *Gospel call to love as Jesus has loved us.*

The significance of the Ten Commandments begins with the way Jesus himself incorporates them into his preaching of the Gospel. The Catechism reminds us, for example, of how Jesus gave the commandments as his first answer to the young man who came to him seeking eternal life (2052), and how the commandments were recalled and renewed by Jesus in the Sermon on the Mount (2054). Thus, even while adding new dimensions to the life of those who seek "perfect fulfillment" as a disciple of Christ (2053), Jesus makes the Ten Commandments an *indispensable part of the Christian moral life.*

The Catechism also highlights the way Jesus links the importance of these commandments to the great commandment to love God and neighbor. Just as we can better understand the demands of the love of God and neighbor by these Ten Commandments, we can also interpret the commandments in terms of love, understanding each of the ten as another way to show our love for God and neighbor and fulfill the Law of God (2055).

The Catechism introduces the Ten Commandments as central to Jesus' preaching about love, and *nothing could have greater importance for the Christian moral life than that.*

CCC 2056-2063
The Decalogue I

When Jesus includes and renews the Ten Commandments in his preaching, he recalls for us the history of the "ten words" given to Moses (2056), and here the Catechism draws our attention to this history in order to express the theological significance of the commandments for the Christian moral life.

From the story of how the commandments were given to Moses on Mount Sinai, the text focuses our attention especially on how *the Ten Commandments are divine revelation given directly by God,* and how they are given in the context of the covenant linked to freedom from slavery in Egypt. In the Gospel, this essential meaning remains. However, now divine revelation reaches new heights when God speaks to us in the Incarnate Word, and the New Covenant frees us from slavery to sin, all of which adds greater significance to the commandments themselves.

The Ten Commandments are the path to freedom from the slavery of sin in a very direct way, in that if we can keep the commandments, our life will have no place for sin in it. However, we do not only receive a set of instructions from God with the Decalogue, but also "the gift of God himself and his holy will" (2059). By revealing himself and his holy will through the commandments, *God gives us a way to be like him, knowing what he knows and willing what he wills.*

The commandments "take on their full meaning within the covenant" (2061), and the text describes keeping the Ten Commandments as the immediate "implications of belonging to God through the establishment of the covenant" (2062). We should think of keeping the commandments as the way in which we can continually accept God's offer of himself through the covenant. These commandments are not simply what God asks of the community that is joined to him by the covenant, but also what he is asking of each of us personally in the intimate relationship he wants with us.

CCC 2064-2074
The Decalogue II

Following the pattern set by Sacred Scripture and by Jesus in particular, the Tradition of the Church has always "acknowledged the primordial importance and significance of the Decalogue" when instructing the faithful on the meaning of the Christian moral life (2064). This section of the Catechism further explains how we should understand the obligations of the Ten Commandments and how they can help us better understand our need for Jesus and God's grace.

The Church has traditionally used the structure of the Ten Commandments to express the requirements of Christian morality, and our Catechism certainly continues that tradition. However, the Church never intends to reduce our morality to a written code, so here the text is again *seeking to link the Decalogue to the Gospel call to love and to our own human dignity*. The Ten Commandments should be recognized as strict obligations in the Christian moral life, but only in so far as they "state what is required in the love of God and love of neighbor" (2067) and "teach us the true humanity of man" and his rights and duties (2070).

To think of the commandments in this way, we will need to recognize *further obligations of each commandment*, concerning what is both "grave" and "light" matter (2072 and 2073), and how *the commandments regulate the interior movements of our hearts as well as our external behavior.*

By seeing the full demands of the commandments, we should recognize our need for Jesus and for grace, making the commandments a *call to conversion*. We might well imagine that we can find a way to avoid the big issues literally mentioned in the commandments, but when we see the interior and detailed demands of the commandments, we may better recognize our struggles and shortcomings. For this reason the Catechism will spend dozens of pages spelling out the depth of what seem, on the surface, to be ten simple rules.

CCC 2083-2094
"You Shall Worship the Lord Your God and Him Only Shall You Serve"

The Catechism begins its teaching on the first commandment by grounding it in the *call to love God with our whole hearts so as to give an adequate response to the love he has shown us*, and this sets the basic pattern for our whole understanding of the commandment.

We fulfill the first commandment by acknowledging that "God has loved us first," and that he deserves to be loved in return (2083). Since God has loved us in an unparalleled way, *our love for God must be expressed in an utterly unique way*, which leads to the notion of the worship that must be given to God alone.

The Catechism first recalls the actions of God in salvation history, where he has revealed himself and the uniqueness of his power and love. The two focal points of this revelation are how God is our *Creator* and *Redeemer*. Consequently, the keys to fulfilling the first commandment will be acknowledging this double role he plays in our lives and cultivating the relationship that he has begun with us.

The text also indicates that *accepting this revelation of God and building our relationship with him are matters of faith, hope, and love* (2086). True to form, then, the Catechism first explains the commandment in terms of what is going on inside the person by way of the theological virtues before discussing the actual behavior of our worship. This also enables us to see the specifically Christian sense of the first commandment, for the theological virtues were already presented as the specifically Christian ways of living out our relationship with God.

In order to keep the first commandment, we need to nourish and protect our faith, entrust ourselves to God's power through hope, and exercise sincere charity in the true worship of God. At the same time, we must avoid any actions and situations that will erode our faith, hope, and charity, and prevent the true worship of God.

CCC 2095-2103
"Him Only Shall You Serve" I

As the Catechism continues its teachings on the first commandment, the text transitions from the theological virtues that form the basis of our relationship with God to the *virtue of religion that leads to the true worship of the one true God*. To keep this commandment, we must properly acknowledge the one true God and worship him in the proper way.

The first key component to the proper worship of God is *adoration*, whereby we acknowledge God as superior to all other entities and acknowledge our dependence on him. Recognizing that we would not exist but for God, we both exalt him and humble ourselves in a spirit of praise and gratitude (2097). The notion of adoration leads quickly to prayer. *Prayer* is turning to God himself in order to acknowledge him, to praise him, and to express our dependence on and gratitude towards him (2098). To further worship God with a sense of adoration, we are required to make acts of sacrifice, both externally and internally, and should especially unite our sacrifices to the sacrifice of Christ on the cross (2100).

The final basic component of worship discussed by the Catechism is our *fidelity to the promises and vows we make to God*. In the Christian life we have general promises, such as those linked to Baptism or Matrimony (2101), and also specific promises that we might make as a matter of personal devotion (2102). Fidelity to these promises is a sign of respect and love for God that acknowledges his unfailing faithfulness to us. Vows within the context of religion take the notion of promise even further by adding a type of deliberate, solemn *consecration to a promise made to God* (2102).

Even while so-called religious vows hold a special place in the life of the Church, we are all obliged to fulfill the first commandment by being faithful to our Baptism and other sacred duties that we have taken on in our relationship with God.

CCC 2104-2109
"Him Only Shall You Serve" II

Throughout this moral catechesis, the Catechism has included the social aspect of our moral lives alongside the personal sense in which we live out our relationship with God, and here the text repeats this pattern, focusing on the *social component* of religion.

Each human person is obliged by the first commandment to worship God in a fitting way, but each person is also a social being, so the "duty of offering God genuine worship concerns man both individually and socially" (2105). However, the logic at work here also leads us in another direction, helping us see that all good societies will have some recognition of the religious duties of its members.

The Catechism begins with the idea that a good human person will offer God genuine worship, and then easily moves to the idea that each human person has a moral obligation and therefore a fundamental human right to practice religion. The logic of the text continues with the notion that *good societies should promote the duty and right of each person to worship God in accord with his or her conscience.* While foreseeing some of the practical difficulties that may arise, the Catechism is simply saying good societies must necessarily promote and protect religious liberty as a fundamental human right, while also enforcing the "due limits" of religious liberty under which *no one has the right to practice religion by doing something contrary to human dignity or the common good* (2106 and 2109).

The Catechism clearly teaches that religious liberty requires Christians to respect those who adhere to other religions and to refrain from forcing anyone to act against the convictions of his own conscience (2106). The text also challenges us to see how this mutual respect does not negate our moral obligation to "awaken in each man the love of the true and the good" and "to make known the worship of the one true religion which subsists in the Catholic and apostolic Church" (2105).

CCC 2110-2122
"You Shall Have No Other Gods before Me"

As a logical consequence of obliging us to offer genuine worship to the true God, the first commandment also prohibits the worship of false gods, the false worship of God, or anything that corrupts the proper worship of God. Therefore, in this section of the Catechism we have *teachings on idolatry, superstition and magic, and irreligion.*

One of the most striking statements of the Catechism is its description of idolatry as "a constant temptation to faith" (2113), because burning incense before golden statues does not usually come to mind when we think of our shortcomings. Yet, as the text explains, idolatry means more than the typical notion of pagan worship and consists in *honoring and revering anything in such a way that contradicts the uniqueness of God.*

We commit some form of idolatry whenever we act as though something (power, pleasure, money, security, health, etc.) is necessary for our happiness, which in effect displaces *God as the sole source of our happiness* (see 1723). This line of thinking also bring us back to the meaning of mortal sin (see 1855), which includes turning away from God out of preference for an inferior good. Once we understand idolatry in these terms, we can admit that this sense of idolatry is our constant temptation.

We can see a similar temptation in superstition and magic or any practices that "contradict the honor, respect, and loving fear that we owe to God alone" (2116). We fail to uphold the first commandment whenever we seek a power source other than God and his plan for the natural powers of the universe. Circumventing God and his plan for creation is the essential problem with these practices, whatever form they take. Of course, even when we engage in the proper worship of God, we need to resist the temptation to "irreligion" (2118), which seeks to manipulate or violate the plan of God for sacred worship.

CCC 2123-2132
Atheism

The first commandment requires us to acknowledge God and our utter dependence on him, which reflects back on our dignity in terms of how we have been created in his image. Because *so much is at stake in the recognition of this bond between our dignity and our Creator*, the Catechism devotes a significant amount of its teaching on the first commandment to the problem of atheism.

The text clarifies that atheism can take various forms and result from a variety of circumstances and motives. For this reason, we should keep in mind that we cannot always know the moral culpability of someone who embraces atheism. Nonetheless, atheism itself always "rejects or denies the existence of God" and is "a sin against the virtue of religion" (2125). The Catechism rightly considers atheism as a way of living one's life rather than merely as some intellectual position on a speculative question. Atheism means acting as though God does not exist, which often leads down a path to other serious evils.

The Catechism indicates that the problems of atheism come from the *false concept of the human person* that necessarily follows the atheistic view of God. In practice, atheism often leads from rejecting the idea of a supreme being to acting as if we humans have supreme control over the world. Paradoxically, by removing God from the picture, *atheism often degrades the human person from someone created in the image of God to a mere thing produced by chance through the forces of the universe.*

If we think carefully about this point, we can see why many atheists would be inclined to accept certain violations of human dignity, such as abortion or euthanasia, since they do not have a clear concept of the human person's origin in the creative love of God. Because atheism degrades the human person in theory and invites such degradation in practice, atheism must be regarded "as one of the most serious problems of our time" (2123).

CCC 2142-2149
The Name of the Lord Is Holy

The second commandment further unfolds the moral requirements of our relationship with God by addressing the *respect that we should show towards the name of God* and the need to avoid using the name of the Lord in vain.

As this section of the Catechism explains, respect for the name of God is "an expression of the respect owed to the mystery of God himself and to the whole sacred reality it evokes" (2144). In others words, the utter uniqueness of God extends to the utter uniqueness of his name and all the sacred things associated with our relationship to him. We have a specific commandment regarding how we speak with God and about God precisely *because speaking is such a fundamental part of any relationship.*

However, the proper understanding of the second commandment begins with the idea that the name of God has been received by us in faith as *a kind of gift*. In turn, using the name of God should be an *expression of faith*, implying that we do not use the name of God "except to bless, praise, and glorify it" (2143). The respect owed to God's name extends to all the sacred names that we use in faith and in our worship of God, such as those of Jesus, the Virgin Mary, and the saints. *Maintaining the attitude of faith in our hearts and words is the key to keeping this commandment in our daily lives.*

By emphasizing the element of faith in the meaning of this commandment, we can see why the Catechism teaches that "blasphemy is directly opposed to the second commandment" (2148). Notice also the full meaning of blasphemy and how difficult it can become to keep this commandment in the midst of difficulties. It would be contrary to faith, and thus blasphemy, to utter against God or reproach him, even inwardly, so we are asked by this commandment to maintain respect for him no matter what trials and tragedies we face.

CCC 2150-2159
The Holiness of the Divine Name and Its Implications

The Catechism concludes its short teaching on the second commandment by addressing the issue of taking oaths in the name of God and also by explaining the sacredness of the Christian name through its connection to Baptism. The teachings on oaths presented here take a balanced approach on the matter, allowing for legitimate oaths while requiring our discretion in calling upon the name of God in this way.

By taking an oath, we take God as a witness to what we are saying and invoke the divine truthfulness as a pledge of our own truthfulness (2150). For this reason, *we must never swear an oath to what we know to be false, for this denigrates the name of God by joining it to a lie.* In the Sermon on the Mount, Jesus reaffirmed the prohibition of false oaths but also asked us not to swear an oath at all when a simple pledge on our part will suffice. The *holiness of the divine name* demands that we do not use it "for trivial matters" (2155).

Consequently, the Catechism affirms that "the tradition of the Church has understood Jesus' words as not excluding oaths made for grave and right reasons" such as in a court of law (2154).

The Catechism concludes its teachings on the second commandment with the sense in which *our own names take on a sacred character through Baptism.* Anything inserted into the sacred worship or our relationship with God demands the same respect owed to the name of God. By virtue of how we enter into God's covenant through Baptism, *our Christian name should be understood as the name by which God calls us, thus making it a fundamental part of that sacred relationship.* Since we are joined to God in Baptism, and given the dignity of his adopted children, the Christian name of each person demands respect "as a sign of the dignity of the one who bears it" (2158).

CCC 2168-2176
The Sabbath Day and the Lord's Day

The third commandment concludes explicit moral obligations of our love of God directly and brings the theme of religion to its high point in the *formal worship of God in the Eucharistic liturgy*.

The Catechism has already highlighted our moral obligation in justice to acknowledge the greatness of God and the need to render God the worship we owe him. The third commandment builds upon this idea, adding the notion that we can do justice to God only by having a whole day that is "holy and set apart for the praise of God" (2171), which also allows for the whole community to be available for that worship and helps fulfill the social component of religion.

The Sabbath is the most logical day to designate for this communal worship since *it recalls the great work of creation*, thus clearly recognizing the *uniqueness of God as our loving Creator*. Dedicating the Sabbath to the worship of God also frees us from "the servitude of work" (2172), enabling us to imitate the way that God "rested" upon the completion of his creative actions.

All of these points add up to make keeping holy the Sabbath the logical way to meet our obligation to render God communal worship, and yet Christians recognize Sunday as the most logical day to fulfill this obligation. As the text indicates, by keeping holy Sunday, we follow the original logic of the commandment but now acknowledge the unparalleled greatness of our "new creation" in Christ (2174). Just as worshiping God on the Sabbath made the most sense because of its connection to Creation, Sunday's "ceremonial observance replaces that of the Sabbath" (2175) because of its connection to the Resurrection and *our re-creation in Christ*.

If we fulfill the third commandment by having a day of worship that commemorates the greatness of God's love, the day of Our Lord's resurrection stands alone among all the days on which we could fulfill our obligation to worship God.

CCC 2177-2183
The Sunday Eucharist and Obligation

The Catechism continues its teachings on the third commandment by outlining why *the Eucharistic liturgy with our parish community is the best way to worship God.*

Gathering as a parish community on Sundays "observes the moral commandment inscribed by nature in the human heart to render to God an outward, visible, public, and regular worship" (2176). However, far from simply being one way in which we worship together, the "Sunday celebration of the Lord's Day and his Eucharist is at the heart of the Church's life" (2177).

The text continues here with the idea that Sunday commemorates the fulfillment of the Paschal mystery in the resurrection of Jesus, while the other holy days of obligation each recall some central event or person in God's work of redemption. In either case, *the key idea is celebrating what God has done for us in the mystery of redemption, which brings us to the Eucharist.*

The Eucharistic liturgy emerges as the best way to worship God because in it we have the unique value of the *adoration, prayer, and sacrifice* (the essential components of worship) *of Christ himself, sacramentally* present and available for us to enter into. Sunday recalls the central event of our redemption, while the Eucharist sacramentally confers the fruit of redemption through Jesus' worship of God the Father, all of which easily make the Eucharist the *most excellent way to worship God.*

Since the Eucharist offers the most excellent way to worship God, Catholics have a serious obligation to participate in the Mass on Sundays and holy days of obligation, and those "who deliberately fail in this obligation commit a grave sin" (2181). While the Catechism clearly mentions how there can be legitimate cases in which a Catholic is unable to attend Mass, or that Mass may be unavailable to the faithful, we should still never lose sight of the utter importance and uniqueness of the Eucharistic liturgy.

CCC 2184-2188
A Day of Grace and Rest from Work

This section of the Catechism presents the moral obligation and the practical complexities of maintaining the practice of rest on Sunday, which for many Catholics has become the greatest challenge in keeping the third commandment.

Being like God is the most fundamental idea of our moral lives and the basis of the practice of rest on the Lord's Day, which gives our lives the rhythm of work and rest found in the biblical account of God's creative activity. Notice, however, that we have here a *positive obligation* to rest on Sunday rather than a *negative prohibition* from work, which in some ways spares us the need to debate what types of work are prohibited.

We are obliged to rest and, consequently, "to refrain from engaging in work or activities that hinder the worship owed to God" and the joy and relaxation that should characterize the Lord's Day (2185). At the same time, we should not just waste our Sunday. Instead, we should use this day to do the "good works" that are "often difficult to do on other days of the week" (2186). As the text mentions, these good works can include *works of mercy, the cultivation of our interior lives, time with our families, and recreation for the mind and body.*

Since we are dealing with a positive obligation, there can be legitimate reasons that excuse someone from the obligation of Sunday rest. The Catechism mentions traditional activities that enable others to enjoy the day, social necessities such as public services, and family needs as examples of what might "require some people to work on Sundays" (2187).

However, we always remain under the moral obligation to make Sunday special in some way. For this reason, we should resist the modern tendency to make work on Sunday a social norm, and we should even be ready, where prudent, to "seek recognition of Sunday and the Church's holy days as legal holidays" (2188).

CCC 2196-2198
The Fourth Commandment I

With the fourth commandment, the Catechism's moral catechesis transitions from the *love of God* directly to the *love of neighbor* as an expression of our *love for God*. The final seven commandments of the Decalogue find their fundamental meaning in Jesus' command to love one another as he has loved us and spell out for us the moral demands of charity in our interactions with each other.

These seven commandments are just as significant on a theoretical level for our relationship with God as the first three, because *they are always concerned with love and the fulfillment of God's law*. Moreover, since they concern the situations in which we find ourselves during our daily lives, on a practical level much of the Christian moral life entails keeping these seven commandments as they are explained in this catechesis.

The Catechism begins by highlighting how the fourth commandment represents the perfect transition from a focus on God to a focus on neighbor in our moral lives. Although the commandment explicitly mentions the authority of parents over their children, "because this relationship is the most universal" (2199), the text indicates that the commandment obliges us "to honor and respect all those whom God, for our good, has vested with his authority" (2197). The fourth commandment helps introduce the other commandments, then, by emphasizing the importance of authority in our lives, which the Catechism then links to the authority of God and the practical role of authority in the establishment of good communities.

This approach clarifies that the love of neighbor should always be grounded in our obedience to God in the practice of Christian charity and directed towards living in communion with others in the fulfillment of God's plan for us. Only by understanding how *our respect for all authority refers back to the authority of God and looks forward to our need to live in community* can we properly grasp the place of this commandment in our lives.

CCC 2199-2200
The Fourth Commandment II

While the Catechism will certainly hold the family up as the premier community to be safeguarded by the fourth commandment, it is also intent on broadening the meaning of the commandment through its application to situations outside the family, such as the relationships between students and teachers, employees and employers, and citizens and those who govern (2199). This wider application expresses the *universality of the fourth commandment*, showing how we are all under the obligations of this commandment in our daily lives. Even those living outside a parent–child relationship have serious moral obligations to consider here.

However, we can also see that the text is clarifying from the outset that this commandment presupposes serious moral obligations on the part of "all who exercise authority over others or over a community of persons" (2199). As such, it is a violation of the fourth commandment any time a teacher, a boss, or a politician abuses authority or fails to do what is best for the communities and persons that they serve. Here the Catechism is trying to avoid the impression that that authority is somehow a good in itself to be obeyed just for the sake of authority by speaking of the *service it renders to the community*.

The text draws all these ideas together by recalling the biblical notion of *promise* and the way in which keeping this commandment produces "temporal fruits of peace and prosperity" while "failure to observe it brings great harm to communities and to individuals" (2200). This also gives us another reason why this particular commandment comes before those that promote life, marriage, property, and truth — namely, that *all of these other goods will be in jeopardy without well-organized communities to protect them.*

In light of how it exhorts us to love our neighbors by promoting the inherent dignity and rights of everyone through our respect for authority, the gravity of the fourth commandment cannot be overstated.

CCC 2201-2213
The Family and Society in God's Plan

From the wider meaning of the fourth commandment, the Catechism now returns to the explicit teaching of the commandment by focusing on *the family and its importance for our lives.*

We can see that the Catechism is intent on resisting contemporary secular trends by emphasizing the *genuine meaning of marriage, the inherent connection between marriage and family, and the unique value that this connection gives to the family.* To preserve this significance of the family, the text clearly defines family in terms of "a man and woman united in marriage, together with their children" (2202). Therefore, while we can legitimately use the word "family" with diverse meanings, such as adopted family or extended family, the community founded through procreation in marriage "should be considered the normal reference point by which the different forms of family relationships are to be evaluated" (2202).

For Christians the natural meaning of *marriage* and *family* takes on greater significance because of how *God's work of creation and redemption take place within the family.* Children come into existence by procreation, which is our cooperation with God's act of creation (see 366), and when parents share the gift of faith with their children, the family also becomes the source of new life in Christ and can be rightly called the "domestic church" (2204).

The Catechism applies these teachings on the special value of the family to the idea that the family deserves special recognition and protection from the societies that it serves. Since the family is "the original cell of social life" and forms the new members of every society, it is only fitting that the family "be helped and defended by appropriate social measures" (2209). The measures *should uphold the utterly unique value of the family* by laws that "acknowledge the true nature of marriage and the family" (2210), and other measures that strengthen marriages and support families, while taking care "not to usurp the family's prerogatives or interfere in its life" (2209).

CCC 2214-2220
The Duties of Children

Since *the family can fulfill its unique role in society only when its members fulfill their roles within the family,* the Catechism now focuses on the duties of family members, beginning with the children, that are addressed directly in the fourth commandment.

This section on the duties of children begins by likening *human fatherhood* and *divine fatherhood* and enjoining children to respect their parents as part of their respect for God, showing "gratitude" to their parents for their role in bringing them into existence and in enabling them "to grow in stature, wisdom, and grace" (2215). Children show this gratitude to their parents by *respect and obedience.*

Children should obey their parents for as long as they live with their parents, but the moral obligation does find its limits in the role of the parents. The obedience of a child to his parents relates to what is good for the child or good for the family and does not extend to that which would be harmful or that which contradicts the judgment of conscience (2217). Since the foundation of obedience is gratitude for the good formation provided by one's parents, if the parents happen to fail in their obligation to promote what is good, the child should not obey a particular order.

Even though obedience "ceases with the emancipation of the children" (2217), *respect towards one's parents is always a moral obligation.* In adulthood, respect is shown by giving one's parents "support in old age and in times of illness, loneliness, or distress" (2218), and in childhood by seeking "harmony" in the family through good relationships between brothers and sisters (2219). This respect makes the tasks of the parents much easier, which brings us back to the main point of these teachings: our respect helps authority to do its job in the community and ultimately benefits everyone who is served by that authority.

CCC 2221-2233
Parents, the Family, and the Kingdom

The Catechism's teachings on the fourth commandment have already emphasized the unique value of the family and the need for children to obey their parents, and now the text turns to the *vital role of the parents in the wellbeing of the family.*

This section focuses on the "moral education and spiritual formation" that children receive when parents fulfill their duties within the family. The role of the parents within the life of the child "is of such importance that it is almost impossible to provide an adequate substitute" (2221); the parents provide an "education in the virtues" (2223) to the child primarily by their example of Christian and marital love lived on a daily basis. For this reason, parents have a grave responsibility to set a good example for their children, lest the behavior of the parents disrupts the home or contradicts the virtues being taught in the home.

Not surprisingly, the text highlights the example of Christian faith that parents are called to give to their children. The fourth commandment requires parents to accept "the responsibility and privilege of evangelizing their children" (2225) and to educate their children in the faith through "family catechesis" and "by the witness of a Christian life in keeping with the Gospel" (2226). We are, in effect, saying that *parents keep the fourth commandment by being educators, catechists, evangelists, and living witnesses of the faith.* In order for the role of the parents to fulfill its grand purpose, parents are obliged to educate their children "in the right use of their reason and freedom" (2228) so that each child can seek out and fulfill "his unique vocation which comes from God" (2232).

In other words, the role of parents culminates in enabling their children to be mature members of society and the Church while pursuing personal holiness in the vocation to which God calls them, allowing parents to *shape the future of the world* by their daily actions in the home.

CCC 2234-2237
Duties of Civil Authorities

In this section, the Catechism begins to consider not only how the fourth commandment concerns the dynamic of authority within the natural society of the family, but also how it "enjoins us to honor all who for our good have received authority in society from God" (2234).

The text starts with the basic idea that those who exercise authority are required to do so "as a service" (2235), because *authority is meant to benefit others* rather than being seen as an opportunity for personal gain; then it describes the mindset with which authority can and should provide this service to the community.

Earlier in the Catechism's moral catechesis (see 1897-1904), we saw that the proper exercise of authority strikes a balance between the *common good of the community* and the *well-being of each individual member of society* on the basis of social justice. Since the purpose of authority is to *help establish a just society*, the genuine exercise of authority can never "command or establish what is contrary to the dignity of persons and the natural law" (2235). Those in authority are obliged to reflect a proper hierarchy of values — which puts spiritual goods above material goods — and should practice "distributive justice wisely" in order to bring about harmony and peace within the community (2236), as well as take special care of families and the disadvantaged.

With these ideas, we have not only the mindset for those in authority but also the basic criteria for distinguishing good authority from authority that has ceased to be legitimate. If authority adopts laws or policies that contradict the natural law, violate the dignity of the human person, denigrate spiritual values, or set the gain of a few against the good of the community, then *that authority ceases to be legitimate*. In such cases, those in authority not only fail in their duties, but also give those under their authority good reason to reject that authority.

CCC 2238-2246
Citizens, the Political Community, and the Church

This section of the Catechism continues the fourth commandment's general theme of the moral obligations of those under authority by focusing on *citizens who are under political authority.*

Although Christians are clearly obliged to respect those in civil authority and to obey just laws, our duties as citizens are actually quite complex and oblige us to take "co-responsibility for the common good" (2240) of the societies in which we live. This co-responsibility requires us to *use our consciences to evaluate the directives of those in authority* and to *contribute in various ways to the actual building up of our societies.*

The text speaks of "submission" to legitimate authorities as a fundamental duty of the citizen, but this teaching emphasizes the collaboration, the contribution, and the co-responsibility that are expected of good citizens. We would fail in our duties as citizens by acting as if those in authority were solely responsible for the well-being of our societies, and we are morally obliged to do our part by paying taxes, voting, defending the community (2240), and even voicing "just criticisms" (2238) when we see those in authority failing in their duties.

The Catechism challenges us to "regard those in authority as representatives of God" whose providence has allowed them to be in authority (2238), but clarifies that we should also be ready to criticize and even refuse obedience to those in authority when their directives are contrary to the *natural law, the dignity of the human person or the doctrines of our faith.* In extremely rare cases, citizens may even need to mount armed resistance to "oppression by political authority" (2243), although this is clearly discouraged by the strict conditions mentioned in the text.

The apparent contradiction between obedience and resistance fades under the logic of the fourth commandment: *all our interactions with authority are meant to serve the good of the community,* and whether that requires obedience or resistance simply depends on the actions of those in authority.

CCC 2258-2262
The Witness of Sacred History

It may seem surprising that the four words of the fifth commandment ("You shall not kill") would need all the pages and pages of explanation offered by the Catechism. However, in light of the way that resisting the so-called culture of death has become a hallmark of Catholic faith, we can readily understand why our Catechism would make such an extensive effort to proclaim the *sanctity of human life and everyone's inviolable right to life.*

The Catechism begins this section with the sacred character of human life via its *special relationship to God the Creator.* Locating the sacredness of human life in the way in which human life "involves the creative action of God" and "remains forever in a special relationship with the Creator, who is its sole end" (2258), this teaching grounds the sacredness and dignity of human life in the human soul. Human life can never be primarily a biological concept, and maintaining the spiritual sense of human life is the first requirement of the commandment.

Recognizing the *dignity of human life through the unity of body and soul,* we should understand the concept of death in equally spiritual terms. The essential meaning of the fifth commandment, then, *prohibits intentionally rupturing the unity of body and soul that serves as the foundation for human dignity,* and by extension it denounces all threats to the human dignity expressed in our bodily life.

The Catechism concludes this section by again shifting our focus to the *inner movements of the human heart.* The violence that threatens human life often reveals the anger and hatred that blind us to the dignity of others. This is why, in the Sermon on the Mount, Jesus speaks so strongly against anger and hatred in the heart. We cannot truly keep the fifth commandment unless we face the threats to human dignity that disturb the heart and seek the peace of heart that neutralizes those threats.

CCC 2263-2264
Legitimate Defense I

At times the protection of human life requires acts of legitimate defense. This section of the Catechism aims to reaffirm the *inviolable right to life of every human being* by explaining how legitimate defense "is not an exception to prohibition against the murder of the innocent that constitutes intentional killing" (2263).

To properly understand this teaching on defense, we must first accurately grasp the meaning of "innocent" in the definition of murder. The term "innocent" is not meant here as the opposite of guilty. Rather, it contrasts directly with *aggressive* or *dangerous* and conveys the sense that a person is *non-threatening* or even *helpless*. The notion of legitimate defense necessarily indicates that someone is acting as an aggressor and can no longer be considered innocent due to the threat they currently pose to others.

However, as the text clarifies, even when taken against an aggressor, the intention of legitimate defense must be the *elimination of the threat we face and not the harm the aggressor may suffer as a result*. The one action results in safety and in harm, but "the one is intended, the other is not" (2263). Additionally, we may not use "more than necessary" force (2264), or else we will be guilty of violence and no longer acting in defense.

The complexity of this teaching ultimately expresses the *incompatibility of violence and the Christian moral life*. We should take steps to prevent violence, but we should never resort to violence as a means or as an end. We can, at times, *tolerate* the harm done to an aggressor, but we can never *intend* it without doing something immoral. By this distinction between intending and tolerating, the Catechism is insisting that we must recognize the inviolable right to life of every human person, even those who pose a threat to others, and be consistent in our respect for life and the dignity of the human body.

CCC 2265-2267
Legitimate Defense II

The Catechism continues applying the same basic criteria for legitimate defense to those cases when civil authorities are seeking to defend the community against criminals.

Those in authority have a *duty to promote and protect the common good*, which includes defensive measures to render criminals "unable to cause harm" (2265) and taking steps to "curb the spread of behavior harmful to people's rights and to the basic rules of civil society" (2266). However, like all cases of legitimate defense, any harm done to criminals can only be the further result of the force necessary to stop them. The criteria of legitimate defense preclude excessive force on the part of the police or the cruel and inhumane treatment of prisoners, even when dealing with those who are clearly a threat to the community.

Further applying the larger concept of legitimate defense, the Catechism addresses the issue of the death penalty as a special concern of respect for life. In theory "the traditional teaching of the Church does not exclude recourse to the death penalty, if this is the only possible way of effectively defending human lives against the unjust aggressor" (2267). *This means that death must be part of the necessary force to stop a criminal in order for the death penalty to be morally acceptable.*

However, if "non-lethal means are sufficient" to defend the community, then "authority will limit itself to such means" (2267). Therefore, cases in which the death penalty would be morally acceptable "are very rare, if not practically non-existent" (2267). Protecting public safety by incarcerating criminals is more in keeping with the dignity of the person and allows us to maintain a *respect for life, even in the case of terrible criminals.*

This teaching not only speaks against the death penalty as it is commonly practiced today, but also proclaims the *universal and absolute right to life of every human*, which also makes *opposition to capital punishment part of our pro-life efforts.*

CCC 2268-2269
Intentional Homicide

Having affirmed the inviolable right to life of every human being in every situation, the text now considers the sense in which "the fifth commandment forbids *direct and intentional killing* as gravely sinful" (2268) and the various ways in which we might sin by "indirectly bringing about a person's death" or endangering lives by action or omission (2269).

Direct and intentional killing is the greatest failure of respect that we owe to human life. Murder and cooperation with it are gravely sinful in all cases. However, the text draws our attention to the idea that some types of murder are worse, and in doing so the Catechism highlights the *personal dimension* of our respect for life.

Every human being is someone in fundamental relationships to others, and *every murder kills someone in violation of these relationships.* While any murder violates the relationship that we all have as neighbors in the great human community, "infanticide, fratricide, parricide, and the murder of a spouse are especially grave crimes by reason of the natural bonds which they break" (2268).

The Catechism continues its teachings on respect for life by asking us once again to *think of the impact that our choices have on the lives of others.* Naturally, intentionally doing something to indirectly bring about someone's death violates the fifth commandment, because it means clearly willing to end a human life. However, the text also points out that we can fail in our respect for life by needlessly endangering others or by "refusing assistance to a person in danger" (2269). Our respect for life even requires us to consider the ways in which we accept situations or problems, such as famine, that cause death without making "efforts to remedy them" (2269).

In other words, *we can violate the fifth commandment in what we fail to do*, such as failing to take reasonable precautions, failing to help those in danger, and failing to care enough about the sufferings of others.

CCC 2270-2275
Abortion

The rationale for this section of the text rests in the notion of innocence with regards to murder, and the high degree of innocence found in the unborn requires us to acknowledge the specific evil of abortion and the obligation to provide special care to the unborn by virtue of their helplessness and dependence on others.

"Since the first century the Church has affirmed the moral evil of every procured abortion. This teaching has not changed and remains unchangeable" (2271); there can be no doubt regarding the evil of abortion in all cases, no matter the circumstances or intentions of those involved.

However, we should also note how carefully the Catechism presents the Catholic understanding of the evil of abortion. Notice how the text refers to "human life" and the "human being" to describe the child in his mother's womb (2270) and carefully avoids basing its moral argument on the philosophically complex concept of personhood, even though it indicates that this new human should be respected as a person from the moment of conception. *Our common humanity is the basis of our respect for all human life, and personhood only deepens that respect.* The teaching further emphasizes that the sacredness of human life is absolute and must not be violated on the basis of good intentions, mitigating circumstances, or rhetoric that appeals to other goods to try to justify the intentional destruction of human life.

Naturally, it will not be enough to refrain from the sin of abortion; we are morally obliged to offer proper medical care to the unborn, giving them the same rights and protections as any other human in the medical field. Specifically, the Catechism condemns the temptation to treat the embryo as an object of experimentation or as "disposable biological material" (2275).

The teachings of this section converge to remind us *that we cannot ignore the dignity and rights of the unborn without making the enormously destructive suggestion that some humans are somehow less than others.*

CCC 2276-2283
Euthanasia and Suicide

Although the sin of euthanasia shifts our focus from the beginning of life to the end of life, these teachings on euthanasia are like those on abortion — they remind us of the *dignity of all humans* and of the *special care that we owe to the most helpless among us.*

The sick and the handicapped "deserve special respect" (2276) due to their special needs and high degree of human innocence. The text clearly condemns any action or omission that in itself or by intention puts an end to the lives of the handicapped, sick, or dying. Even if done for noble reasons and with consent, this "constitutes a murder gravely contrary to the dignity of the human person and to the respect due to the living God" (2277). However, this condemnation of euthanasia equally seeks to reaffirm that the dignity of human life cannot be lost through a so-called diminished quality of life and to exhort us to maintain Christian hope in the face of suffering.

By allowing for the discontinuation of medical care that can be deemed burdensome, extraordinary, dangerous, or disproportionate to its benefits, these teachings permit us to accept our inability to impede death in some cases. However, *ordinary care is owed to every patient, while palliative care is a special form of charity that shows our respect for life and concern for suffering.* Both are essential to morally sound healthcare.

Our respect for human life extends to ourselves and requires a grateful recognition of the *stewardship that God has given us with the gift of life.* Suicide is clearly contrary to this respect, gratitude, and stewardship. Moral responsibility can be diminished in cases of suicide, so we "should not despair of the eternal salvation of persons who have taken their own lives" (2283). Nonetheless, we can never condone suicide, for this would bring us back to the destructive suggestion that some lives are not worthy of living, which is diametrically opposed to our respect for life.

CCC 2284-2287
Respect for the Souls of Others: Scandal

The Catechism's teaching on the respect owed to human life is grounded in its *sacredness* and how human life *originates with God* and remains *destined for eternal life with him* (2258). This approach emphasizes the importance of the human soul for our concept of human dignity. For this reason, the Catechism's teachings on human life include a section on the respect owed to the souls of others and our moral obligation to avoid the sin of scandal.

We can harm the souls of others when we lead them to do evil, diminishing the practice of virtue and damaging their relationship with God. At times we may even lead them into "spiritual death" (2284). Harming another's soul in this way is called *scandal*, and we commit scandal by any attitude or action that "leads another to do evil" (2284). Even without any intention of encouraging that person's sinful behavior we may be guilty of scandal, but scandal becomes a grave sin only when we deliberately lead another into a grave sin.

We should see in this teaching of the Catechism that *harming someone's soul hinders that person's moral and spiritual life the same way harming someone's body would hinder someone's physical life.* Harming someone's soul diminishes that person's life, fails to respect the dignity of the human person and violates the fifth commandment in much the same way as physical harm does.

Scandal can be a particular concern for those who have responsibility for the well-being of others, and scandal is grave "when given by those who by nature or office are obliged to teach and educate others" (2285). Yet, we should also recognize that scandal can be caused by laws and social trends, and in order to avoid being complicit in this kind of scandal, we must *resist these trends and work towards a just society.* We all have some responsibility for the way in which our culture influences the moral lives of our neighbors.

CCC 2288-2291
Respect for Health

This section of the Catechism expresses how the fifth commandment obliges us to see health and physical integrity as "precious gifts" and to take "reasonable care of them" (2288).

Before private individuals can properly take care of their health, the societies in which they live need to establish the basic conditions of good health. Here we see the Catechism applying its general teachings on social justice to the specific issue of health, which requires all of us, and especially those in authority, to *promote the conditions of human flourishing* (see 1906). Here the text mentions "food and clothing, housing, health care, basic education, employment, and social assistance" (2288) as vital to the promotion of health in our societies. At the same time, this teaching clarifies that by failing to promote these healthy living conditions we fail not only in our obligations to work for social justice, but also in our respect for life. Conversely, it tells us that *in being pro-life we necessarily commit ourselves to working for social justice.*

On the basis of these societal conditions, we have a *moral obligation to maintain our health by the choices we make on a daily basis.* The key idea expressed here is our need to practice the virtue of temperance and "avoid every kind of excess" (2290). Our pro-life commitment needs to be expressed in moderation with regard to food and alcohol, for example, and by the refusal to needlessly endanger ourselves or others. It also includes recognizing the destructive nature of drugs used for recreational rather than medicinal purposes (2291).

At the same time, these moral demands of the fifth commandment prohibit making the life of the body "an absolute value" (2289) or making health and beauty necessary conditions for a meaningful life. We certainly need to reject the "neo-pagan" notion that illness or disability can make life not worth living, since that contradicts the sense of inherent human dignity at the heart of the fifth commandment.

CCC 2292-2298
The Person: Scientific Research and Bodily Integrity

Advancements in scientific knowledge and medical technology play a central role in the promotion of health, and for this reason the Catechism includes them in its teachings on health and respect for human dignity.

The pursuit of advances in medical science and technology take place according to our understanding of the laws of nature, but they must also adhere to the moral law and respect the dignity of the human person. They cannot "claim moral neutrality" or be measured simply by the results they produce (2294). Medical advances should never come at the cost of violating the dignity of some for the well-being of others, and all research and experimentation must respect the health and dignity of any humans involved, remaining "in conformity with the plan and the will of God" (2294).

Our respect for human dignity and for the human body does allow for medical experimentation and even organ transplants, provided these are done with the informed consent of those involved and do not expose them to "disproportionate or avoidable risks" (2295), or diminish their health for the sake of others.

This section of the text concludes by condemning the violence associated with terrorism and torture, since, whatever the motives and means are, these forms of violence are contrary to "respect for the person and for human dignity" (2297). The principle at stake in the fifth commandment requires us to recognize that the immorality of violence used to threaten, punish, or pressure its victims cannot be negated by extenuating circumstances or noble intentions. The central issue with these practices remains the *need to maintain a clear sense of the dignity of every human being in all situations* and to resist the temptation of trying to justify violations of human dignity because of the circumstances or the persons involved. Regarding violent practices "used by legitimate governments to maintain law and order," the text challenges us "to work for their abolition" (2298), making more clear than ever that Christians denounce all violations of human dignity.

CCC 2299-2301
Respect for the Dead

The Catechism continues its teachings on the fifth commandment by addressing the *sanctity of life in its final moments*, which requires us to acknowledge once again the *great significance of death within our Christian understanding of the human person.*

The respect owed to human life includes giving attention and care to those who are facing the end of life by helping them "live their last moments in dignity and peace" (2299). The help we offer those facing death includes the "palliative care" needed to alleviate suffering, which was "encouraged" earlier in the text (2279), but it also includes attending to their spiritual needs, especially by offering prayers and the sacraments in preparation for death (2299). Here we see the Catechism following an established pattern by highlighting that *our respect for life applies to both the body and the soul,* with a special emphasis on the soul.

Recognizing the great significance of the death of a human person includes respecting the body of each person after death has occurred. The dignity that the human body has by virtue of its substantial unity with the soul in this life morally obliges us to respect the body even after that unity is broken by death. Respect for the bodies of the dead and the burial of the dead are regarded by the Church as *expressions of faith* and even as "a corporal work of mercy" (2300). As the text points out, the respect owed to the human body after death does not morally prohibit autopsies, research, organ donation, or even the practice of cremation, so long as these actions do not imply a lack of respect for the body or "demonstrate a denial of faith in the resurrection of the body" (2301).

This section of the text provides another great example of how our moral truths intersect and how our respect for human life can be integrated into our practice of religion and the proclamation of our faith in Jesus Christ.

CCC 2302-2304
Peace

The moral catechesis of the Catechism has often expressed the sense in which the Christian understanding of God's law extends the precepts of the law by following the teachings of Christ, epitomized in the Sermon on the Mount. Taking up that basic pattern, this section of the Catechism summarizes the way in which the fifth commandment *prohibits anger and hatred in the heart and morally obliges us to work for peace.* At the same time, we are reminded how our respect for life challenges us to see every human as *worthy of our respect and fraternity.*

The Catechism defines anger as "a desire for revenge" (2302) and describes hatred as the deliberate desire that evil befall someone (2303). Anger amounts to desiring to do evil as a form of vengeance on someone who is deemed in need of punishment, whereas hatred is a more straightforward desire for some harm to come to a person. Even though they may differ somewhat in origin and character, both lead to a desire to harm someone in a way that contradicts the respect owed to every human. As the text indicates, anger and hatred can be mortal sins when they take the form of a deliberate desire to kill or seriously harm someone, even when these desires are not acted upon in a physical way.

Clearly, the main issue here concerns how anger and hatred in the heart *break down human solidarity* and can often lead to the physical violence that harms individuals and further erodes social bonds. As such, we can understand the immediate moral obligation of the fifth commandment as requiring us to *maintain peace in our hearts* so as to preclude anger and hatred. However, the commandment also morally obliges us to work for peace in our societies as a way of safeguarding the respect owed to every human life. *Being peacemakers in our hearts and in our societies truly is central to the Christian moral life.*

CCC 2305-2308
Avoiding War

Understanding that anger, hatred, and violence can emerge from the experience of injustice or from a lack of human solidarity, we can understand that here the Catechism is recalling our basic obligation to work for social justice, but now specifically as *a means to protect the dignity of human life from the threats of violence.*

If we fail in our obligations to promote social justice, we are indirectly exposing the good of life to threats that come from anger and hatred, whereas *promoting peace as the fruit of social justice* helps us fulfill our duty to defend life. The text also makes special mention of the value of those "who renounce violence and bloodshed" in their work for social justice and in their defense of the weak (2306). Using only nonviolent means to seek social justice sets a consistent example of the respect owed to all human life in every situation and can sometimes prove decisive in our efforts to be peacemakers.

Earlier the text mentioned that peace "is not merely the absence of war" (2304) in order to expand our notion of peace to include all elements of social justice and human solidarity. Now the text is clarifying that we can, however, regard war as an especially intense threat to peace and the respect for human life that comes with it. Even though the use of military force can at times be morally justified, "the evils and injustices that accompany all war" (2307) oblige us to pray for an end to all war, and "all citizens and all governments are obliged to work for the avoidance of war" (2308). In other words, although there can be such a thing as a "just" war, there really is *no such thing as a good war.*

CCC 2309-2317
Defense and Armed Conflict

The Catechism concludes its teaching on the fifth commandment by outlining the conditions for legitimate defense by military force, often called the "just war" doctrine, and the *need to maintain respect for all human life even in the midst of war.* The key to understanding this doctrine is maintaining a clear sense of how "the fifth commandment forbids the intentional destruction of human life" (2307), no matter the circumstances, and allows for harm to be done to another only as a further effect of actions that are defensive in nature and intention (see 2263-2267).

There are strict conditions for legitimate defense by military force that go beyond the simple requirement that it always be defensive in nature and purpose, because "the gravity of such a decision makes it subject to rigorous conditions of moral legitimacy" (2309). Even when the use of military force meets these conditions, "the mere fact that war has regrettably broken out does not mean that everything becomes licit between the warring parties" (2312).

In order for acts of war to maintain the respect owed to human life, "non-combatants, wounded soldiers, and prisoners" must never be the targets of military action and must be "treated humanely" (2313). The text unequivocally condemns acts of genocide and the use of weapons of mass destruction that target "vast areas with their inhabitants" as "crimes" that have no place in the legitimate use of military force.

Having earlier challenged us to be peacemakers, the text does here clarify that all citizens would have a moral obligation to serve our community in wartime, but also requires public authorities to make provisions for those who "for reasons of conscience refuse to bear arms" (2311), such as allowing those persons to fulfill non-combat roles.

These complex teachings on military force have value in themselves, but they also allow the Catechism to state, yet again, that *the respect owed to human life is absolute* and *human dignity endures even in the most extreme situations.*

CCC 2331-2336
"Male and Female He Created Them ... "

Catholic doctrine on the sixth commandment is perhaps the most misunderstood and misrepresented of all the teachings of Catholic morality. While many people misunderstand this teaching as a negative stance on a series of controversial issues, in truth *Catholic doctrine on sex, love, and marriage is a very positive, profound, and dignified expression of what it means to be man and woman created in the image of God.*

The Catechism begins its teaching on the sixth commandment by recalling the Genesis account of the creation of man and woman as the image of God, thus setting the *deeply theological foundations* for our understanding of sexuality and recalling the original theme of this entire moral catechesis (see 1701-1709). Linking it to our creation as the image of God grounds all of our statements on sexuality in the truth that "God is love and in himself he lives a mystery of personal loving communion" (2331). This perspective also links sexuality with the center of the Christian life by making sexuality inseparable from our "capacity to love" and "for forming bonds of communion with others" (2332). These criteria of *personal loving communion* and the *Gospel command to love one another* will serve as the primary basis of our entire understanding of the sixth commandment.

The other foundational idea here concerns how sexuality "affects all aspects of the human person" (2332) and *cannot be reduced to a trait of the body.* This prevents us from mistakenly thinking of sexuality merely in terms of the body, and explains why it is so important for each person to "acknowledge and accept his sexual identity" since it belongs to one's personality. The sexual identity is found in the complementarity and equality of man and woman, which "are oriented toward the goods of marriage and the flourishing of family life" (2333). Being true to one's sexual dignity and fulfilling that meaning of complementarity in marriage will be the other basis of our understanding of the sixth commandment.

CCC 2337-2345
The Vocation to Chastity I

The Catechism began its teachings on human sexuality by highlighting the connection between sexuality and our identity as the image of God, and the text recalls our basic *need for grace to live up to our inherent dignity* by presenting the Christian sense of chastity.

Since human sexuality belongs to our creation as the image of God, we can readily understand why our sexuality needs the healing power of redemption in Jesus, who "came to restore creation to the purity of its origins" (2336). Restoring creation in this case refers to restoring "the integrity of the person" and "the successful integration of sexuality within the person and thus the inner unity of man in his bodily and spiritual being" (2337), which is how the text defines *chastity*. This provides a positive meaning of chastity as opposed to a defective sense of chastity that limits it to the ability to "say no" to certain forms of sexual behavior.

As a virtue, chastity enables a person to maintain "the integrity of the powers of life and love placed in him" (2338) by a self-mastery over sexual desires, shaping that person's sexual desires and actions according to what is known to be true in the conscience. Above all, we must not think of the chaste person as one who represses himself or simply refuses to act on certain desires.

The Catechism certainly acknowledges that this kind of self-mastery is a "long and exacting work" that requires "renewed effort at all stages of life" (2342). This personal effort should be supported by a "cultural effort" (2344). However, the decisive factor in the practice of chastity will be a "gift from God" in the form of grace and the active presence of the Holy Spirit, who enables those regenerated in the waters of Baptism "to imitate the purity of Christ" (2345). In other words, *our chastity can become a dramatic witness to the powers of redemption in Christ and a fundamental sign of our discipleship.*

CCC 2346-2350
The Vocation to Chastity II

Because of the difficulty in achieving chastity and because of its *supernatural source*, the Catechism can say that the Christian who practices chastity becomes a "witness to his neighbor of God's fidelity and loving kindness" (2346). This section of the text links chastity with the *work of the Holy Spirit in us* and with the *theological virtue of charity*, which serves as the basis of our entire Christian moral life.

To fully understand the connection between chastity and charity, we need to first see in chastity *a call to love in and through our sexuality* and then recall how the moral catechesis of the Catechism has consistently emphasized our *need for grace* in order to love as God calls us to love. This connection between chastity and love also serves the Catechism's teaching that from the moment of his Baptism "the Christian is pledged to lead his affective life in chastity" (2348). If to be Christian is to love through charity, and to be chaste is to love through charity, *being Christian becomes interwoven with being chaste.*

All Christians are called to chastity, but there are various forms of chastity, just as there are various states of life among Christians. As the text points out, within the Christian community we have the chastity of single people and the chastity of those who are consecrated for the sake of the Kingdom — both of which live chastity as continence — and the chastity of married people (2349).

These various forms of chastity, however, point back to the universal meaning of chastity and its link to love. Chastity varies in practice according to the type of love or relationship that characterizes a person's life. The basic idea that we "should reserve for marriage the expressions of affection that belong to married love" (2350) expresses the larger truth that *chastity always serves the love that we truly have for a person.*

CCC 2351-2356
Offenses against Chastity

Whatever state in life we have or form of chastity we live, *we are all called to avoid lust*, which the Catechism here addresses.

The Catechism locates the essence of lust in the reduction of sexual desire and activity to the pleasure that sexuality offers, or when the enjoyment of sex is "isolated from its procreative and unitive purposes" (2351). The constant pattern that we will see in lustful behavior is the *absence of the communion and fruitfulness that characterize the true meaning of sexuality*. Lust is always the narrow approach to sexual activity, seeking the *smallest portion* of what human sexuality has to offer us.

While physical pleasure and release may be the main issue with lust, we should not strictly limit the meaning of pleasure to the physical level. There are also emotional senses of sexual enjoyment that we can seek in a lustful way, such as having sex for the sole purpose of feeling good about our sex appeal. Additionally, we should note that the text in no way implies that sexual pleasure or the desire for satisfaction are problematic in themselves, but rather only that they become disordered *apart from the procreative and unitive aspects of marriage*.

The text offers a short catalogue of offenses against chastity, listing such actions as masturbation, fornication, the production or use of pornography, prostitution, and sexual assault as examples of how lust manifests itself in action. While each of these sins is described by its own specific disorders, they all are examples of sexual activity that cannot fulfill the marital meaning of sexuality and that reduce sex to the experience of satisfaction in some form.

Sadly, sociologists confirm for us that most of these lustful acts are common in our world, with many of them openly embraced by our culture. Yet, this also serves to make our chastity more important and more worth pursuing, so that it can *serve as a kind of light in the darkness*.

CCC 2357-2359
Chastity and Homosexuality

Within the general discussion of offenses against chastity, but set apart in its own smaller section, the Catechism offers a concise statement of Catholic doctrine on homosexuality and homosexual acts. With this approach, the text is seeking to strike a balance whereby homosexual acts are considered one among the many offenses against the sixth commandment but are also deserving of special consideration.

On the one hand, we can see that homosexual acts fit the pattern of other offenses against chastity because they, too, *lack the expression of marital love found in the procreative and unitive aspects of sexuality*. On the other hand, since homosexual acts also lack the fundamental values of "genuine affective and sexual complementarity" (2357), they seem to represent a *further displacement of the marital meaning of human sexuality*.

The Catechism also gives this issue special consideration because of the question of homosexuality or homosexual tendencies, which the text describes as "an exclusive or predominant sexual attraction to persons of the same sex," for which the "psychological genesis remains largely unexplained" (2357). The experience of same-sex attraction does not yet reach the level of sexual immorality, while homosexual acts are deliberate choices to act on that attraction and must be regarded as gravely immoral, contrary to the natural law and incompatible with the virtue of chastity.

By distinguishing homosexuality from homosexual acts, we can coherently say that homosexual acts can "under no circumstances" (2357) be approved, and that we must accept those who experience homosexual tendencies "with respect, compassion, and sensitivity" (2358). Moreover, "every sign of unjust discrimination in their regard should be avoided" (2358), because we must view the homosexual person as having the *same call to chastity as anyone else*. The pastoral solution to the issue, then, envisions the kind of chastity that enables those with same-sex attraction to refrain from acting on their homosexual desires by the "inner freedom" to act according to the truth of human sexuality (2359).

CCC 2360-2361
The Love of Husband and Wife I

The Catechism now turns our attention to the *love of husband and wife* as the only context in which sexual acts can embody the truth and meaning of human sexuality, meet the criteria of chastity, and fulfill the moral demands of the sixth commandment.

Implicitly referring back to the theological foundation set by the opening section of this catechesis on the sixth commandment (see 2333), the Catechism begins with the basic truth that sexuality "is ordered to the conjugal love of man and woman" (2360). As such, marriage not only *gives moral legitimacy to sexual acts,* but also really does *fulfill the inner truth and purpose of human sexuality.* The main point of the theology here is that sexual intercourse in marriage does not simply have a different moral value than sex outside of marriage, but rather that sexual intercourse in marriage is in itself *radically different* from any other sexual act.

The uniqueness of sexual intercourse in marriage rests in the way that through the marital commitment "the physical intimacy of the spouses becomes a sign and pledge of spiritual communion" (2360). We can see that the text is drawing upon the fundamental Catholic vision of the human person and human sexuality, which focuses on the bodily and spiritual unity of the human person to present sexuality as multi-dimensional and something that "concerns the innermost being of the human person as such" (2361).

In these terms we should understand the value of sexual intercourse in marriage by how the physical act embodies the spiritual goods of conjugal love itself, "by which a man and woman commit themselves totally to one another until death" (2361). However, we can also see how *sexual intercourse in marriage runs counter to lust by uniting the pleasure of sexual intercourse to the procreative and unitive aspects of sexuality,* thus uniting the pleasure of sex with the call to chastity.

CCC 2362-2363
The Love of Husband and Wife II

The Catechism continues its teaching on marital intimacy by strongly affirming that, far from being lustful, acts of marital sexual intercourse are "noble and honorable" and meant to be a "source of joy and pleasure" for the husband and wife (2362). However, the text also clarifies that "the truly human performance of these acts" (2362) ensures their nobility and enables the spouses to experience them as acts of mutual self-giving as well as joyful and pleasurable. In other words, sexual intimacy in marriage enables husband and wife to experience all the values and truths of human sexuality *only through the practice of chastity animated by Christian charity.*

This teaching of the Catechism brings together various elements of the meaning of the sixth commandment in order to emphasize the *uniqueness of marital sexual intimacy,* while also clarifying that the attitude with which husband and wife have sex makes all the difference. Like so much of Catholic teaching on sexuality, these statements about marital intercourse integrate the physical and the spiritual while making the *inner movements of the human heart the decisive element of the human and moral significance of the act.* As we have seen throughout this moral catechesis, the Catechism is emphasizing the role of the human heart, and the human will in particular, to explain the meaning of our behavior. The key to grasping the significance of sex in marriage, then, is to focus more on what the husband and wife *will in their hearts* than on what they do with their bodies in sexual intercourse.

In order to correspond to the human dignity and marital identity of the husband and wife, *the sexual intimacy of a married couple must express love rather than lust.* In other words, their physical intimacy must be directed in their hearts to the procreative and unitive aspects of human sexuality made decisive earlier in the teachings on lust.

CCC 2364-2365
Conjugal Fidelity

Having sought to emphasize the *uniqueness* and *nobility* of marital intercourse, the Catechism begins to offer further details on the fidelity and fruitfulness that are central to the *chastity of the married life*. Avoiding lust in marriage means keeping the procreative and unitive aspects of human sexuality in sight, and the text now addresses these aspects in terms of the *obligations of fidelity and fecundity*.

Husband and wife stand under "the twofold obligation of fidelity and fecundity" (2363), and only by meeting this obligation can the sexual life of husband and wife attain the nobility to which it is called. However, we should not think of fidelity and fruitfulness merely as obligations of Christian morality and marital chastity. Instead, we must recall the connection that the Catechism made earlier between chastity and love and see that the love of a husband and wife represents the ultimate source of these obligations. *To speak of the requirements of chastity always refers us back to love, which in turn refers to the human dignity of the one we love.*

We can see this dynamic with the obligation of fidelity addressed in this section. By their irrevocable marital consent, husband and wife "give themselves definitively and totally to one another" (2364), becoming one flesh in the words of the Genesis account referenced at the outset of these teachings on the sixth commandment. The marital covenant "imposes on the spouses the obligation to preserve it as unique and indissoluble" (2364). However, the obligations of the marital covenant, like the sixth commandment in general, only reiterate the moral demands of authentic love. The love of husband and wife leads them to affirm each other's utter uniqueness and to form an exclusive relationship, while *marital chastity serves to protect that love in the heart of the man and woman.*

Man and woman freely enter the marital covenant, and by that same choice they freely give themselves exclusively to each other. *The obligation to fidelity only confirms that free gift.*

CCC 2366-2367
The Fecundity of Marriage I

Well aware that many people today regard having children as a burden, the Catechism begins its teachings on the fruitfulness of marriage by striking a positive tone, describing children as "a gift," an end or purpose to which the self-giving of conjugal love naturally tends (2366). This section further strikes a positive tone by highlighting the *great dignity of parenthood as cooperation with the creative power of God.*

On the surface, the key teaching here is the moral requirement for each and every marriage act to remain "ordered *per se* to the procreation of human life" (2366). The rationale for this openness rests in the *total self-giving* that should mark the marital relationship. Sexual intercourse will not be fruitful on all occasions, but married couples should give their true and full selves to each other in every marriage act. *This total giving includes the fertility of the sexuality of the body.*

However, the deeper teaching here concerns the way that a child "springs from the very heart" of the mutual self-giving of husband and wife and should not be thought of as an accessory to be "added on to the mutual love of the spouses" (2366). Having children together is a way for man and woman to love each other and to give each other motherhood or fatherhood through their openness to life.

The Catechism also wants to emphasize that by being open to life man and woman "share in the creative power and fatherhood of God" (2367), bringing the love of the Creator into their own love through the fruitfulness of human sexuality. Again, we see the text concentrating on the *deeper theological origin of the child*, while avoiding a merely biological sense of the transmission of human life. By "cooperating" (2367) with God in the transmission of life, man and woman fulfill a sacred role, and this explains why husband and wife must be open to life "with a sense of human and Christian responsibility" (2367).

CCC 2368-2372
The Fecundity of Marriage II

Being under the obligation to remain open to life and to cooperate with God in the transmission of life, married couples also have a moral obligation to practice responsible parenthood. The Catechism continues its catechesis on the sixth commandment by addressing how responsible parenthood is practiced in spacing births, especially in light of the possibilities offered by modern technology.

Responsible parenthood can mean spacing births for *just reasons*, but in such cases it must also mean spacing births by *just means*. When married couples have just reasons for spacing births, and not motives of "selfishness" (2368), the biological, personal, and moral truths of human sexuality allow them to practice "periodic continence" (2370), which is also often called *fertility awareness* or *natural family planning*.

Periodic continence is a form of "birth regulation based on self-observation" (2370) of the woman's fertility cycle, but it is also based on self-discipline through the choices made as a result of these observations. This practice *respects the dignity of the body* and *encourages the kind of self-mastery* that the text earlier described as *essential to the practice of chastity*. In addition to effectively spacing births, periodic continence can enhance the marital relationship with "tenderness" and "the education of an authentic freedom" (2370).

Responsible parenthood cannot, however, be practiced by choices that seek "to render procreation impossible" (2370) by altering the sexuality of the body or the sexual act. This means that contraception fails to meet the criteria of responsible parenthood even when a couple has just reasons to space births. Contraception not only renders the sexual act infertile, but also treats the human body as a mere object or, in animalistic terms, erodes the practice of self-mastery, and it entails a grave violation of the sixth commandment. Even if not by conscious intent, *the use of contraception negates the procreative and unitive aspects of the sexual act and reduces it to an act of lust* by limiting its value to the satisfaction of desire.

CCC 2373-2379
The Gift of a Child

Although the question of spacing births tends to dominate modern discussions of responsible parenthood, we must not forget that responsible parenthood also means *seeking new life within the true spirit of conjugal love* and according to the objective criteria of the moral law.

Conjugal love naturally tends to bear fruit, and those in conjugal love naturally desire to be mother and father together. We should certainly regard children as the natural end and "supreme gift of marriage" (2378), but we must never view a child as "something" owed to a married couple. Instead, a child is "someone" with personal dignity to be *received as a gift from God*, brought into existence by a direct creative act of God with the right "to be the fruit of the specific act of the conjugal love of his parents" (2378).

The Catechism recognizes why "couples who discover that they are sterile suffer greatly" (2374), and we must sympathize with that sadness and frustration. For this reason, "research aimed at reducing human sterility is to be encouraged" (2375). At the same time, we would have to reject medical techniques that replace marital intercourse as the source of conception, since these *disassociate conception from conjugal love* and establish "the domination of technology" over the transmission of human life (2377). *Medicine can serve the love of husband and wife, but it must not replace their act of love with biological manipulation.*

We can rejoice when couples find morally acceptable medical help in overcoming infertility, but we should also recognize that "physical sterility is not an absolute evil" (2379), and *infertile couples still fulfill the meaning of marriage by their openness to live in fidelity to the sixth commandment.* Moreover, they may be able to not only have a *spiritual fruitfulness* through their marriage but also find practical ways to help children in need.

CCC 2380-2386
Adultery and Divorce

The Catechism now shifts our focus to failures in fidelity by actions that violate or deny the uniqueness and irreplaceability of one's spouse.

Adultery is an obvious violation of marital fidelity. While adultery refers to sexual relations between those "of whom at least one is married to another party" (2380), it can also be a matter of "mere desire" (2380) for someone other than one's spouse. All forms of adultery *violate the marital commitment* and *contradict the sexual dignity and worth of one's spouse*, implying at some level that one's spouse is inadequate in fulfilling those sexual desires.

Despite generally having more cultural acceptance, the sin of divorce follows the basic pattern of adultery by *violating one's marital commitment* and *negating the unique value of one's spouse*. Here divorce refers not to a simple legal matter, or "civil divorce" (2383), but rather claims to break the marriage covenant by which the spouses promised "to live with each other till death" (2384). Such a claim is a grave sin because it does harm to the "deserted spouse" and "the children traumatized" by the divorce of their parents (2385). This teaching clearly acknowledges the "considerable difference" between the spouse who is "unjustly abandoned" through divorce and the one who, through his or her "own grave fault," chooses to end a marriage by divorce (2386). The notion of *abandonment* here gets to the root of the evil of divorce.

The serious difficulties that allow for a "separation of spouses while maintaining the marriage bond" (2383) cannot negate the enduring nature of the mutual self-giving of the marital covenant. We can note that a "civil divorce" may be tolerated when legally necessary to protect rights and property during a separation (2383). However, in such cases *the marriage remains*, and any attempt to contract a second civil marriage after a civil divorce would be a grave violation of the sixth commandment and result in a state of "public and permanent adultery" (2384).

CCC 2387-2391
Other Offenses against the Dignity of Marriage

The Catechism concludes its teachings on the sixth commandment by considering other offenses against the dignity of marriage, which primarily gives the text reason to once again affirm that the meaning of human sexuality "demands a total and definitive gift of persons to one another" (2391).

Polygamy has a long history and has taken various forms, and the core issue of this problem has emerged in the contemporary period in the trend of polyamory or so-called open marriages. The practice of claiming to have more than one spouse or having additional lovers alongside one's true spouse "directly negates the plan of God," which calls husband and wife to "give themselves with a love that is total and therefore unique and exclusive" (2387).

Having more than one marital or sexual relationship contradicts the dignity of the person by implying the inadequacy of one person to fulfill the meaning of spousal love. By these relationships, men and women essentially deny each other's worth by saying, with their actions, that they are not enough, and for this reason additional lovers must be introduced into the relationship.

We can see the Catechism expressing a similar concern for human dignity in its teaching on so-called free unions (2390) or sexual relationships without a juridical and public marital commitment. As the text reminds us, even for those couples who have "the intention of getting married later" (2391), *sex before marriage exposes the man and woman to the threat of being discarded and replaced since there is no formal commitment to a permanent relationship.*

Sexual relationships outside of marriage are grave offenses against the dignity of marriage because *they suggest that the exclusive and permanent self-giving of conjugal love is not essential or important for sexual fulfillment,* which contradicts everything we have heard about human sexuality and human dignity in this catechesis.

CCC 2401-2406
The Universal Destination
and Private Ownership of Goods

The seventh commandment *explicitly prohibits theft*, but the Catechism introduces the commandment by explaining that its meaning extends to *any situation that concerns the material goods of the human person*, seeking to ensure both a "respect for the universal destination of goods and respect for the right to private property" (2401). We need material goods to preserve our lives, as called for by the fifth commandment, and to provide for our families, as called for by the fourth and sixth commandments, and even just to imitate and carry on the creative action of God, which brings us to the seventh commandment itself.

God's providence has provided for the material needs of everyone through the *universal destination of goods*, meaning that "the goods of creation are destined for the whole human race" and entrusted "to the common stewardship of mankind" (2402). By highlighting this universal destination of the goods, the Catechism grounds the moral obligations of the seventh commandment in the *stewardship we have over the gift of creation* and the need to ensure that each person gets his or her just share of the gift and a share of the stewardship, which brings in the notion of private property.

The legitimate right to private property does not negate the universal gift of creation to everyone. Anyone who has private property "should regard the external goods he legitimately owns not merely as exclusive to himself, but common to others also," in the sense that "the ownership of any property makes its holder a steward of Providence, with the task of making it fruitful and communicating its benefits to others" (2404).

Political authority has the right and duty to help us by regulating the ownership and use of property, but ultimately *we must take personal responsibility for this stewardship* by moderation in our use of material goods and by seeking to help others, especially our families, the sick, and the poor, to meet their material needs.

CCC 2407-2414
Respect for Persons and Their Goods

While it obliges us to exercise good stewardship over our property, the seventh commandment explicitly requires us to *respect the property of others and to refrain from interfering with their call to stewardship*. For this reason, the seventh commandment forbids theft but also other sins such as the unjust retention of lost items, fraud, and enslavement, or the reduction of others to the mere means of production.

The Catechism carefully articulates the meaning of theft in order to maintain the universal destination of goods without displacing the idea of a moral absolute against stealing. Theft is "usurping another's property against the reasonable will of the owner" (2408), and this is absolutely prohibited at all times in every situation.

However, there are times when we can take another's property without committing theft, such as when consent can be presumed, when the other is doing evil with the property, or "when the only way to provide for immediate, essential needs (food, shelter, clothing ...) is to put at one's disposal and use the property of others" (2408). Taking someone's property to meet an urgent need corresponds to the *universal destination of goods* if it truly is the only way to meet that need. This precludes rationalizing the taking of another's property just to avoid the trouble of meeting that need in another way, which would constitute theft.

The Catechism also mentions a number of other ways that we can fail to keep the seventh commandment, such as fraud, doing shoddy work, tax evasion, and refusing to honor contracts or pay debts, but the moral issue is always the *need for commutative justice*, "which regulates exchanges between persons ... in accordance with a strict respect for their rights" (2411).

The seventh commandment requires justice in the exchange of goods and services, and anytime we take advantage of someone or give them less than what they deserve we have failed to keep the commandment and have failed in both *justice* and *charity*.

CCC 2415-2418
Respect for the Integrity of Creation

As a matter of gratitude for the gift we have received from God, "the seventh commandment enjoins respect for the integrity of creation" (2415), which brings us to the way in which ecology enters Catholic morality.

Our moral obligation to *protect the integrity of creation* is an extension of the stewardship already explained in the Catechism's statements on the universal destination of goods. This section simply applies that fundamental principle to our use and management of the earth's mineral, vegetable, and animal resources. The Catechism reminds us that we really do have dominion over the earth, and *we are not merely one among the many creatures on the planet.* However, our superiority over the rest of the creatures of the earth includes a concern for our neighbors as well as "a religious respect for the integrity of creation" (2415), and this prevents us from being wasteful with the resources that God has given.

Our *stewardship over creation* includes a special concern for animals and the need to recognize how causing them to suffer or die needlessly contradicts our own human dignity. While we can have a kind of love for animals, we "should not direct to them the affection due only to persons" or "spend money on them that should as a priority go to the relief of human misery" (2418). We can put animals at the service of human needs, and this includes the ability to use animals in research that will benefit us. Any research done on animals must remain within "reasonable limits" (2417), and we should maintain our dignity by not causing the animals unnecessary suffering.

The great insight of these teachings on the environment is how the Catechism shows that our concern for the world does not lead us to deny our superiority over the rest of the world, as many modern ecological movements suggest, but rather leads us to *recognize our stewardship precisely as a requirement of our superiority over the world.*

CCC 2419-2425
The Social Doctrine of the Church

Since it regulates our stewardship over the goods of the earth, the seventh commandment also guides the social and economic policies that we make in order to govern how we will share in God's universal gift of the world to all mankind. The Church does not claim to offer concrete solutions to the practical challenges of social dynamics and economics, but it does provide *principles of reflection, criteria for judgment and guidelines for action* that express the moral demands of the seventh commandment (2423).

As the text explains, the social doctrine of the Church expresses the dignity and vocation of the human person in light of "the truth about man" that has been revealed in the Gospel (2419). The Church proclaims social doctrine in order to *protect the dignity of the person* and to *seek the salvation of souls*, but never to usurp the rightful place of legitimate political authorities.

Even though it is rooted in the Gospel, much of the social doctrine of the Church "developed in the nineteenth century when the Gospel encountered modern industrial society" and its new ways of organizing economic and social activity (2421). Without naming specific examples, the Catechism teaches that the moral demands of the seventh commandment are incompatible with systems that make profit the exclusive norm and ultimate purpose of economic activity, and with those systems that subordinate the individual to the collective organization of production (2424). For this reason, the moral obligations of the seventh commandment include the reasonable regulation of the marketplace and the protection of the human rights of workers.

Above all, *our Christian faith should lead us to promote economic activity that serves the good of the human person and the various values needed for human flourishing.* Just as we need more than money to flourish, the economy should do more than simply increase wealth. It should be designed to give everyone an opportunity to participate in responsible stewardship over the goods of the earth.

CCC 2426-2430
Economic Activity and Social Justice I

Continuing its presentation of the seventh commandment's relevance for our understanding of economic activity, here the Catechism offers a *thoroughly Christian view* of the personal meaning of economic activity, especially the "work" done by the human person.

The Catechism bases these teachings on the fundamental idea that work is our way to "prolong the work of creation by subduing the earth, both with and for one another" (2427), and thereby manifest our having been created in the image of God the Creator. This approach to work prevents us from merely thinking of work as a punishment for sin by instead *locating its essential meaning in the stewardship over the earth that God gave us from the beginning.*

We can understand that the primary value of work rests in how it enables us to honor the "gifts and talents" given to us by God (2427) by putting them to good use in shaping the world to be better and at the service of others. For the Christian, work can also be a "means of sanctification and a way of animating earthly realities with the Spirit of Christ" (2427).

When we persevere in the work God has given us, we imitate the work of Christ in the carrying of the Cross for the benefit of others.

Since work has such fundamental importance in the life of the person, everyone has both *the right to work and the duty to put his talents to good use* (2429). Here, however, we are operating with a two-fold meaning of work. Work can be anything we do to *make the world a better place*, whether that be in a profession, in the home, or elsewhere. Work can also be understood as that which explicitly has an economic value in the marketplace.

With these teachings, the seventh commandment requires us to value both meanings of work and to resist thinking that work is meant "solely to multiply goods produced and increase profit or power" (2426).

CCC 2431-2436
Economic Activity and Social Justice II

Since economic activity relates directly to the dignity of the human person and the good of the human community, the Catechism continues its teaching on the seventh commandment by addressing the *responsibility of the state to regulate economic activity* and the *moral obligations of business leaders to exercise social responsibility.*

The state has a responsibility to regulate economic activity to *promote human dignity and the flourishing of the community,* and we should expect our political leaders to enact laws that promote the security needed for successful economic activity (as outlined in the teachings on the common good, see 1910) and defend human rights in the economic sector. However, the Catechism clearly states that the burden of creating a just and sound economy does not rest on political leaders alone. Business leaders also "have an obligation to consider the good of persons and not only the increase of profits," and must take responsibility "for the economic and ecological effects of their operations" (2432).

To fulfill the moral obligations of the seventh commandment, politicians and business leaders must seek to ensure that access to employment in various professions is "open to all without unjust discrimination" (2433), allowing men and women, people of all races, the disabled, and immigrants to find suitable work.

However, simply finding work is not enough; people also need to be paid a just wage, and *paying just wages is a moral requirement of the seventh commandment.* The practical determination of a just wage may pose a challenge, and "both the needs and the contributions of each person must be taken into account" (2434); yet the amount paid as wages can never be morally justified simply by an agreement between a worker and the employer.

Social justice and the seventh commandment require that there be a meaning to just wages beyond simply what people are willing to accept for their work and that there be provisions in the economy that protect workers from unjust treatment.

CCC 2437-2442
Justice and Solidarity among Nations

Economic activity does not merely take place within a single community, but also concerns the relationship between nations; here the Catechism expresses how the moral demands of the seventh commandment include *justice and solidarity among nations.*

In order to establish justice and solidarity among nations we will need to address the inequality, or "gap," between "those nations possessing and developing the means of growth" and "those accumulating debts" (2437). However, we must not think of justice simply in terms of *economic development* but also *moral and cultural development* embodied in the concept of social justice. For this reason, the seventh commandment obliges us to work towards a global recognition of the true dignity of the human person and to promote the proper hierarchy of values in the economic arena.

In this pursuit of a sound global economy, "rich nations have a grave moral responsibility toward those which are unable to ensure the means of their development by themselves or have been prevented from doing so by tragic historical events" (2439). We cannot stand by with indifference towards the economic and cultural development of other nations or look upon other nations, even those with whom we have historically had tensions or hostility, as adversaries in the global marketplace. Although it can include direct aid to struggling nations, this solidarity should primarily be expressed by efforts "to reform international economic and financial institutions so that they will better promote equitable relationships with less advanced countries" (2440).

The Church does not offer concrete solutions to the practical challenges posed by these teachings of the seventh commandment, but rather reminds us of our *moral obligation to promote human dignity and social justice in the economic sphere.* We can recognize the complexity and difficulty of global solidarity, but the moral demands of the seventh commandment prevent us from using these as an excuse for not trying to bring the message of the Gospel to bear on the realities of the global economy.

CCC 2443-2449
Love for the Poor

The Catechism concludes its teaching on the seventh commandment on an especially Christian note by reminding us to *practice a love for the poor* as a matter of our moral obligations. Rather than thinking that helping the poor amounts to some special form of charity, we need to acknowledge that justice and the universal destination of goods require us to share our goods with the poor.

As the text points out, both Scripture and the Tradition of the Church seek to promote a preferential love for the poor. God blesses those who come to the aid of the poor, and it is "by what they have done for the poor that Jesus Christ will recognize his chosen ones" (2443). Being able to help the poor can even be a motive for the work we do, which gives fuller meaning to what the text has already said about work and the seventh commandment.

However, *sharing our goods with the poor should be understood in light of the universal destination of the goods of the earth* upon which this whole catechesis on the seventh commandment is based. By virtue of the principles underlying the seventh commandment, we can rightly conclude, in the words of Saint John Chrysostom, that not allowing "the poor to share in our goods is to steal from them and deprive them of life. The goods we possess are not ours, but theirs" (2446).

At the same time, we should not think of helping the poor merely in terms of giving up some of our money. *In order to truly show our love for the poor we need to engage in a variety of works of mercy*, "by which we come to the aid of our neighbor in his spiritual and bodily necessities" (2447). There are many forms of poverty, and the seventh commandment morally obliges us to help alleviate poverty in all its forms according to our abilities and the opportunities presented to us.

CCC 2464-2470
Living in the Truth

The Catechism now turns to the eighth commandment, which explicitly prohibits bearing false witness against our neighbor, but in its deeper meaning "forbids misrepresenting the truth in our relations with others" (2464). With this catechesis on the eighth commandment, the text highlights the intersection of our relationship with the truth and our relationship with others. The moral obligations of the eighth commandment regulate our relationship to the truth, but, more importantly, *respect for the truth serves our relationships with other people.*

The text first expresses the need to be truthful in terms of our vocation to bear witness to the truth about God and his love for humanity. *If we prove ourselves to be untruthful in mundane things, we will lose the credibility that we need to proclaim the Gospel.* For the sake of our Christian vocation, we need to avoid offenses against the truth and maintain truthfulness in every situation.

The text also mentions the fundamental human need for truth. We cannot flourish or even maintain the goods protected by the Ten Commandments without access to the truth, since falsehoods are bound to lead to all sorts of harm in the political, medical, or economic spheres.

However, our moral obligations to respect the truth do not simply amount to telling all the truth all the time to all people, for that is bound to cause harm as well. Instead, we need to practice the *virtue of truthfulness,* "which consists in showing oneself true in deeds and truthful in words, and in guarding against duplicity, dissimulation, and hypocrisy" (2468). Truthfulness means giving "another his just due" and "keeps to the just mean between what ought to be expressed and what ought to be kept secret" (2469).

In other words, keeping the eighth commandment is much harder than just telling the truth and refusing to lie. Truly keeping this commandment obliges us to *express the right truth at the right time in the right way and for the right reasons.*

CCC 2471-2474
To Bear Witness to the Truth

Just as Jesus came into the world "to bear witness to the truth" (Jn 18:37), the followers of Jesus have a fundamental duty to *bear witness to the faith and proclaim the truth of the Gospel.* These teachings of the eighth commandment remind us that offering a credible witness to the Gospel requires us to avoid all offenses against the truth so that we can be faithful disciples of Jesus, have good relationships with others and maintain our credibility before the world.

All Christians have a duty to take part in the Church's mission that "impels them to act as witnesses of the Gospel" and to bear witness to the faith "in words and deeds" (2472). Martyrdom is "the supreme witness given to the truth of the faith" (2473). The martyrs remain an example of the duty we all have to be willing to make sacrifices for the sake of proclaiming the truth and to be always unwilling to deny the truth, even to avoid great suffering.

However, our commitment to the truth extends to all our daily situations, not just dramatic moments like those faced by the martyrs. In tomorrow's reading, we shall see how the Catechism recalls the various ways, big and small, that we may be tempted to commit offenses against the truth. From such issues as *false witness and perjury,* which publicly and formally contradict the truth, to *detraction and boasting,* which express the truth for the wrong reasons or at the wrong times, offenses against the truth remind us of the *need to practice the virtue of truthfulness in all situations.*

As we will see, the text clearly concentrates on how *offenses against the truth introduce various injustices into society, harm the reputations of others, and corrupt our relationships with others.* Nonetheless, it is not only for respecting someone's good name or maintaining healthy relationships that we should practice truthfulness, but also precisely for the sake of *having credibility in our Christian witness.*

CCC 2475-2487
Offenses Against Truth

In this section, the Catechism first establishes that the eighth commandment obliges us to practice the virtue of truthfulness. Then the text addresses the immorality of lying, "the most direct offense against the truth" (2483), and the harm done by lying.

The proper definition of lying has two parts in that "a lie consists in speaking a falsehood with the intention of deceiving" (2482). Since a lie must be *both false and deceptive*, speaking falsely without being deceptive, such as on stage during a play or as part of a game of pretend, is not a lie in itself. At the same time, speaking truthfully but also deceiving or misleading your listener is immoral if not done for grave reason (addressed by the Catechism in the next section), but still not a lie.

Lying is always a sin in every situation, but the gravity of a lie can vary greatly from case to case. In order to assess the gravity of a lie we must take into account "the nature of the truth it deforms, the circumstances, the intentions of the one who lies, and the harm suffered by its victim" (2484). These criteria certainly leave room for lies to be venial sins in some cases; however, "by its very nature, lying is to be condemned" (2485) because of the harm it does to individuals and to relationships.

The Catechism highlights how lying "does real violence to another" and is "destructive of society" (2486) by depriving people of the truth they need to make decisions in accord with reality and to form healthy relationships. Since lying is a form of injustice that does real harm, *the virtue of justice requires us to make reparation for any lies that we have told.* Depending on the circumstances and the requirements of prudence, the reparation can be made publicly or privately and be material or spiritual, but the eighth commandment does require us to take responsibility for harm done by lying.

CCC 2488-2492
Respect for the Truth

Although lying always causes some harm, at times telling the truth can be harmful or unwise due to the nature of the truth or the situation at hand; for this reason the Catechism explains the sense in which "the communication of the truth is not unconditional" (2488).

While *prohibiting lying in all cases*, the eighth commandment requires us to *judge whether we should reveal the truth* to someone who asks for it in a given situation. The "good and safety of others, respect for privacy, and the common good are sufficient reasons for being silent about what ought not be known or for making use of a discreet language" (2489).

Silence may work in some situations, but in other situations we can also see the prudence of using what the text calls *discreet language*, which means saying something that is true but also either uninformative or misleading. This enables us to avoid the sin of lying while also adhering to the obligation to speak the right truth at the right time for the right reasons. So, here we have the solution to those hypothetical situations where telling the truth would be dangerous, making lying seem acceptable. *Catholic morality offers the middle road of silence or discreet language to avoid the extremes of lying or revealing a dangerous truth, since both extremes would contradict the respect for the truth required by the eighth commandment.*

The teaching on secrets follows a similar logic by placing our *commitment to the truth within the context of prudence.* Information received under the seal of secrecy cannot be shared unless sharing it is the only way to prevent grave harm. Even when there is no official seal of secrecy, we should all "observe an appropriate reserve concerning persons' private lives" (2492), because some truths are private and should not be sought after or shared with others.

Again the text is reminding us that respect for the truth often requires limited access to the truth.

CCC 2493-2503
Truth and Beauty: Media and Sacred Art

This section of the Catechism presents how Catholic moral teachings relate to modern media and the *need for the media to adhere to the moral demands of truthfulness, especially in light of the enormous influence that the media has in the modern world.* The proper assessment of the media takes a typically Catholic middle road by seeing the great potential for good found in the media's ability to reach millions and by recognizing the dangers associated with the misuse or overuse of the media.

Modern means of communication have a *positive role to play in the transmission of truth*, and "the information provided by the media is at the service of the common good" (2494). The media can provide information that we have a right to know and thereby empower us to make better decisions. However, the media can serve this positive role only when it fulfills the requirements of truthfulness, which means that the media must not only communicate the truth but also communicate it in the right way, at the right time and for the right reasons. *Our freedom of expression is perfected rather than diminished by the moral boundaries that truthfulness places on us.*

The modern means of communication become problematic when they are not used in service of the truth and justice, when they violate charity and the respect owed to others, or when they gain too great an influence in the lives of individuals. The text seems especially concerned with cases in which the media engages in defamation for false information and when individuals fail to practice moderation in how much time and importance they give to mass media.

Of course, media is at its best when it serves a sacred purpose by expressing the truth about God and the beauty of God and his creation. Sacred art expresses "what is beyond words" (2500) and *should hold a special place in the life of the Church and in each of our lives.*

CCC 2514-2519
Purification of the Heart

Although the ninth commandment explicitly mentions the marital covenant and the need to respect the spouse of another, the Catechism clarifies that *the ninth commandment forbids all carnal concupiscence and requires us to practice purity of the heart in all our relationships.*

Since the ninth commandment forbids carnal concupiscence, this section begins with the proper meaning of "concupiscence" and its significance for our understanding of the human person. The term "concupiscence" here means any "movement of the sensitive appetite contrary to the operation of the human reason" (2515). In other words, concupiscence refers to sensual desires that contradict what we know to be good through the natural moral law and conscience.

We know in our conscience that acting on these disordered desires would be wrong, and this leads us to condemn the disorder within our own mind, creating opposition or tension between our passions and desires. In turn, this *tension between disordered passions and conscience* is often experienced as a *tension between flesh and spirit*, which corresponds to the tension in our composite being that "belongs to the heritage of sin" (2516).

The ninth commandment specifically concerns how this tension between spirit and flesh shows itself in the sphere of human sexuality.

In order to keep the ninth commandment, we cannot simply refrain from acting on disordered sexual desires, but instead must work towards a *purity of heart* where we are free of these desires and experience peace between the spirit and the flesh. Although purity of heart has meanings outside the sexual sphere, the ninth commandment focuses our attention on the purity of heart that "lets us perceive the human body — ours and our neighbor's — as a temple of the Holy Spirit, a manifestation of divine beauty" (2519). Far from condemning the body, the Christian call to resist "the flesh" means recognizing the *personal dignity of the body* and refusing to reduce the body to an object meant to serve our disordered desires.

CCC 2520-2527
The Battle for Purity

The purity of heart that we need to keep the ninth commandment requires us to *overcome the consequences of sin*, and now the Catechism begins to speak of how God's grace enables us to win the "struggle against concupiscence of the flesh and disordered desires" (2520), which leads to the practice of *modesty*.

Within our baptismal vocation we have the commitment to reject sin and resist concupiscence. In order to fulfill this commitment, *we need to see the potential for purity given in God's grace, base our relationships in love rather than use, make fulfilling God's will our top priority, and practice discipline in what we see or imagine.* Prayer will be the path along which we can progress in the other elements, and modesty will both express and develop our purity of heart.

Although modesty will be expressed externally in how we dress, speak, and look at others, the Catechism once again focuses our attention on how modesty "protects the intimate center of the person" (2521) by the attitudes and intentions within our hearts. Modesty can be expressed by the body, but *it resides in the heart.* The "forms taken by modesty vary from one culture to another" (2524), or even from one situation to another, such as the acceptability of complete nakedness in front of a doctor during a medical examination when nakedness would be otherwise prohibited with that same person in a different context. However, in all cases modesty means *protecting the dignity of the person* and displaying the "consciousness of being a subject" (2524) as opposed to the willingness to objectify the body.

The way we display ourselves or look at each other, whether in real life or in the media, has an enormous impact on the *development of modesty in those around us.* For this reason, the battle for pure hearts requires a communal effort to create cultural norms that favor the practice of modesty in all our relationships.

CCC 2534-2540
The Disorder of Covetous Desires

The tenth commandment completes the whole dynamic of God's law by once again calling us to focus on the "intentions of the heart" (2534) and by reminding us of the subtle ways in which we can fall into idolatry by acting as though created goods hold the keys to our happiness. Recalling the desire for God that should shape our whole lives, the tenth commandment not only "summarizes all the precepts of the law" (2534), but also brings us back to the very foundations of Christian morality laid at the outset of this whole moral catechesis, which "invites us to purify our hearts of bad instincts and to seek the love of God above all else" (see 1723).

The tenth commandment directly concerns our desires for created goods, desires that are good in themselves but often exceed "the limits of reason and drive us to covet unjustly what is not ours and belongs to another or is owed to him" (2535). On the one hand, then, we are obliged to moderate our desires for good things, resisting greed and "the desire to amass earthly goods without limit" (2536). At the same time, we are called to recognize the way greed creates discord in our relationships with others, making the other a kind of enemy in the pursuit of earthly goods; thus the commandment "requires that *envy* be banished from the human heart" (2538).

This section of the text concludes by calling attention to the *deeper evils at work in envy*. In addition to the further evils that can be spawned by envy, such as lying and stealing, envy expresses "sadness" and "pride" that *contradict the movements of charity in our hearts* (2540). We are envious when we are discontent and think that we deserve more than our fair share. Envy, then, shows not just an excessive love of created goods but also a defective love of the Creator, who alone could satisfy our hearts, if only we let him.

CCC 2541-2550
The Desires of the Spirit

This final section on the meaning of the tenth commandment allows the Catechism to conclude its entire moral catechesis with a final reminder of the *perfection in God* that it has been calling us to every step of the way. Restating the essence of Christian morality, *the tenth commandment exhorts us to enkindle in our hearts the desire for God, who alone can satisfy the deep longings of the human spirit.*

The Catechism links the tenth commandment's prohibition of greed and envy with the Gospel call to poverty, where "Jesus enjoins his disciples to prefer him to everything and everyone" (2544). This teaching of Jesus obliges us to practice "detachment from riches" in order to enter the Kingdom of Heaven (2544), but more importantly it requires us to *get our priorities and affections in order so that love for God can reign supreme in our hearts.* As the text points out, the "desire for true happiness frees man from his immoderate attachment to the goods of this world so that he can find his fulfillment in the vision and beatitude of God" (2548). Being poor in spirit "frees us from anxiety about tomorrow" (2547) through an abandonment to the providence of our heavenly Father, and prepares our hearts to be content in God alone, which brings us back to the essence of Christian morality.

Called by Jesus, led by the Holy Spirit, and assisted by God's grace, we may need to "struggle" and "mortify" our cravings in order to "prevail over the seductions of pleasure and power" (2549) and to keep our hearts set on God. This entire moral catechesis of the Catechism has been able to keep our focus precisely on this practice of discipleship, while assuring us that the divine adoption in Jesus by which God loves us, and the eternal communion in heaven to which God calls us, far surpass anything that he demands of us.

PART FOUR
Christian Prayer

CCC 2558
Prayer in the Christian Life

The mystery of faith has been revealed to us for the sole purpose of our entering into, and abiding in, it. The fourth and final part of the *Catechism*, on Christian Prayer, instructs us on this abiding. Let us begin by considering the painting which introduces this section. In an ancient miniature, we see the disciples watching Christ, who is turned towards the Father in prayer. Christ's posture reveals the *essence of who he is*, and the *essence of prayer*. The Gospel of John tells us: "In the beginning was the Word, and the Word was *with* God" (literally, "*turned towards* God," Jn 1:1). The Son, from all eternity, is turned towards the Father. He is eternally *with* the Father, in the communion of the Holy Spirit.

When Jesus' disciples ask him to teach them to pray, Jesus responds, "Our Father ... " He introduces them to his own relationship with the Father, inviting them to share in it. Prayer, then, is fundamentally *a relationship* — "a vital and personal relationship with the living and true God" (2558). This first definition of prayer is a clue that we must approach Part Four a little differently than the other three parts of the Catechism. We will not find here the same kind of organization or precision that we found in them. Rather, the beautiful and often lyrical language of Part Four that circles around and goes deeper into the meaning of prayer serves to *draw us into its object, inviting us to go and spend time with the One who waits for us.*

The difference in approach in Part Four is also due to its *distinct authorship*. It was written primarily by Fr. Jean Corbon, a priest of the Melkite Greek Catholic Church in Lebanon, and will incorporate some of the rich heritage of Eastern Catholicism. Section One focuses on the nature and ways of prayer in the Tradition, while Section Two comments on each line of the Lord's Prayer.

CCC 2559-2561
Prayer as God's Gift

The Introduction to Part Four begins with two quotations from saints, for the saints are the most eminent teachers of prayer throughout the Tradition. These particular citations have in common that prayer is a *movement which happens when we explicitly turn our hearts towards God and give him our attention.*

The foundation of prayer is *humility*, CCC 2559 tells us, referencing Saint Luke's story of the Pharisee and the tax collector (Lk 18:9-14). The tax collector acknowledges that he is unworthy and thus goes "to his house justified" (Lk 18:14). But the prayer of the Pharisee goes unheard because he is turned, not towards God, but towards himself, listing all the holy deeds he has performed. *Self-righteousness and pride are perhaps the most serious obstacles to real prayer.* They keep a man from admitting his need of God — his condition as sinner — and close him to the *gift* of prayer. Ponder as you read this truth that prayer is a *gift*.

In a most beautiful paragraph we learn that prayer begins not with us, but with God (2560). *Our desire to pray is but a response to the deepest desire of God's heart* — that we may come to him, and drink of his Life. God first seeks us out, as he did the Samaritan woman at the well. He thirsts — yearns — to love us, and to receive our response of love. Jesus' cry on the cross, "I thirst," reflects the Father's thirst to have us with him, eternally. The citing of Jeremiah 2:13 in paragraph 2561 reminds us that our temptation is to find other "wells" — other sources of satisfaction that do not offer true happiness. *God alone quenches the thirst of the human soul.*

CCC 2562-2565
Prayer as Covenant and Communion

Prayer arises from the *heart* of the human person (2562). The biblical understanding of heart encompasses much more than emotions; it is the *seat of our whole being.* At that core (from the Latin, *cor*, for "heart"), where we are most aware of our needs, desires, hopes, and fears, God comes to meet us. In the heart, we are moved, towards him or away from him. There we can wrestle with God, as Jacob did (Gn 32:24-31). *If we do not descend to the level of the heart, our prayer risks remaining superficial or impersonal.* CCC 2563 notes that the heart is the place of "covenant," a term which appears several times in these paragraphs. "Covenant" evokes a relationship initiated by God but requiring man's response, specifically the relationship reflected in marriage (see 1612). Prayer, then, consists of a mutual partnership, where the human person is not passive but a true agent.

Christian prayer, like the liturgy, is always Trinitarian, both in its form and in its goal. We who pray always do so *"in Christ," to the Father, with the Holy Spirit.* We can note here (2564) that prayer has a twofold source — ourselves and the Holy Spirit. The goal of our Christian life is union with the whole Trinity, and that goal has already begun to be realized in the person who prays (refer here to 260). Prayer accustoms us to being in the presence of the Trinity and, we will see later, gives us a taste of the delights of that perfect communion for which we were made. So prayer has a quality of the "already" and "not yet" characteristic of the Kingdom. We do not have to wait to experience the communion of love shared by Father, Son, and Spirit — it is available to us every time we sit down to pray.

CCC 2566-2568
The Universal Call to Prayer

All human beings seek to connect with the one who brought them into being. Whether or not we are aware of it, *we were made to relate to God.* The desire to acknowledge God is present even after the Fall, and it is a fruit of grace, of God's initiative. He is tireless and faithful in inviting us to "that mysterious encounter known as prayer" (2567).

In a wonderful phrase, the Catechism describes prayer as a "covenant drama" (2567). Be attentive to the theme of *prayer as a drama* — it will undergird the whole fourth part, especially Chapter One. Salvation itself is a drama, in which God engages with man and man with God through the events of history. This drama is reflected and expressed in prayer, because *prayer, as we have seen, is the arena where God calls to man's heart and man responds from the heart.* And it is in the heart that covenants are made, broken, and renewed.

The "stuff" (the contents) of the drama of prayer is taken from our history, both as God's people and as individuals. Let no one argue that Christian prayer is detached from life! Like history and drama, therefore, our prayer has direction, meaning, movement, and entails our full participation. Every drama is composed of words and deeds, and the story is revealed gradually, over time. The reality and understanding of prayer grow as God interacts with his people — we see again the divine pedagogy at work (see 53). The Catechism will look at this drama of prayer first in the Old Testament, then in the Person of Jesus, in whom the response to God is finally fulfilled and perfected, and finally in the life of the Church.

CCC 2569-2573
Prayer, Creation, and God's Promise

The first traces of prayer are found in simple acts — an offering of an animal, an unspecified "calling upon the name of the Lord," and living an upright life (summed up in that marvelous biblical phrase "walking with God"). The Catechism recognizes these prayers of the righteous as present in many religions. But prayer, strictly speaking, cannot be revealed until the dynamic of relationship is established, in the call of God and the response of man — in this case, Abraham. Abraham is our father in faith, so he is also the one who first teaches us about prayer. (Note the many side references to the Catechism's section on faith here.) For Abraham, prayer is a *continual dialogue with God*, for he both walks and talks with God.

Abraham's prayer is a model for us, *because his heart is attentive to God*, and he *obeys what he hears there*. His first words of prayer, ironically, are a complaint, which illustrates his level of comfort with God and trust in the relationship, and reveals that *in prayer, faith is tested*. Because of his faith, Abraham is receptive to God, and here the Catechism makes a beautiful parallel between the responses of Abraham and Mary, and between their two *sons of the promise*. Because of his obedient faith, Abraham comes to share God's own heart of compassion for men and "dares" to intercede for the men of Sodom and Gomorrah. And when Abraham accepts the call to sacrifice his son, his faith in God's promises conforms him to the Father himself, who does not spare his own beloved Son. Prayer makes us like God and enables us "to share in the power of God's love that saves the multitude" (2572).

Recalling Jacob wrestling with God, we hear the first intimations of *prayer as a battle*, to which a whole section will later be devoted (2573).

CCC 2574-2579
The Prayers of Moses and David

The account of Moses and the burning bush gives us crucial lessons about prayer, especially the *power of intercession*. Content in keeping the flocks of Jethro, Moses is not actively seeking God. Rather, God comes to him and initiates a relationship, calling him by name. *In every instance of prayer, God is already calling out to us by name.* He reveals himself to us, as he did to Moses, so that we may participate in his plan of salvation, for ourselves and for all of humanity. We learn to pray as Moses did, in dialogue and even debate, by being honest with God about our questions, reservations, and fears. God's response to Moses' questioning — the revelation of his Holy Name — demonstrates that it is appropriate and even desirable to pray in this way.

The Catechism identifies Moses' intimate conversations with the Lord, occurring frequently and at length, as *contemplative prayer*. Such "face to face" communication is possible because of Moses' marked humility (2576). In the context of prayer, God reveals himself to Moses as *abounding in steadfast love and as faithful, trustworthy, constant* — these divine attributes will be recalled again and again in the prayer of his people (see 214). Confident in his knowledge of God's nature, Moses is willing to engage in the battle of intercession. After the people abandon God for the molten calf, Moses argues with God on their behalf, calling (and trusting) God to be faithful to whom he has revealed himself to be.

The prayers of King David hold a special place here because of his integrity of heart; even after sinning grievously, he repents and is submissive to God. His joyful praise of God (one thinks of him dancing naked before the ark) resounds from the Psalms.

CCC 2580-2584
Elijah, the Prophets, and Conversion of Heart

With Solomon, the Temple emerges as a privileged place of prayer for the People of God, even as "the place of their education in prayer" (2581). Note the many expressions of prayer that surrounded the Temple, which remain in the age of the Church, albeit transformed. Solomon's dedication prayer cited here (2580) is a long and detailed supplication that the Lord's forgiveness will extend far into the future.

In time, the external practices involved with Temple worship became dissociated from a corresponding interior devotion of heart. The role of the prophets was to call the people back to faith and conversion, and to proclaim the Lord as the one God. The prayer of Elijah, who is an exemplar of all the prophets, is expressed first in his zeal for seeking God's face. Like Moses, he comes to know God one-on-one and experiences God's presence, albeit in a veiled way. Only in the New Covenant will both of these holy men behold the full splendor of Christ, his Transfiguration. *This glorious response to their long waiting and hoping fuels our own hope in prayer.*

We see Elijah zealous, again, in the prayer of intercession. Through his pleas, the Lord performs miracles. The writings of the prophets reveal a *connection between intimacy with God in prayer and effectiveness in works.* The prophet's relationship with the Lord and his attentiveness to God's Word were the source of his strength and direction for mission, as they are for ours.

In all these biblical figures, we see the outlines of a person of prayer emerging: he or she is one who walks uprightly, who gets to know God in personal encounters and struggles with him, who believes what God reveals about himself, whose heart becomes like the heart of God, who makes God's people his own and intercedes for them, and, finally, who yearns for the One who is to come.

CCC 2585-2589
The Psalms, the Prayer of the Assembly

The *high point of prayer in the Old Testament* is the collection of prayers known as the Psalms. These prayers are unique in two ways. First, they are both "personal" and "communal." They give voice to the prayers of an individual believer, to the prayers of the People of God, and to the prayers of all humanity. Second, the Psalms are unique in that they span all time, and all history. While the Psalms can be prayed alone or in community, they were originally intended to be prayed by the assembly in the synagogues and in the Temple. They were taken up as the primary content of the Liturgy of the Hours (see 1177), which remains the "Prayer of the Church."

The Psalms become even more powerful for us when we understand them as prayed by Christ himself. The *General Instruction of the Liturgy of the Hours*, cited in footnote 38, provides a beautiful explanation of how the Body of Christ prays the Psalms.[4] The Psalms express our response to God and his saving works, and as such they constitute a "school of prayer" for us, as they have been used for centuries in abbeys and monasteries and convents.

The Psalms reflect both *God's deeds in history* and the *human experiences of the Psalmist*, who is struggling to respond in faith in his own situation. Their genius is that they address every situation the human being can find himself in, and show us how to bring that situation before God. The prayer which begins with the distress of the Psalmist moves to an act of trust in God's love and fidelity, and ends with praise (see 304). Praying them, we learn how to make this same movement, and to come to rest in the song of praise that honors God and brings us joy.

---

[4] This extract from the *General Instruction* can be found in *The Companion to the Catechism of the Catholic Church: A Compendium of Texts Referred to in the Catechism of the Catholic Church* (San Francisco, Ignatius Press, 1993).

CCC 2598-2601
Jesus' Filial Prayer

Prayer takes on a radically new dimension when it is God himself, in the Person of his Son, who is doing the praying. Jesus' prayer reflects his identity as both God and man, two natures in one person (see 470-473 for a deeper understanding of the union of human and divine natures in Jesus). Thus Jesus' prayer stems both from his *human formation* — from his mother (how wondrous!) and his people — and in a much deeper way from the *communion he experiences with his Father*. These two sources of prayer are not separate, but are united in the mystery of the Incarnation.

Because the Son of God joined himself ineluctably to all humanity, *his prayer expresses, on our behalf, the perfect response of all humanity to the Father*. That which none of the great "pray-ers" of the Old Covenant could realize Jesus embodies in his "filial prayer," as the Catechism terms it (2599). In the fullness of time, Jesus lives this filial prayer in his human flesh, *that we might observe it, imitate it, and participate in it*.

Jesus' filial prayer is "a humble and trusting commitment of his human will to the loving will of the Father" (2600). The Catechism draws on the Gospel of Luke here, for this evangelist speaks most about Jesus at prayer (see footnotes on 2600). It is not just in Gethsemane that Jesus entrusts himself to the Father's will, but throughout his life. Jesus' prayer before the crucial events of his mission prepares him for the revelation of the Father's plan and obedience to it. Filial prayer, then, *disposes* one to receive and carry out the will of the Father. We will see later that when we pray, *we prepare ourselves for the gifts our loving Father wants to give us*.

CCC 2602-2604
Contemplating Jesus in Prayer I

The Catechism notes, tersely, Jesus' penchant for drawing apart to pray *in solitude*, on a mountain, preferably at night. All of these contexts, deeply steeped in biblical allusions, enable Jesus to focus exclusively on communicating with the Father. A similar solitude is essential for all who pray — if we are to respond to God's desire to be with each of us in a unique and exclusive way.

CCC 2602 points out a twofold consequence of the Incarnation which is brought out by the references to Hebrews (see footnotes 47 and 63). First, when Jesus prays, he prays *with us* (in the midst of us, as one of us — our brother). Second, as our Head, the new Adam, Jesus prays *for us* (see 616). He incorporates us into his offering to the Father. Because he shares in all that we do in our lives, even our weaknesses, excepting sin, Jesus carries us in his heart in prayer and makes our cries his own.

The little phrase "Yes, Father," in Jesus' prayer in Matthew 11:26 sums up the response of Jesus' very being to the Father and his will. The parallel passage in Luke adds, "He rejoiced in the Holy Spirit and said ..." (Lk 10:21-23). Jesus experiences joy as he confesses the mysterious ways of his Father. He begins his prayers by thanking the Father, establishing a pattern for all petitions. Here, even petition becomes an entrustment to the Father, who rewards the petitioner not only with what he asked, but with infinitely more: *the treasure of God himself.*

CCC 2605-2606
Contemplating Jesus in Prayer II

In 2605-2606, we contemplate Jesus' *fiat* in Gethsemane and especially his "seven last words" as he dies on the cross. We see there a *union of word and deed, prayer and sacrifice*. The words which reveal the heart of the Savior, his last testament, are completed in the laying down of his life, into the hands of his Father, on behalf of us sinners. *The perfect expression of filial prayer is filial love — total gift of self out of love for the other.*

Jesus' prayer is not just a model for us, but is the "way" into which we are inserted, through baptism in his death and resurrection, into communion with the Father. By remaining in Christ, our prayers of surrender become visible in deeds of love.

Take a moment to ponder the first two sentences of 2606. At long last, the Father receives from his Son the perfect response he has awaited from humanity since creation. Jesus' complete offering of himself in intercession is accepted and confirmed by the Father in the Resurrection, and the drama of prayer is fulfilled. Here the Catechism draws on the mystery of faith hidden in Psalm 2 and developed in the Acts of the Apostles and the Letter to the Hebrews. As Hebrews tells us, Christ's plea — his prayer to be saved from death — is answered, not by preventing his physical death on the cross, but by *raising him to eternal life*, even in his humanity. The "begetting" in Psalm 2 is understood as the Father's act of raising Jesus from the dead. As a result of Jesus' "godly fear" and perfect obedience to the Father's will, the Father puts all things ("the ends of the earth") into Jesus' hands. For this reason, the Father will answer every prayer uttered in his Son's name.

CCC 2607-2611
Learning from the Master

Having contemplated Jesus in prayer, we now consider his specific counsels on the subject. As righteousness of heart made the prayers of the prophets and patriarchs effective, so the children of the New Covenant must be "committed to conversion" (2609) to pray in faith. (Note: the phrase here is "committed to," not "already completely" converted.) For the prayer of a Christian is not isolated from the other actions in his life. How can I ask the Father to grant my requests if my ways contradict the ways of my heavenly Father (see 1430-1432)?

The Catechism speaks in 2609 of praying "in faith," which is believing the truth about the One to whom we pray and surrendering with docility to him and his will. Such prayer requires "a filial adherence to God *beyond what we feel and understand*" (2609, see also 153). The supernatural virtue of faith enables us to believe when our thoughts and emotions do not give us sufficient ground for belief or are even contradictory to the reality faith puts forth. It is an act of trust in God's truth over my own perceived "truths." We will see later how crucial this aspect of faith is in the battle of prayer. *Faith is promised to us if we remain in the Son, for whom trust in the Father is at the core of his being.*

The Gospels are clear: God wants our prayer to be bold! Why? Because a son should be bold in asking his father whatever he wills, for he knows his father loves him and desires his good (Mt 7:7-11). Recall that as Moses learned what God was like, he dared to ask him big things. The prayer of the one who believes makes it possible for God to act in his life, to do miracles. The Scriptures cited in 2611 remind us that prayer is not just about us and our plans, but about helping *align us with God's plans.*

CCC 2612-2616
Characteristics of Prayer

Why does Jesus place so much emphasis on our keeping watch in prayer? It is worthwhile to read Mark 13 and Luke 21:34-36 (footnote 73). First, *vigilance in prayer is necessary,* because we do not know the hour of the Master's return. When he comes, we cannot make ready in an instant to stand before him; either we will have prepared through long hours of being with him in prayer, coming to know his ways and living them out, or we will be caught off guard, unable to receive him or even recognize him. Second, *prayer fortifies us* both against the temptations of the hour and against the colossal struggles of the end times, when our faith will surely be put to the test.

The first two parables from Luke in CCC 2613 emphasize prayer that is insistent, continual, and with the patience of faith. Why must we keep asking? Not for God's sake, but *for ours.* Persistent seeking and asking develops certain characteristics in us; they force us to exercise the muscle of faith and *acknowledge our dependence on the Father.* The patience of faith enables us to wait, not in a resigned way, but *with humble trust that God will come through for us.*

Asking in Jesus' name and abiding with him emphasize the truth which underlies all of the Catechism's treatment of prayer. Christian prayer always means relating to God "in the place" of the Son, the filial place. We pray *in* Jesus Christ, and only there can we receive the Spirit, the Counselor, who enables us to know the Father. When we abide in this Trinitarian communion, we can be confident that anything we ask in Jesus' name will be granted. *For we will ask only what God desires, what is in accord with his gracious will, and we will receive his gift rejoicing.*

CCC 2617-2619
The Virgin Mary's Prayer

Mary's prayer exemplifies all the characteristics of Christian prayer we have seen in the New Testament. Her response to Gabriel's message is *humble and trusting* (beyond what she can see or understand); like that of her son, and because of him, it is *perfectly filial*. In her *fiat*, the quintessential prayer, she expresses her willingness to adhere totally to God's will, through the gift of her whole self. How beautifully the Catechism describes the Virgin Mary's prayer as our own: "to be wholly God's, because he is wholly ours" (2617). In prayer we seek to offer our whole selves to God because he has first placed his whole Being at our disposal. How many saints have echoed this desire in their prayers! Think of Saint Ignatius' *Suscipe* ("Take, Lord, Receive"), for example.

Mary's prayer, the Catechism points out, is crucial to the coming of the Kingdom — in its inception in the Incarnation, and in its fullness in the outpouring of the Spirit at Pentecost. Her free and perfect alignment with the Father's plan makes her both the Mother of God and the Mother of his Body, the Church. And so the Church makes Mary's song of praise and thanksgiving its own every evening at vespers.

Mary intercedes at Cana by pointing out the need of the people to her son. It seems so simple, to point out a need. *But this act is done in complete and utter faith that the Lord will fill the need.* Mary models for us a simple yet profound way of prayer, of petition and intercession: going to the place of need, and telling Jesus what it is. Because Mary is "Mother of all the living" (2618), we can ask her to present all our needs to Jesus, too.

CCC 2623-2628
Forms of Prayer: Adoration and Blessing

We have examined prayer in the Old and New Covenants, and in this third article of Chapter One, we look at prayer at the time of the Church. The Church's prayer is based on the "forms" (2625) or kinds of prayer which are used throughout Sacred Scripture, in a pronounced way in the Psalms. In fact, these forms of prayer are fundamental "movements" of the human spirit vis-à-vis God; they are, in a sense, the content of our prayer. You may be familiar with a version of these taught traditionally to children as "ACTS" (Adoration, Contrition, Thanksgiving, Supplication). It is the Holy Spirit, the memory of the Church, who forms the Church in the life of prayer (2623). The Spirit revealed these forms in Scripture — thus they remain normative — and he provides continually for the development of new "formulations" (2625) within the great traditions of spirituality, religious orders, and rites of the Church.

As in every prayer, *it is God's initiative that precedes our prayer of blessing.* God blesses us — he showers us with his gifts, he shows us his favor. And we in turn are moved to respond by declaring his goodness — blessing him and then invoking his continued favor, or blessing, upon us. The movement of blessing takes place in the Holy Spirit, through Jesus Christ, and has its origin and end in the Father. The Catechism references three great prayers of blessing by Saint Paul (see footnotes on 2627).

In the prayer of adoration, we acknowledge our littleness, yea, our nothingness, in relation to the One who created us, and who redeemed us. We bow down before God's greatness, his almighty power, and his holiness. Adoration is pure worship and enjoined by the first commandment — for God knows how desperately we need it.

CCC 2629-2631
Petition and Supplication I

The term *petition* refers to a broad category of asking God for help. Under this category, the Catechism distinguishes between a narrower understanding of *petition*, which is supplication *for one's own needs*, and *intercession*, which is requesting help for others. The prayer of petition is an admission that we are in need, and that we believe there is someone who can help us. It requires humility, faith, and especially hope — that God will fulfill his promises.

Petitioning is a work, which at times may take the form of what Saint Paul calls "groaning" (Rom 8:22) — an intense, even physical, yearning for God to save us, both in our immediate concerns and definitively for eternal life. The Catechism points out the special role of the Spirit here, *who takes over when we cannot voice our needs, especially our deepest longings.* The most profound prayers may be unutterable — these are testimony to the Spirit within us.

Petition is the first movement of the heart which has strayed: it leads us back to God and into dialogue with him. In fact, the Catechism establishes an order: before we ask for our other needs, we often need to ask for mercy. In fact, *we are not ready to adore or thank or praise if our conscience is weighed down with something we have put between ourselves and God.* Prayer is based on honesty before God, on truth: "But if we walk in the light, as he is in the light, we have fellowship with one another, and the blood of Jesus his Son cleanses us from all sin (1 Jn 1:7). We see this pattern also in the Mass: we ask for forgiveness and mercy on multiple occasions *before* we actually go forward to receive the Body and Blood of Christ.

CCC 2632-2633
Petition and Supplication II

When we request God's help, our first priority is not to focus on our evident personal needs. The Catechism emphasizes in 2632 that we must *pray first for the kingdom*. This means, first of all, that we desire his reign in our hearts and in our lives. (Indeed, this is one of the primary ways that Vatican II speaks of the kingly role of the laity, see *Lumen Gentium*, 36.) His reign is, very simply, his will and plan for us and for the whole Church. When God does not seem to answer a petition of ours, it may be because his sights are on filling our greater need: our *salvation*. Do we believe Jesus' promise that if we seek first his kingdom, all else will be ours as well? If we pray that way — placing the loving will of our Father first — we will grow in trust that all that is necessary will be provided.

It is clear in CCC 2632 that the prayer of petition extends to prayer for ourselves as the community of believers, the Church. *The members of the Body depend on one another to pray for the graces each person needs to obtain salvation and sanctity.* In his prayers, Saint Paul models how we should pray for one another — for growth in grace, hope, love, wisdom, discernment, righteousness, and maturity in Christ (see footnotes on 2632).

The Catechism emphasizes that there is no need too small — or too great — to be included in our prayers (2633). The reason for this truth can only be the comprehensive nature of God's love for us: he takes an interest in every dimension of our lives, no matter how seemingly insignificant. Christ came to redeem *all* things, and when we give him the "opportunity" to do this, the Father is glorified in him.

CCC 2634-2638
Intercession and Thanksgiving

Intercession — our prayer on behalf of others — is a *participation in Jesus' prayer,* for he is, as the Letter to the Hebrews points out, *the* Intercessor to the Father. He lives not for himself but to lay down his life for others. And, as Scripture makes clear, we have two advocates, for the Spirit of the Father and the Son also intercedes for us.

If we share in the heart of Christ, we will place the needs of others before our own, even in prayer. In communion with Christ, we will also share his desire for the salvation of all people. Our intercession includes not only the people we like or are close to: it must also extend to our enemies, and even to those at whose crimes we shudder. We are to pray that their sins be forgiven!

We give thanks both individually and corporately, in the Eucharistic liturgy. CCC 2637 reveals that our thanksgiving is a participation in Christ's returning of all creation to the Father. Saint Paul exhorts us to give thanks in *all* circumstances, which means the negative as well as the positive ones. There is a great spiritual lesson here. Practicing being thankful — and it is a discipline which must be practiced! — enlarges our hearts and gives rise to joy. And when we give thanks to God for even the hard things, *we find our perspective changing, and we are able to welcome his grace in the situation.*

In the two Scripture passages cited in 2638, we see a link between thanking God and praying continually (see also 1 Thes 5:17). To be thanking God at all times is a way to pray always.

Thanksgiving and petition go together, as Philippians 4:6-7 makes clear. In fact, *we should preface and close our petitions with thanks.* The humble doorkeeper and miracle worker Blessed Solanus Casey advised the needy who came to him with their requests, "Thank God ahead of time."

CCC 2639-2643
Prayer of Praise

Praise is the most *selfless* form of prayer, the most *pure*, and perhaps the *most often neglected*. We are meant to live, to use an expression Saint Elizabeth of the Trinity borrows from Ephesians 1:14, "to the praise of his glory." God's glory is "the radiance of his majesty" (see 2809), the sheer splendor of his Being. The *Gloria* we sing at Mass is a perfect illustration of the prayer of praise. We might say that praise *expresses outwardly* what is *interior to the heart silent in adoration*.

The Catechism highlights the *Trinitarian reality* of the act of praising. Praise calls down the Holy Spirit, who manifests to our spirits our sonship in Christ, by which we praise the Father of all. Saint Luke highlights that the people responded both to Jesus' miracles in his lifetime and to the wonders worked by his apostles through the Spirit by "glorifying" God. It is a spontaneous response to how amazing God is. Praise, we have seen, constitutes the basis of the Psalms, and in the New Testament is expressed in the form of what were originally hymns or songs, all celebrating the great work of salvation.

The Book of Revelation is filled with praise, for praise is the life of heaven. *Our praise here on earth trains us for eternity.* The Catechism concludes 2642 by saying, "Faith is pure praise." How much it must mean to God when we choose to acknowledge his greatness even when not seeing it. *Praising God in the midst of any distress is one of the most powerful prayers* — it lifts us right out of ourselves into the truths of revelation. If we recognize who God is, and exalt him for it, our faith is strengthened, and our hope enlivened, and the distress we experience no longer overwhelms us.

CCC 2650-2660
At the Wellsprings of Prayer

We turn now from Sacred Scripture to hear what Sacred Tradition has to teach us about prayer. The Catechism beautifully integrates the *major sources of prayer*: Christ and his Spirit; the Word of God; the sacred work of the liturgy; the supernatural powers operating in the soul; and the stuff of our daily lives.

The Holy Spirit will figure largely in these sources. *He is our teacher in prayer, the drink of our spirits, and the one who leads us to Christ.* He enables us to hope, and he pours out love, the very essence of prayer. He is present at all times, to transform the moments of each day into prayer.

In prayer, Scripture is to be read specifically as *a means to encounter the living God*, for prayer, we recall, is *a relationship*. The quote given in CCC 2654 refers to the ancient practice of *Lectio Divina*, or prayerful reading of the Bible, which continues to be a fundamental method of prayer today.

Our personal prayer deepens the saving work of God in us which began in the liturgy. Thus the liturgy forms my prayer, which is never strictly my own, but always that of the whole Church.

The supernatural virtues of faith, hope, and love are given to us that we may pray. We cannot pray without hope, and prayer, in turn, fuels our hope. Love is the heart of prayer — God's bestowal of love on us, and our offering of it in return. The beautiful citation from Saint John Vianney does not portray a too lofty ideal; *if we practice prayer faithfully, we too may reach the summit of love* (2658).

Prayer is intended, by the power of the Holy Spirit, to become the yeast which makes even the minute realities of our days a participation in the Kingdom (2659-2660). We recognize here one aspect of the drama of prayer: *nothing in our lives is outside of our communication with God.*

CCC 2663-2672
The Way of Prayer

Prayer is authentically Christian if it calls upon the Lord through his "sacred humanity" — that is, "in the name of Jesus," who lived among us, who died and rose for us (2664). *Our prayer, like our faith, is grounded upon the God who entered history in order to save us, and who has brought our bodily humanity into the heavenly places.* Other spiritualities that seem to call upon Christ but ignore this factor will not lead us to the Father. Note that the teaching on the Father here is brief because of the section exclusively devoted to him in the Lord's Prayer (2779-2793).

The name of Jesus has a particular power, which the Catechism beautifully explains in 2666. Uttering his name with devotion *is* prayer. It is the only name which "contains the presence it signifies" (2666). *Jesus' name brings us into immediate communication with him*; by it, we "welcome" him into our hearts. The Catechism highlights the use of the "Jesus prayer," for its simplicity and depth, and because it can be repeated ceaselessly in our hearts regardless of the activity in which we find ourselves engaged (2667-2668).

The Holy Spirit is always operative in Christian prayer. Indeed, his prevenient ("coming before" or "anticipatory") grace makes our first movement towards Jesus possible, and then continues to reveal him as the Lord (2670). The Catechism encourages us to address the Spirit consciously and deliberately in our prayer, and to seek his aid in each significant event in our lives. Two petitions to him are given, which might be used at the start of our time of prayer (2671). Reflect on the second, a Byzantine prayer less familiar to those in the West. Its words make us more conscious of what the Holy Spirit can do in us and for us as we pray.

CCC 2673-2679
Prayer and the Holy Mother of God

Because of her unique cooperation with the Holy Spirit in the plan of God, Mary exercises a vital role in Christian prayer. The Catechism clarifies what is often confusing about prayer to Mary. The Mother of God is "wholly transparent" to her Son (2674). She cannot but lead us to Jesus. In the icon referred to here — that of the "*hodigitria*" — Mary is depicted as holding the child Jesus at her side with her left hand while pointing to him with her right, indicating him as the way to salvation. This representation has been used in the West in icons such as Our Lady of Perpetual Help and Our Lady of Czestochowa. This truth about Mary undergirds the spirituality of *total consecration to Jesus through Mary* developed by Saint Louis de Montfort.

The Catechism offers a lovely catechesis on each line of the Hail Mary, which is equally a meditation. Gabriel's greeting, "Hail," or "Rejoice," is presented as a way of *our sharing in God's joy* in his most esteemed creature — but a creature like us, nonetheless (2676). Mary is called "full of grace" — literally, superabundantly overflowing with grace — because she is the dwelling place of the Most High God. Should it be any wonder, then, that *we who make our home in her encounter God there*?

When we pray to Mary, we enter into the mystery of her maternity, which is a participation in the mystery of the divine economy. Her maternity flows from her *fiat*, and when we entrust our prayers to her, they are, in a sense, "purified," because *in her hands God's will alone is done*. Like a true mother, Mary comes alongside us in our prayer, both individually and as the entire Church, of which she is the heavenly image.

CCC 2683-2691
Guides for Prayer

Who helps us on our journey of prayer? In addition to the Mother of God with her unique role, there is the whole communion of those who, by their perfection in love, have joined Christ in heaven, yet are still active here on earth. In our formation in prayer, we gain enormously from the writings and example of the saints, and the Catechism identifies intercession as "their most exalted service to God's plan," and instructs us to seek their assistance (2683).

Many of these holy witnesses possessed charisms meant not just for their own spiritual family, but equally for the *formation of the whole Body of Christ*. Saint Francis, for example, endows the Church with a particular spirituality, as does Saint Thérèse of Lisieux with her Little Way. The Catechism also refers to spiritual traditions based on the theology, liturgy, and culture of a particular people, such as those of the Eastern Catholic churches (2684; see 1202). *It is the creativity of the Holy Spirit which gives rise to all of these spiritualities, providing the whole Church with what is needed in each time and place.*

The Catechism speaks of ordained ministers, religious, and spiritual directors as "servants" in the growth of the Church in prayer. Consecrated life is "one of the living sources of contemplation" bearing fruit for the spiritual life of the whole Church (2687). The first place for formation in prayer is the family, as the *domestic church*; this may be supplemented by catechesis. It is very significant that the Catechism emphasizes that catechesis — for all ages — is to have as its focus *meditation on Scripture in personal prayer* (2688). Even young children can learn to meditate, to internalize the Word in their hearts, and thus to come to know the Lord early in their lives. The Catechism will speak of meditation in the next chapter.

CCC 2697-2704
Vocal Prayer

The third chapter of Section One treats of how we pray — the three "expressions" or ways of prayer — as well as an examination of our struggles in prayer. We are *enjoined by Scripture to pray always*, but this does not usually happen because of our natural tendency towards "forgetfulness of God." *We must acquire the habit of prayer by setting aside times devoted exclusively to that purpose.* Whether our prayer takes the form of words or meditation or contemplation, it must begin with "composure of heart" (2699). We attain composure by bringing together, or recollecting, all our interior faculties in order to be attentive to the presence of God. Getting to this place, especially in our age of distraction, may require effort and practice, but *real encounter with God cannot happen without it.*

Vocal prayer may be words spoken aloud, or those uttered in the mind, such as the Rosary or the Liturgy of the Hours prayed silently. The Catechism notes that *Jesus expressed himself freely out loud in prayers arising from his heart,* modeling a way for us to do so as well (2701). Whether spontaneous or in established forms, vocal prayer is essential, and we never move completely beyond it. For we, like the Word made flesh, are incarnate beings, and we need to relate to God with our whole selves, in that mysterious union of body and soul. Only then will our *whole being be transformed.*

Vocal prayer — the prayers of the Church or the saints — can be especially helpful when we find it difficult to pray — when we are fatigued or distracted or without fervor. *When we pray with our lips, our hearts must be in communication with God, too*; otherwise we "heap up empty phrases" (Mt 6:7). And if we combine the attentiveness of the heart with our vocal prayer, God can raise us even to the prayer of *contemplation.*

CCC 2705-2708
Meditation

The Catechism encourages all Christians to take up the method of prayer known as *meditation* (2707). There are many diverse approaches to meditation, stemming especially from the great schools of spirituality — Ignatian, Benedictine, and Carmelite, for example. The Catechism makes reference here (for the fourth time) to the 1500-year-old monastic tradition of *Lectio Divina* (2708), though it does not confine its treatment to this one way.

In meditation, we actively engage the mind by reflecting on a spiritual text (or sometimes an image) in order to *better know God and his ways with us*. (Return now to 158 and read the first sentence.) Our faith quickens and grows as we engage in meditation.

In *Lectio Divina*, to meditate is to ruminate, or chew, on the words in order to digest them and extract nourishment from them, so that their "strength can pass into our innermost heart" (Guigo the Carthusian, see footnote to 2654). Meditation may begin with the mind, but it is directed towards *stirring* the heart, the seat of prayer. In meditation, we do not seek to acquire general spiritual truths, but to perceive "what God is saying to me" in this text. We meditate to meet Christ, who is "the one way of prayer" (2707). Thus a privileged subject for our meditation is "the mysteries of Christ" (2708). Saint Teresa of Avila counsels us to *choose those mysteries which relate to our current situation in life*. She says, for example, that if I am sad, I should reflect on Jesus on the way to Gethsemane, or if joyful, reflect on Jesus as risen. The prayer of meditation, practiced consistently and properly, will lead us beyond itself, to deeper prayer, and ultimately to union with Christ.

CCC 2709-2712
Contemplative Prayer

We approach now the height of Christian prayer. The expression of prayer known as contemplation deals with the *deepest mysteries of the soul's communion with God.* There are various understandings of contemplation within the Catholic spiritual Tradition, and the Catechism borrows widely from these in order to shed light on this way of prayer. In the text, one can distinguish between a broad meaning of contemplation, sometimes called in the Tradition "acquired contemplation," and a narrower, more precisely defined meaning, usually identified as "infused contemplation."

In the broad sense, contemplation means a process which may begin with meditation but moves towards prayer which is *less focused on the meaning of the text and its application,* and *more centered on communicating with a person: Jesus himself.* In this kind of contemplation, we may still use a few words or contemplate mysteries of Christ's life (as in Ignatian contemplation). We are still the ones actively engaged in seeking God, but our desire is now to be with God and to attend to his desire for our time of prayer.

As with all prayer, *contemplation requires preparation.* We dispose ourselves to being with God by first recollecting ourselves and turning towards him in our hearts; we cultivate an awareness of his presence. We call to mind his love for us and "let our masks fall" (2711). What a beautiful thing, to come before him just as we are, trusting in his acceptance of us! Then, just as in the Mass, we offer ourselves to him and await transformation.

Contemplation is above all a *space of love.* God invites us, to use Teresa's phrase, "to be alone with him who we know loves us" (2709).

CCC 2713-2719
"Infused" Contemplative Prayer

The quote from Saint Teresa of Avila which begins this section refers to "mental prayer" (the exact translation of Teresa's phrase), or "inner prayer," another term the Catechism uses. Both of these are expressions referring to contemplation in the broader sense, which serves as preparation for the prayer of infused contemplation. *Infused contemplation is pure gift from God*; we cannot attain it by our own efforts — we can only dispose ourselves to receive it. In this prayer, we become aware of our poverty (mentioned in this section three times), not as an obstacle, but as a *necessary condition*. It is an acknowledgment that *we cannot move further unless God acts*.

When God bestows the grace of this deeper prayer on us, our prayer becomes simpler, with our attention wholly fixed on God. We gaze upon the Lord. We are no longer seeking to understand, but rather, content to *abide*, to remain in his love. The Catechism quotes from the *Song of Songs*, for this kind of prayer is an encounter between the lover and the beloved (2709). *Contemplation is the highest expression of prayer as communion with the Trinity*. And this communion is transformative — by it we come to resemble Christ more and more.

CCC 2719 brings up several rich topics. First, contemplative prayer is fruitful, "bearing Life for the multitude." Contemplation is not just for the person praying, but for the Church and the world. How is this so? Such deep prayer is always intimately connected to the Paschal mystery (2718-2719). The one praying undergoes a "night of faith," a time of testing and trial, which is a participation in Jesus' own night. By remaining faithful to God and to prayer in this time ("keeping watch"), the soul shares in Christ's triumph as well, and brings his grace to countless other souls.

CCC 2725-2728
The Battle of Prayer

The Christian life is a battle; the journey to the heights "passes by way of the cross" (see 2015). This spiritual battle is fought intensely in the arena of prayer, as Christ himself bears witness. Following in the tradition of the saints, the Catechism devotes an entire article to examining the struggles that prayer entails. Here we find keen insight and practical advice.

Progress in prayer is not automatic, like the physical growth of a tree. Prayer takes *consistent, concerted effort* on our part. There are three forces which draw us away from our pursuit of God in prayer (and in life): the "mentality of this present world," "ourselves," and "the tempter" (2725, 2727). Readers may recognize here the classic triumvirate of *the world, the flesh, and the devil*. Not to be aware of these influences, and how they operate, is to be spiritually at risk.

One of the false concepts of prayer is meditation that seeks to free the mind of any thoughts or images (2726). This technique is prevalent in the non-Christian religions of the East, but has also been mingled with Christian prayer. It is crucial to remember that Christian prayer is *always directed to a person* (see 2664). Christ can never be left behind for some "state of being." Also problematic is the prayer of the believer who only "goes through the motions" exteriorly, as if to check off a duty from a list, without ever descending into *the heart*.

The Catechism exhorts believers to vigilance in the face of the multiple secular philosophies which would persuade them that prayer is unnecessary or useless. CCC 2728 offers a list of penetrating reasons that we give up on prayer. Some will be treated in the following pages, but take time in the Lord's company to see if any "strike home." The following sections of this article will show how we can gain ground in the battle through *humility, trust, and perseverance*.

CCC 2729-2731
Distractions and Dryness

The Catechism offers clear advice about distractions in prayer, and a profound insight about the *roots* of our distractions. "A distraction reveals ... what we are attached to" (2729). My attention in prayer might be on various tasks, on relationships, on pleasures, or on concerns of my daily life. Am I placing these before seeking God? My prayer must become a *renewed commitment to place God first* and a *humble request* that he cleanse my heart of these attachments. The battleground lies in the will, in my freedom to choose, yet again, what will be my god. And this choice must be made over and over, without indignation at my own weakness and sinfulness. Distractions will decrease to the extent that I learn, in my daily walk, to gain "sobriety of heart" — an interior detachment from what would turn my heart away from God (2730).

Dryness in prayer can have at least two causes, and it requires discernment to distinguish between them. First, one can feel empty and unenthused about God or prayer because one has actually drawn away from him, through sin. If, for example, I have neglected prayer for a week in order to watch television, or have deliberately pursued some other venial sin, when I go to prayer I may find it difficult to enter into conversation with God and experience his touch in my heart. The answer then is *conversion* — that is, *repentance*. If, on the other hand, I am being faithful to my life in Christ and to seeking God in prayer, and yet experience dryness, this is an indication that I am being called to *deeper prayer* and to a *purification* that God is directing. This dryness is salutary; it is part of the dying to self that the Christian life requires, and a necessary preparation for union with God. My task in this time of darkness is to be faithful to the Lord, accepting this suffering and *continuing to trust even when he seems absent.*

CCC 2732-2733
Lack of Faith and *Acedia*

The disciples' lack of faith was always a concern of Jesus in the Gospels. CCC 2732 looks at the motives for our prayer and how they reveal our unbelief. Do we only call on God when we are desperate? Do we ask for his help but don't really think we need it — because we see ourselves as self-sufficient? Do we assume that of course he will forgive us and bless our plans (see 2092)? We lack the faith that *authentic prayer requires* when we are not humble enough to accept our *radical dependence on God*. We may be addressing him in words of prayer, but we have not surrendered our hearts to him. Do we really desire a relationship with God?

Another temptation, very prevalent in our modern world, is *acedia*, or "spiritual sloth" (see 2094). *Acedia* is not the same as laziness, though it shares some aspects; it is a kind of indifference to the things of the spirit, a lukewarmness in our Christian life. The person caught in this vice sees only the negative in the life that God offers and turns away from prayer with distaste. The flesh (mind and body) is ruling the spirit, which has become complacent and self-indulgent. A return to "ascetical practice" — that is, the disciplines that undergird the spiritual life — is called for. We tend to forget that *self-denial is not an option in the Christian life. Acedia* can lead to abandoning prayer and God himself, and may also lead to discouragement. Here, the discernment of spirits is helpful, to seek out the root of the discouragement and work against it. The remedy: *come back to prayer, humbly seeking God's mercy, and renewing our trust in him.*

CCC 2734-2737
Unanswered Petitions

When we think God does not hear our prayers, our faith is *being tested*. God wants our relationship with him to be authentic, and not based solely on our desire to get something from him. If we are willing, he purifies us from this selfish love towards a love of God simply *for who he is*. We may also question why we must petition him for our needs at all, if, as Scripture tells us, he knows them already. Here, too, God has our growth in mind, the maturing of our freedom. The quote from Saint Augustine (2737) indicates that our capacity for God grows if, undaunted by the trials, we continue to seek him and trust in his help. Indeed, each time we petition him, we can reaffirm our trust in him again, and our faith increases.

There is another reason we do not receive what we ask: we have asked for the wrong things, and in the wrong way. The Letter of James puts it boldly: such petitioners are "adulterers" (2737). This is the language of the covenant, of a God who loves fiercely, jealously, and will not stand to see his beloved forsaking him for what is in fact destructive. James is clear about the *antidote to a divided heart*: "Submit yourselves therefore to God. Resist the devil.... Cleanse your hands ... and purify your hearts.... Humble yourselves before the Lord and he will exalt you" (Jas 4:7-10; see footnotes on 2737). When we surrender once again to God, and let the Holy Spirit take over, our petitions are heard.

An important point is implied here. The fact that our prayer does not go the way we intend does not mean that God is absent. God is *always* at work in our sincere prayer, he is always seeking our good, he is always bringing us to salvation, and he is always preparing us to receive the riches he has for us.

CCC 2738-2745
The Efficacy and Necessity of Prayer

Our prayer is effective because it is *based on faith* and *united with Jesus' prayer* in us and for us. Its first fruit is the change that it brings in our hearts. CCC 2738 points out another significant fruit of prayer: our *cooperation in God's plan* of salvation for humanity. It is a remarkable truth of our Catholic faith that every Christian can, by his prayer, become a "fellow worker" of God (see 307). United to Christ in his prayer and sacrifice, we creatures can be instrumental in changing the course of history.

The section on "Persevering in Love" (2742-2745) is a beautiful exhortation on the place of prayer in the Christian life. First, Saint Paul urges us to *persevere in prayer*. Prayer can be arduous, as we have seen, and we need to keep at it. But our courage to keep going in prayer comes not merely from a sense of duty or sheer force of will, but from love. Second, *nothing separates us from prayer*, as Saint John Chrysostom reminds us in words that could be contemporary, although they date from the fourth century (2743). One can also interpret the Catechism's line "It is always possible to pray" as meaning that there is no situation in which prayer is not possible (2743). As Saint Thérèse has told us, even a "simple look turned toward heaven" suffices (2559).

Third, the Catechism is clear on what happens if we do not pray: enslavement by sin and damnation. No light prospect. On the other hand, for those who do pray, everything is possible, even *complete freedom from sin* (which is the height of sanctity). Fourth, "Prayer and Christian life are inseparable," because prayer and love are inseparable (2745). If we pray rightly, we will not fail to love our brother with the same love we have received from Jesus.

CCC 2746-2751
The Prayer of the Hour of Jesus

Section One of Christian Prayer fittingly concludes with a catechesis on the long prayer which completes Jesus' Farewell Discourse. Jesus' prayer in John 17 is his own, not meant for imitation, but for our enlightenment. In this "priestly" prayer (2747), we see again that Jesus' prayer (word) is perfectly united to the sacrifice (deed) he will soon make. *Both the prayer and the sacrifice endure until the end of time.* The power of the prayer is such that it "carries" the end times "towards their consummation" (2749)!

In the prayer of John 17, Jesus exhibits what the Catechism calls "a sovereign freedom" (2749). Fully aware of the power the Father has handed over to him, Jesus petitions his Father on behalf of his disciples: "Keep them in your name ... that they may be one," "that they may have my joy," "that they may be consecrated in truth" and "that they may be with me where I am" (see footnote on 2749). Indeed, in Jesus' priestly prayer, all the petitions of the Our Father find their *perfect expression.*

In CCC 2751, the Catechism highlights one of the most important truths Jesus has revealed to his disciples: "And this is eternal life, that they know you, the only true God, and Jesus Christ whom you have sent" (Jn 17:3). Eternal life begins on earth in this gift, covenant, drama, and battle we call *prayer*, when the Spirit draws us into the communion of love which *is* the Father and the Son *endlessly pouring out themselves for the other.* Prayer begins in, proceeds in, and ends in love. In the final petition of his priestly prayer, Jesus says: "I made known to them your name, and I will make it known, that the love with which you have loved me may be in them, and I in them" (Jn 17:26).

CCC 2759-2760
The Lord's Prayer: "Our Father"

The first thing to notice is the historical reference point in the scriptural text, indicated by the phrase "at a certain place" (2759). The actual place is not important to the Gospel writer now, but this definite event affected the disciples so powerfully it could not be forgotten. *Imagine watching Jesus praying in his utter love, intimacy, and abandonment to his Father in heaven.* The most suitable response must be exactly that of the disciples, "Lord, teach us that!" Teach us how to experience what we've just watched.

The next point is startling, too. The prayer is almost entirely made up of *petitions*. We've been taught the different kinds of prayer, such as praise, intercession, contrition, thanksgiving, and so forth, and we might have expected Jesus to show us how to praise and thank God in this prayer, or how to be sorry, but he doesn't; he reveals to us that the perfect prayer to our Father in heaven is to *ask*. The rest of this section goes through the seven petitions of this most perfect prayer, perfect because it came from the very Son of God himself.

CCC 2760 gives us the ancient historical origins of additional words sometimes added to the Lord's Prayer. These words are of praise. The source called the *Didache* ("Teaching") is possibly as old as the first century, and the *Apostolic Constitutions* come from the third or fourth century. These are important early Christian writings, even though not chosen by the Church as part of the inspired Word of God, the New Testament.

Finally, note the reference to the Roman Missal and the side reference to 2854. In that paragraph you will find, in full, the beautiful words of the prayer that concludes the Our Father in the Roman Missal, which you will recognize as very similar to the words in the current liturgy.

CCC 2761-2764
At the Center of the Scriptures

Jesus says, "Ask and you will receive," and in the petitions of the Lord's Prayer, he gives us what to ask for as the "foundation" (2761) of all our personal desires. This foundation gives "new form" (2764) to the desires for which we plead. This is why it would be good to begin all our petitionary prayer by praying the Lord's Prayer first, so that our Father in heaven can form us first in *how* to ask and *what* to ask for.

In this sense the Lord's Prayer is already a summary of the Good News, which is that we have a Father in heaven who wants us to ask him for what we desire, who guides our asking and re-forms our desiring, even giving us the right order in which we should desire things (2763).

The next claim may at first seem a surprising one — that being a "summary of the whole gospel" (2761) also means being a *summary of the entire Scriptures*; that everything is "included in the Lord's prayer" (2762), especially the Psalms; and if the Scriptures are all found in the Lord's Prayer, then the Lord's Prayer is at the *center* of the Scriptures.

How do the Psalms, for example, "flow together in the petitions of the Our Father" (2762) so that when reading the Psalms one can see the Lord's Prayer echoed there at their center? Saint Augustine's meditations can show us, but we can begin to find this for ourselves, too. For example, in the first line of the Lord's Prayer, although God is not called "Father" in the Psalms, he is called "My God" and is spoken of *as* a Father, in such phrases as, "He is their help and their shield. The Lord has been mindful of us; he will bless us," and "The heavens are the Lord's heavens" (Ps 115:11-12, 16). And it is enlightening to find, in all the Psalms, the same sentiments as those of the Lord's Prayer.

CCC 2765-2766
The Lord's Prayer

These two paragraphs explain how unique this prayer is. Of all the prayers of all religions, there is nothing to compare with this prayer that is "of the Lord," the Lord's own prayer. It is "of the Lord" because it is *from Christ the Lord* who received the words *from the Lord God his Father*, for us. The Catechism reminds us of another prayer of Christ to his heavenly Father where he says, "I have given them the words which thou gavest me, and they have received them" (Jn 17:8).

The Lord Jesus, who has become man, knows both how to pray *to* his Father and how to pray as man, knowing "in his human heart the needs of his human brothers and sisters" (2765). The Catechism goes on to explain that this prayer is "of the Lord" in a third way. The Lord Jesus gives us the prayer, and he gives us the Holy Spirit who is also *Lord* and God, to enable us to pray it in accordance with its fullest meaning, of which we have only yet grasped a tiny fraction.

The Lord's Prayer, then, engages the Blessed Trinity every time we pray it, which is why we must try not to repeat the words mechanically, but with *the mind, the will, and the heart open to the Lord's greatest work*, because it is the Lord's greatest prayer. It is "of the Lord," because the "Lord God," the Blessed Trinity, gives us the words we need for our deepest self to engage in the Lord's deepest desires for us.

CCC 2767-2772
The Prayer of the Church

We have seen that the Lord's Prayer is a double gift: "of the Lord's words and of the Holy Spirit" (2767). Now we are told the gift is *indivisible*, so the Spirit is *always* present when we begin to pray, prompting the words in us and "giving life to them." What does it mean to "give life" to words? Life makes words real.

The key reason why the Lord's Prayer is the prayer "of the Church" is because it is "essentially rooted in liturgical prayer" (2768). As you will remember, "liturgy" is a "public work" (1069). To be "rooted" in liturgical prayer means that the Lord's Prayer begins in liturgical events, always "dwells" there, and draws its strength from there. When we say the prayer alone and in silence, we can remember that its roots are elsewhere, in the congregation where it manifests itself most fully.

It is at its zenith in the Eucharistic liturgy. Notice what happens: the Lord's Prayer "sums up ... all the petitions and intercessions ... of the *epiclesis* and ... knocks at the door of the Banquet of the kingdom" (2770)! Consider some of these petitions that lead up to the *epiclesis*, when the priest calls upon the Holy Spirit:

"Lord ... accept this oblation of our service ... order our days in your peace, and command that we be delivered from eternal damnation and counted among the flock of those you have chosen" (Eucharistic Prayer I).

The petitions of the Lord's Prayer sum up these petitions and at the same time "knock at the door" of the "banquet" which is the Kingdom. We know from the Scriptures that the Kingdom will be a wedding banquet, and we know from the parable of the ten foolish virgins that the "door was shut" to them (Mt 25:10). When we pray the Our Father liturgically, we join the Holy Spirit with the whole Church to knock and ask for the door of the banquet, which is Jesus himself, to be opened.

CCC 2777-2778
"We Dare to Say"

We have seen how the words of the prayer and the Holy Spirit are a double, indivisible gift. Here we read how the Spirit helps us with the words. He helps us to say them with "filial boldness" (in Greek, *parrhesia*).

There are two sides to this sense of daring. Since the Garden of Eden, *man does not dare*. When Adam and Eve "heard the sound of the Lord God ... they hid themselves.... But the Lord God called to the man and said to him, 'Where are you?' ... and Adam said 'I was afraid ... and I hid myself'" (Gn 3:8-10). Many people do not dare to approach God, expecting in some sense to "dissolve into dust" (2777); we each, often, continue to hide, knowing our sinfulness, our lack of purity, our lack of worthiness.

We can see that if we were simply to *presume* that we could approach the eternal God with boldness, there would be something deeply wrong with such a presumption. How *can* we, human and sinful as we are, approach the All-Holy God? At the burning bush, God says to Moses, "Do not come near." The Jews knew that "man cannot see the face of God and live" (Ex 33:20).

God must *himself* provide the way for such daring to take place. "Only Jesus could cross that threshold of the Divine holiness." Only *he* could bring us "into the Father's presence" (2777). Only in *him* are we adopted "as sons ... no longer a slave but a son, and if a son then an heir" (Gal 4:5-7). It is *the Spirit* in our hearts who enables us to cry, "Abba! Father!" with *parrhesia*. It is worth taking time over the meaning of this wonderful word, especially by looking up the Scripture references in the footnote; you will find it at the end of paragraph 2778.

CCC 2779-2785
Father

The Church has so much to say about the exclamation "Father" that under these next two subheadings of "Father" and "Our Father," there are fifteen paragraphs — that is, fifteen vital things to know and to tell others, about *the reality and the privilege* of being able to call God "Father."

The first point the Catechism makes is that to compare our *heavenly* Father with any father on this earth would lead us far away from the truth. We are not to impose our own experience or idea of fatherhood onto our Father in heaven but to, by purifying our hearts and learning about him from Jesus, his one and only Son, "enter into his mystery" (2779).

- Notice the key points, made in italics, in each of the six paragraphs that follow.
- God as "Father" is *revealed to us* by his Son.
- We are *in communion with him* to whom we pray and with his Son.
- By *adopting us* as his children, the Father incorporates us into his Son.
- The Lord's Prayer *reveals us to ourselves.*
- Through praying to our Father we should find ourselves *desiring to be like him.*
- Through praying to our Father we should come to develop *a humble and trusting heart.*

The last point the Catechism makes here is that by calling God "Father," which *he truly is*, we put ourselves in the position of children, which is what *we truly are*. We are little and we are loved. Without recognizing this, we cannot call the God of all kindness our Father. The Father begs us to "harden not your hearts" (Psalm 94), to keep them soft, to keep them kind *with the kindness the Father lavishes on his children.*

CCC 2786-2793
"Our" Father

Who would expect there to be so much to say about the little word "our"! We are warned in the first paragraph that "Our Father" "does not express possession" in the way one might say "our house." The "entirely new relationship" with God the Father which it signifies is described in the following paragraphs.

The next two paragraphs give us the beginning of the covenantal promises in the Old Testament and the fulfillment of them in the *Book of Revelation*, that we have become *his* people. So it does "express possession," but it is rather *we* who are God's possession, rather than him being ours.

CCC 2789 takes the mystery of the "our" deeper, into the relationships of the Persons of the Blessed Trinity. Here we find that it is Christ who gives us the ability to say "our" Father to "his" Father by *uniting us to himself* and *sharing the Holy Spirit* with us. "Our" is the "our" of Christ and the Holy Spirit.

The next paragraphs show us that the "our" also means the communion of the whole *Church* with the Blessed Trinity, the deep communion in Christ of all the baptized "in spite of the divisions among Christians" (2791). The "our" is widened further by the love the Father has for "all those for whom he gave his beloved Son" (2793). The Our Father prayed sincerely makes us "leave individualism behind, because the love that we receive frees us from it" and "excludes no one" (2792).

CCC 2794-2796
Who Art in Heaven

"In heaven" "does not mean a place ('space'), but a way of being" (2794). What simple clarity! What a surprise! We speak similarly when we say that someone is "in peace," or "in tune," or "in misery." Also, when we see a child who is very happy, we too can say, "Look at him, he's in heaven, in that sandpit, or when he's swimming!" So, when is God "in heaven" like the child? Or, when is God happiest? Of course, God is permanently, infinitely, and unwaveringly happy, but, at the same time, one could answer, "When he is in the hearts of the just and the humble" (see 2794).

The next paragraph returns to the idea that heaven is God's dwelling place, but we must now remember that God dwells "in happiness"; *our homeland* is God's happiness, which is also God's majestic holiness. Sin "exiled us from the land of the covenant" (2795). The "land of the covenant" is the "way of being" which is one of loving, trusting obedience to God's Word.

Sin destroys true happiness, which is *to be obedient to God's Word.* God's Word will only *ever* lead us to happiness in him. God only wants us with him in his happiness. So, when "heaven and earth are reconciled" in Christ (2795), it means that the earth is brought back into God's happiness which it lost through sin.

Christians are "citizens of heaven" (2796). What does this mean? They spend their lives on earth but are "citizens" of God's happiness, his joy, by their loving obedience to God's covenantal plan. To be a citizen is to be a "city-dweller" or to belong to a nation. Our city is the New Jerusalem, a city of God's own love and happiness.

CCC 2803-2806
The Seven Petitions

These paragraphs explain that there are two groups of petitions in the prayer of the Our Father and that they are all *blessings*. The first side reference, to CCC 2627, helps us understand how this can be. There we find two movements of the Holy Spirit in blessing: first, our prayer *ascends* in the Holy Spirit to bless the Father for having blessed us. In the Our Father, God has blessed us with his "name," his "kingdom," and his "will." In the second movement, we plead, in the Holy Spirit, for God's blessing to *descend* upon us in our necessities.

This ascending and descending movement of the Holy Spirit, as we pray the Our Father, may remind us of Jacob's ladder (Gn 28:10-17) linking earth and heaven. Jesus speaks of this ladder when he meets Nathaniel (Jn 1:51), saying that "you will see heaven opened, and the angels of God ascending and descending upon the Son of man" — which happens *every time* we pray the Lord's Prayer.

The first group of three petitions or blessings do not mention ourselves, but only "*thy* name, *thy* kingdom, *thy* will!" (2804). These words are *from the heart of the Son*, in his love for his Father's glory. The Catechism links these petitions to Jesus' "burning desire, even anguish," which reminds us of his agony in the garden. There, he himself, in our name, begs the Father "Thy will be done" (see Lk 22:42).

The second group of four petitions is linked to the work of the Holy Spirit in the liturgy where he "descends" at the *epiclesis*, and then the petitions for our life *ascend* with him to the Father of mercies.

The last paragraph here explains that when we say the Our Father, the first three petitions strengthen the theological virtues that we received at Baptism, and the next four plead for the work of the Blessed Trinity "for us and for the whole world" (2806).

CCC 2807-2812
Hallowed Be Thy Name I

The opening text of CCC 2807 explains the *grammar* of the phrase "hallowed be thy name," using technical language: "causative sense," "evaluative sense," "optative" sense. Without having to understand fully the grammatical formulation, the meaning comes alive and loses the confusion that this phrase sometimes causes when we realize that we cannot "make" God's name holy; "only God hallows." "Hallowed" is a plea; it is to pray, "May your name be held holy by the world," "May I hold your name holy." As the text says, to ask God our Father "that his name be made holy" means asking him to "make" us *recognize it and hold it firmly.* When we ask God to do this in us, he never refuses, and we become "immersed in the innermost mystery of his Godhead" (2807) — that is, his holiness.

The paragraphs move on to the history of when God's name was revealed, beginning with Abraham, to whom God reveals himself but does not give his name. He comes to be called the "God of Abraham, Isaac, and Jacob" since he is clearly a God who outlives generations of men and has committed himself to a *people,* not to a geographical area of land.

Notice that the Catechism says, "He begins to reveal it to Moses" (2810). Moses asks for God's name and God says, "Say this to the people of Israel, 'I AM has sent me to you'" (Ex 3:14). This is only a *beginning* because the name *Jesus,* meaning "God saves," "fully manifests the supreme power of the 'name which is above every name'" (434).

"Hallowed be thy name," then, also means "May thy name, fully revealed in the name 'Jesus,' a name given to us in the flesh, as Savior, be held holy in my heart and my mind, in all hearts and all minds."

CCC 2813-2815
Hallowed Be Thy Name II

There is nothing to compare with this first petition, this first blessing, because it "embodies all the others" (2815), and it is urgent! It is urgent because God's glory and our life "depend on the hallowing of his name in us and by us" (2813). It is not difficult to see how we depend on it, because this is the only name that "gives salvation to a lost world" (2814). How, though, can we say that God's glory depends on it?

This question takes us back to CCC 2809, which explains that only what God has *revealed* of his holiness, *in creation and history*, is called his "glory," "the radiance of his majesty." Notice the footnote to Psalm 8, which begins: "O Lord, our Lord, how majestic is thy name in all the earth" (Ps 8:1). "In all the earth" is a reference to God's *glory* that has been revealed "in creation and history," while the utter and complete *holiness* of God is "the inaccessible center of his eternal mystery" (2809). We can conclude from this that it is we who prevent God's holiness from being revealed as glory when we turn creation into ugliness and do not allow God's reign, his majesty, his peace and righteousness to be reflected in the historical deeds of our lives.

Praying this first petition of the Our Father is to pray that he may radiate his majesty again and restore us to his image and likeness (see 2809). In the beginning, man and woman were endowed, "crowned," with God's glory, but lost this "radiance of his majesty" that shone on them and in them by sinning. Christ takes up our prayer in his own prayer. Our prayer "is fulfilled by the prayer of Christ" (2815).

CCC 2816-2818
Thy Kingdom Come I

Just as "in heaven" does not mean a place but a "way of being," so the "Kingdom" is not so much a place but "the reign of God" replacing the reign of sin. Where God is allowed to be "Lord" in someone's life, he reigns — that is, he governs, nourishes, and protects. This is why we pray *Maranatha* — "Come Lord Jesus" (Rv 22:20). We pray it especially during the Advent liturgies. That is where "the Spirit and the Bride," which is the Church, cry out together every year (2817).

Interestingly, the Old English word "Lord" is derived from two words meaning "bread-keeper" or "warden of the bread." A good "Lord" keeps the peace and ensures the just distribution of life's necessities, such as bread. Jesus, who is the Good Shepherd, is also the *Good Lord* above all others, who gives his own body and blood as food for his people.

"The Kingdom of God" — that is, of the good "Lord Jesus, — *has been coming* "since the Last Supper" (2816). This means that it is established by the Paschal mystery, the passion, death, resurrection, and ascension of Christ. This is where the reign of sin begins to be definitively overcome. The kingdom of God is also *in our midst* in the Eucharist, there where the Word of righteousness and peace is made flesh. It has come in Christ's death and resurrection, and it *will come* "in glory when Christ hands it over to his Father" (2816).

In fact, the Catechism says that the petition is primarily for what is still to come — that is, "the final coming of the reign of God through Christ's return" (2818). The final coming is the work of the Holy Spirit "bringing to perfection" Jesus' work of sanctifying creation to the full (see 2818).

CCC 2819-2821
Thy Kingdom Come II

The text continues, reminding us that the "kingdom" is not so much a place but the reign of God in "righteousness and peace and joy" (2819), and it comes about through the "outpouring of the Spirit." It is the end-times — that is, the time after the resurrection and ascension of Christ and the descent of the Spirit at Pentecost, the time of the Church.

We have spoken about the reign of God replacing the reign of sin. Where there is one "Lord" reigning (the Lord of lies — a created, not a divine, Lord — Satan) and another desires to win back his people that they might come under his lordship again, there will always be a battle. This is another reason why we must pray this prayer and beg for the *reign of God* to establish a kingdom of righteousness, peace, joy and all the fruits of the Spirit (see Gal 5:22-23).

The next article makes sure that we do not think *praying* for the kingdom of God is all that we do in the battle (2820). Our engagement in "the progress of culture and society" are *essential avenues* for putting the reign of God, the lordship of Christ, into practice. The side reference, to 1049, takes us to a helpful quotation from the Vatican II document *Gaudium et Spes*. Here we are helped to see that "we must be careful to distinguish earthly progress ... from the increase of the kingdom of Christ," but also that "such progress is of vital concern to the kingdom of God, insofar as it can contribute to the better ordering of human society" (1049).

This petition "bears its fruit in new life in keeping with the Beatitudes" (2821). This is where we can see the fruit of our constant praying of the Our Father. Lives will be renewed and converted; they will be mourning, meek, thirsting for righteousness, merciful, pure, and peacemakers (Mt 5:3-11).

CCC 2822-2824
Thy Will Be Done on Earth As It Is in Heaven I

We have pondered on the first two petitions relating to God's *name* and his *kingdom*. This is the third petition of the seven and the last of the three relating directly to our heavenly Father.

That God's will is done in heaven is not a surprise. What we need is a strong sense of what that *means*, otherwise we cannot pray properly for his will to be done on earth "as it is in heaven." So, how is it done "in heaven"? What can we know?

We read here from Saint Paul's Letter to the Ephesians (see footnote 98) that God "has made known to us the mystery of his will, according to his good pleasure that he set forth in Christ" (2823). We know that those in heaven have "come to the knowledge of the truth" (2822), which is that God is lovingly gathering everything and everyone up, into his beloved Son, Jesus, purging away everything that isn't worthy. We know that those doing God's will in heaven love one another as Christ has loved them (see 2822). Also, as we have seen previously, they are embraced in the holiness and happiness of the Father's infinite reign of peace, righteousness, and joy. In heaven, then, God's will is knowingly, freely, totally, and lovingly followed, *with great joy and deep happiness.*

This, then, is what we pray to be "done on earth," and only *Christ* has done this. "In Christ, and through his human will, the will of the Father has been perfectly fulfilled once for all" (2824), and it was fulfilled on earth knowingly, freely, totally, and lovingly, with great joy and deep happiness, through his life with Mary and Joseph, his public ministry, and the agony of his passion and Cross.

CCC 2825-2827
Thy Will Be Done on Earth As It Is in Heaven II

We cannot know how to do the will of God our Father on earth without looking at how Jesus the divine Son of God did it, "through his human will." Jesus is God, so he also has the divine will of the Godhead. Nonetheless, he follows the will of his Father — that is, the divine will that he also shares — with his human will. Jesus held his human will in *constant and perfect alignment* with the will of the Father, and he learned to do this through *obedience*.

We are "radically incapable" of what we are praying unless we are "united to Christ" (2825)! Our will needs *bending* by the Holy Spirit who gives us the grace from on high to "surrender our will ... and decide to choose ... what is pleasing to the Father." To help us, we have the Church's prayer, above all in the Eucharist, and we have the intercession of the "all-holy Mother of God and all the saints who have been pleasing to the Lord" (2827). All the help I need is available to me so that I can will what pleases the Father; but am I really interested in this? If I'm not, then what can I do? I can ask! I can ask the Holy Spirit and ask Mary the Mother of God for this *conversion of heart* and know that it will be given.

The quotation from Saint Augustine helps us to see that, even though we are "radically incapable" when we ask "thy will be done on earth," it *is* actually done on earth, "in the Church as in our Lord Jesus Christ himself," in Mary and the Church as the Bride, and in Christ the Bridegroom (2827).

In each of these first three petitions we have read that this prayer prays for the whole world, "for everyone, even our enemies" (2814). This is emphasized here even more by the words "on earth" — that is, everywhere and in every age.

CCC 2828-2834
Give Us This Day Our Daily Bread I

Can you see that these next four petitions, which relate more directly to our life on earth, cannot be fulfilled unless the first three precede them — that is, unless we desire God's will, his kingdom and the hallowing of his name? The first three sum up everything; these four *cannot be separated* from them.

We read earlier in CCC 2803 that these next four "commend our wretchedness to [God's] grace. 'Deep calls to deep' (Ps 42:7)." The "deep" of our human wretchedness calls to the deep of God's grace, and the Psalmist continues:

> All thy waves and thy billows have gone over me.
> By day the Lord commands his steadfast love
> and at night his song is with me. (Ps 42:7-8)

In other words, God *overwhelms* with his abundant grace when we have the courage to commend to him our wretchedness, *when we ask him to give,* and we ask with the "trust of children who look to their Father" (2828). So much does God want us to ask, so that he might provide for us without forcing our will, that this petition "glorifies our Father by acknowledging how good he is, beyond all goodness" (2828).

The paragraphs go through each word of this phrase, "give," "us," "our," "bread." And the word "daily" is explained in detail at the end of this section. The paragraphs root us first in the covenant, in our belonging to God our Father: "We are his and he is ours, for our sake" (2829). The paragraphs then take us out into the needy world of hunger, injustice, and poverty, and the need for "all appropriate goods and blessings, both material and spiritual" (2830).

We are reminded that Jesus "is not inviting us to idleness" (2830), but to pray and work so that the whole earth may "rise" by the Spirit of Christ, to the Father (2832).

CCC 2835-2837
Give Us This Day Our Daily Bread II

There is "another hunger from which men are perishing" (2835), and it is a famine. This is the serious subject of these next paragraphs. The plea for "our daily bread" is also because of the "famine on earth" for the "Bread of Life: the Word of God accepted in faith, the Body of Christ received in the Eucharist" (2835).

The Catechism then reveals to us that the word *daily* in Greek "occurs nowhere else in the New Testament" (2837). It refers to the "'today' ... of our mortal time, but also the 'today' of God" (2836). The side reference to CCC 1165 will remind you of the depth of meaning this carries. In this prayer it is an "expression of trust taught us by the Lord" (2836). We can find the scriptural basis for this in footnotes 126 and 128.

In Matthew's Gospel Jesus tells us not to be anxious about tomorrow, "for tomorrow will be anxious for itself" (Mt 6:34), and the reference to the book of Exodus takes us to the instructions for gathering the manna in the desert: "Each gathered according to what he could eat. And Moses said to them, 'Let no man leave any of it till the morning'" (Ex 16:18-19). Our Father is leading us *to trust in him daily* to take care of all our needs.

"Daily" in Greek *is an extraordinary word.* As well as the biblical meanings we have followed above, we are now given the philosophical meaning: "super-essential." It is essential (in Greek, *ousios*). It also has the prefix *epi* (in Greek, "super" in the sense of "from above" or "over," as in *epi-scopos*, "over-seer" — that is, the bishop). So this "daily bread" for which we are asking is that which is *essential to our earthly life,* but also *essential for eternal life.*

CCC 2838-2841
And Forgive Us Our Trespasses

The Catechism describes this petition as "astonishing," while it is more often seen as confusing and obscure because the petition *seems to be written the wrong way*. Surely, I need *God* to forgive me first *so that* I can forgive others. This petition seems to suggest that we have to be forgiving "on our own" and without help first, before receiving the forgiveness we need from God. Clearly, it is the little word "as" that joins the two parts of the petition together that we need to ponder and understand more fully.

Before we reach the word "as," these next few paragraphs take us into the "daunting" wonder of the path of forgiveness. In CCC 1697 we have already read how we need to be able to acknowledge that we are sinners in order to know the truth about ourselves, but "without the offer of forgiveness [we] would not be able to bear this truth." In other words, we all need to know that we are offered forgiveness before we can even *see*, let alone admit, our trespasses.

Those who do not know the Father's *infinitely loving forgiveness* cannot admit their trespasses and so *cannot ask* for forgiveness. This is the tragedy we see in any decline in Christianity — without knowing Christ, where do people turn with their guilt and sin? Guilt is a signal to us of the "shipwreck which is the loss of grace" (1446), urging us to return to our heavenly Father for his forgiveness.

The "efficacious and undoubted sign" for us of this forgiveness from God himself is found "in the sacraments of his Church" (2839). This does not limit God's forgiveness to the sacraments alone, but there we are *sure*, without doubt, that the forgiveness of God is available to us if our hearts are open.

CCC 2842-2845
As We Forgive Those Who Trespass Against Us

The Catechism reminds us first of all that the word "as" is not unique here. We have already considered it in the previous petition "thy will be done *as it is in heaven*." There we needed to know what "in heaven" meant before we knew what we were praying for on earth. Similarly, we need to know *what it means to forgive* those who trespass against us, as the saints in heaven know, before we can know for what we are asking. The other examples the Catechism gives are the same: "You, therefore, must be perfect, *as* your heavenly Father is perfect" (2842). For this we need to consider the perfection of God before we can ask him to make us like that.

The kind of forgiveness that we all need is total, and it can only come from Christ. When he tells his disciples "Love one another as I have loved you," they know how he has loved them; they have experienced the kind of love themselves that he desires for them, in order for them to love one another. But as the Catechism reminds us, "Only the Spirit by whom we live can make 'ours' the same mind that was in Christ Jesus." In Christ, we can pray this petition because *in Christ* "the unity of forgiveness becomes possible" (2842) and we can learn to give and to ask for forgiveness "as God in Christ forgave us."

CCC 2846-2849
And Lead Us Not into Temptation

This can be another petition. We know God would never *lead* us into temptation. However, we do need him to "lead us" always. At every moment we beg for his leading. As you can see, the word "lead" in Greek is rich and full of meaning. In another sense it also means "allow." We are asking God *not to allow us to enter into temptation*: "In your leading of us, Lord, don't let us yield to temptation. Lead us towards the good and don't let us follow our normal tendencies and be tempted to treat your precious creation badly."

The role of *discernment* is highlighted. In God's leading of us he can allow us to face great difficulties; we have challenges that can seem overwhelming. Sometimes God's leading allows this because he knows that they are "necessary for the growth of the inner man" (2847). Sometimes he allows temptation so that we can know ourselves better, know our need for his grace, and so that he can "unmask" what we find tempting. Only resistance and battle reveal the power of temptation, since as soon as we give in to it we no longer need to face it. Our freedom is only gained when we have formed the habit of constantly "giving in" to *grace* rather than to the temptation.

Temptation, then, can become the occasion for being *more closely united to Christ*. Note how the final paragraph is concerned with *Christ's* battle with the Tempter and with his victory, with Christ's vigilance of heart and his ultimate struggle. When we pray this petition to our heavenly Father, *Christ unites* us to "his battle and his agony"; he *urges* us to keep vigilance *with* him; and the Father sends the *Holy Spirit* to *awaken* us. Then it is no longer we who fight alone. It is *Christ* who fights with us, in us, and for us against the Tempter, "for vain is the help of man!" (Ps 60:11).

CCC 2850-2854
But Deliver Us from Evil

This petition begins from the point we noted with regard to the prayer not to be led into temptation — namely, that we do not pray alone. It is as "us" that we seek deliverance. This tells us to both widen our prayer, not thinking of ourselves alone as needing deliverance, and to remember that we pray within the Church, within the communion of saints. Our prayers are made in union with the whole Body (2850).

We are next alerted to the reality that a created will opposes us and opposes God's Kingdom. Evil has a name — Satan is "the Evil One, the angel who opposes God" (2851). The cross-reference to 391 reminds us to review the Church's teaching on the nature and purpose of Satan and the fallen angels and their real but limited power. Whereas God is the one who leads you "beside still waters" (Ps 23:2-3), restoring your soul and leading you "in paths of righteousness," the devil "is accustomed to leading into sin," in the words of Saint Ambrose (2852). He leads us into sin because sin leads in turn to death, and the devil is a murderer.

The devil is real, but his power is limited. He is the "prince of this world" (Jn 14:30; CCC 2853), not the King. He is the pretender who seeks the throne. He has no hold wherever Jesus is present as the good Lord. The Catechism asks us to remember that the *evidence of Jesus' complete victory* is already in the Woman, full of grace, whom the devil could not harm, for she was "preserved from sin and the corruption of death" (2853).

This is a prayer for deliverance from *all evils*, "present, past, and future" (2854), of which the devil is the instigator, and for the *gift of peace* — Christ's peace, which is the final peace of the Kingdom.

CCC 2855-2856
The Final Doxology

So we reach the conclusion of this, *the most perfect of all prayers*, with the "doxology." "*Doxa*" in Greek is "glory," and a doxology is a praise of God's glory that is often placed at the end of a hymn or canticle. It is fitting that the prayer that Jesus taught concludes with praise of the Father's glory. Look back to 2760 for an earlier comment on the linking of the doxology to the Lord's Prayer.

The simple phrase parallels the opening of the Lord's Prayer, with its leading three petitions that "draw us toward the glory of the Father" (2803). In this way we are returned to the beginning point; but now, the Catechism teaches, it is different. "These prayers are now proclaimed as adoration and thanksgiving, as in the liturgy of heaven" (2855). It looks as though we have gone full circle, but in fact we have moved from *petition* to *adoration*, from the needs of the *earth* to the thanksgiving that is offered forever in *heaven*.

After a brief reminder of the liar and of his false self-attribution of the titles to himself, our hymn of glory focuses on that final moment when the Kingdom, the Power, and the Glory are definitively restored to the Father at Jesus' second coming. "For all the promises of God find their 'Yes' in him. That is why we utter the 'Amen' through him, to the glory of God" (2 Cor 1:20).

The final scriptural reference of all returns us to the Blessed Virgin, to her "fiat," which we have already learned is the *very definition* of Christian prayer (2617). The Blessed Virgin's words are the perfect response to the whole loving plan of the Blessed Trinity: "Let it be to me, according to your word" (Lk 1:38).

ADDENDUM

READING FOR LIFE

Congratulations! It is a great thing to have read the whole of the Catechism, to have engaged seriously with the heartfelt desire of Saint John Paul II that each person "seek and receive Christ's love which surpasses all knowledge" (*Fidei Depositum*). You have "run with perseverance the race that is set before us" (Heb 12:1)!

Now that you have completed your reading of the whole text, *different kinds* of reading can truly begin. You have embraced the whole text in a comprehensive way. Now you can begin to use some of the riches in the text that the Church has placed there to assist you with deeply satisfying readings of other kinds.

You can read *across* the text, following the cross-references from one section of the text to another. The Catechism calls this an "organic" reading, since it helps us to see how the faith is a *living whole*. You will remember that CCC 18 proposed this as the main "practical direction" for reading. This kind of reading, beginning with one topic, and following the links to other subjects, helps us to see the glorious unity of the faith and of the one plan of God's loving kindness.

You can read *the sources of the text* that are referenced here — the holy Scriptures, and the selections from some of the great writings of the Sacred Tradition of the Church. You may remember that Saint John Paul thanked God for the publication of the Catechism which, he said, would renew catechesis "at the living sources of the faith!" (*Fidei Depositum*). To begin, when you are reading on a particular topic, look up the Scripture references and spend time with these. You can also read *from* the scriptural index at the end of the Catechism, following the references back into the Catechism. This is a particularly good way to prepare for readings at Mass, to allow the Church's understanding of the text, as found here, to instruct you.

About the Contributors

Dr. Donald Asci is professor of theology at Franciscan University of Steubenville. His academic degrees include a Licentiate in Sacred Theology in systematic theology and a Doctorate in Sacred Theology in moral theology from the Pontifical Università della Santa Croce in Rome, Italy, and a Masters in Sacred Theology from the Pontifical John Paul II Institute for Studies in Marriage and the Family in Washington, D.C. He is the author of *The Conjugal Act as a Personal Act* (Ignatius Press, 2002).

Fr. Dominic Scotto, TOR, is professor of theology at Franciscan University of Steubenville. He gained his Licentiate in Sacred Theology (STL) from the Catholic University of America, an MA in Liturgical Research from the University of Notre Dame and STL and Doctor of Sacred Theology (STD) degrees from the Pontifical Institute of Sant'Anselmo in Rome. He is author of *Liturgy of the Hours* (Franciscan University Press, 2001) and *The Table of the Lord* (Fordham University Press, 2002) and numerous articles on the religious life.

Elizabeth Siegel has an MA in philosophy from the University of Texas at Austin and completed coursework for the STL at the University of Fribourg, Switzerland. She began working with the Catechism in 1995, developing a new catechist formation program for the Archdiocese of Washington, D.C., and serving in the Offices for Religious Education in Washington and Bridgeport, Connecticut. Over the past twenty years, she has continued to teach, write and edit material for adult formation, including the creation of a neophyte program at her home parish of Christ the King in Ann Arbor, Michigan.

Dr. Petroc Willey, married to Katherine and with four children, is professor of theology (catechetics) at Franciscan University of Steubenville and director of the Catechetical Institute at the University. He is also a reader in the New Evangelization at the School of the Annunciation, Buckfast Abbey, in Devon. In 2011 he was appointed a consultor for the Pontifical Council for the Promotion of the New Evangelization. He holds doctorates in philosophy from Liverpool University and the Lateran Pontifical University and a Licentiate in Sacred Theology from Maynooth.